International Economic and Financial Cooperation: New Issues, New Actors, New Responses

Geneva Reports on the World Economy 6

International Center for Monetary and Banking Studies (ICMB)

International Center for Monetary and Banking Studies
11 A Avenue de la Paix
1202 Geneva
Switzerland

Tel (41 22) 734 9548
Fax (41 22) 733 3853
Website: www.icmb.ch

Centre for Economic Policy Research (CEPR)

Centre for Economic Policy Research
90-98 Goswell Road
London EC1V 7RR
UK

Tel: +44 (0)20 7878 2900
Fax: +44 (0)20 7878 2999
Email: cepr@cepr.org
Website: www.cepr.org

British Library Cataloguing in Publication Data
A catalogue record for this book is available from the British Library

ISBN: 1 898128 84 7

International Economic and Financial Cooperation: New Issues, New Actors, New Responses

Geneva Reports on the World Economy 6

Peter B Kenen
Council on Foreign Relations and Princeton University

Jeffrey R Shafer
Citigroup and former US Under Secretary of the Treasury

Nigel L Wicks
CRESTCo and former Head of HM Treasury

Charles Wyplosz
Graduate Institute of International Studies, Geneva and CEPR

ICMB INTERNATIONAL CENTER
FOR MONETARY
AND BANKING STUDIES

CIMB CENTRE INTERNATIONAL
D ETUDES MONETAIRES
ET BANCAIRES

International Center for Monetary and Banking Studies (ICMB)

The International Center for Monetary and Banking Studies was created in 1973 as an independent, non-profit foundation. It is associated with Geneva's Graduate Institute of International Studies. Its aim is to foster exchange of views between the financial sector, central banks and academics on issues of common interest. It is financed through grants from banks, financial institutions and central banks.

The Center sponsors international conferences, public lectures, original research and publications. It has earned a solid reputation in the Swiss and international banking community where it is known for its contribution to bridging the gap between theory and practice in the field of international banking and finance.

In association with CEPR, the Center launched a new series of *Geneva Reports on the World Economy* in 1999. The four subsequent volumes have attracted considerable interest among practitioners, policy-makers and scholars working on the reform of international financial architecture.

The ICMB is non-partisan and does not take any view on policy. Its publications, including the present report, reflect the opinions of the authors, not of ICMB or of any of its sponsoring institutions.

President of the Foundation Board   Tommaso Padoa-Schioppa
Director   Charles Wyplosz

Centre for Economic Policy Research (CEPR)

The Centre for Economic Policy Research is a network of over 600 Research Fellows and Affiliates, based primarily in European universities. The Centre coordinates the research activities of its Fellows and Affiliates and communicates the results to the public and private sectors. CEPR is an entrepreneur, developing research initiatives with the producers, consumers and sponsors of research. Established in 1983, CEPR is a European economics research organization with uniquely wide-ranging scope and activities.

CEPR is a registered educational charity. Institutional (core) finance for the Centre is provided by major grants from the Economic and Social Research Council, under which an ESRC Resource Centre operates within CEPR; the Esmée Fairbairn Charitable Trust and the Bank of England. The Centre is also supported by the European Central Bank, the Bank for International Settlements, 22 national central banks and 45 companies. None of these organizations gives prior review to the Centre's publications, nor do they necessarily endorse the views expressed therein.

The Centre is pluralist and non-partisan, bringing economic research to bear on the analysis of medium- and long-run policy questions. CEPR research may include views on policy, but the Executive Committee of the Centre does not give prior review to its publications, and the Centre takes no institutional policy positions. The opinions expressed in this report are those of the authors and not those of the Centre for Economic Policy Research.

Chair of the Board   Guillermo de la Dehesa
President   Richard Portes
Chief Executive Officer   Stephen Yeo
Research Director   Mathias Dewatripont

About the Authors

Peter B Kenen is a Senior Fellow in International Economics at the Council on Foreign Relations and Walker Professor of Economics and International Finance Emeritus at Princeton University, where he also served as Director of the International Finance Section from 1971 to 1999. He taught at Columbia University from 1957 to 1971. A specialist in international economics, he earned his BA from Columbia and his PhD from Harvard. He has written several books, including *Exchanges and Policy Coordination, Economic and Monetary Union in Europe*, and *The International Financial Architecture: What's New? What's Missing?* He has been a consultant to the US Treasury and other US government agencies and to the International Monetary Fund, and he has held research fellowships awarded by the Center for Advanced Study in the Behavioral Sciences, the Guggenheim Foundation, the Royal Institute for International Affairs, and the Bank of England. He is a member of the Council on Foreign Relations and the Group of Thirty.

Jeffrey R Shafer dealt with international financial and monetary issues during 25 years at the Board of Governors of the Federal Reserve System, the Federal Reserve Bank of New York, the Organization for Economic Cooperation and Development and the US Treasury, where he was Assistant Secretary and subsequently Under Secretary for International Affairs. He joined what is now Citigroup in 1997, where he is Vice Chairman, Public Sector Group. Mr Shafer holds a PhD in Economics from Yale University and an AB in Economics from Princeton University.

Sir Nigel L Wicks joined HM Treasury in 1968 after working for the British Petroleum Company. He worked for Prime Ministers Harold Wilson, James Callaghan and Margaret Thatcher. He has been the UK's Executive Director at the International Monetary Fund and World Bank, the Prime Minister's representative ('Sherpa') for the Economic Summits of the Group of Seven Industrialized Nations and G7 'Deputy' for five Chancellors of the Exchequer. From 1989 to 2000, he was the Treasury's Second Permanent Secretary responsible for international financial matters, during which time he was for five years Chairman of the EC Monetary Committee. The UK Prime Minister appointed him as Chair of the Committee on Standards in Public Life for the period March 2001 to April 2004. He is now Deputy Chairman of the securities settlement company Euroclear. He studied Business Administration at Portsmouth College of Technology and holds degrees in History from the Universities of Cambridge and London.

Charles Wyplosz is Professor of International Economics at the Graduate Institute of International Studies in Geneva where he is Director of the International Centre for Monetary and Banking Studies. An expert in monetary affairs, currency crises and the international monetary system, Charles Wyplosz has written numerous books and papers. He is a member of several advisory committees to the French government and to the European Commission and Parliament and an occasional consultant to the European Commission, the IMF, the World Bank, the United Nations, the Asian Development Bank, and the Inter-American Development Bank. He holds degrees in Engineering and Statistics from Paris and a PhD in Economics from Harvard University.

Contents

List of Conference Participants

Oliver Adler	Managing Director, Head of Investment Strategy UBS WEALTH MANAGEMENT, ZÜRICH
Edmond Alphandéry	Chairman of the Supervisory Board CNP - ASSURANCES, PARIS
Markus Arpa	Deputy Head, Foreign Research Division OESTERREICHISCHE NATIONALBANK, VIENNA
Thomas Atkins	Journalist REUTERS, GENEVA
Jeanne Barras-Zwahlen	Senior Economist CRÉDIT SUISSE PRIVATE BANKING, GENEVA
Vít Bárta	Adviser to the Vice-Governor CZECH NATIONAL BANK, PRAGUE
Ric Battellino	Assistant Governor RESERVE BANK OF AUSTRALIA, SYDNEY
Rémy Bersier	Managing Director, Head Market Group II CRÉDIT SUISSE PRIVATE BANKING, GENEVA
Gavin Bingham	Head of International Liaison, Monetary and Economic Department BANK FOR INTERNATIONAL SETTLEMENTS, BASEL
Marc Büdenbender	Director, Head Public Policy Analysis UBS AG, ZÜRICH
Richard Buhler	Senior Vice President SARASIN & CO LTD, GENEVA
Ariel Buira	Director G-24 LIAISON OFFICE, WASHINGTON, DC
Benoît Coeuré	Deputy Chief Executive MINISTRY OF THE ECONOMY, FINANCE AND INDUSTRY, PARIS
Jon Cunliffe	Managing Director, Macroeconomic Policy and International Finance HM TREASURY, LONDON
Jean-Pierre Danthine	Professor ECOLE DES HAUTES ETUDES COMMERCIALES, LAUSANNE
Pierre Darier	Partner LOMBARD ODIER DARIER HENTSCH & CIE, GENEVA
Olivier Davanne	Associate Professor Université Paris-Dauphine DPA CONSEIL, PARIS
Stella Dawson	ECB Correspondent REUTERS, GERMANY

Jean-Marie de Charrière	Chief Executive Officer FERRIER LULLIN & CIE SA, GENEVA
José De Gregiorio	Vice President BANCO CENTRAL DE CHILE, SANTIAGO
Jacques Delpa	Director, Economist BARCLAYS CAPITAL, PARIS
Slobodan Djajic	Professor, Economics GRADUATE INSTITUTE OF INTERNATIONAL STUDIES, GENEVA
Benoit Dumont	General Director JP MORGAN (SUISSE) SA, GENEVA
Georges Gagnebin	Chairman UBS Wealth Management and Business Banking UBS AG, ZÜRICH
Olivier Garnier	Head of Strategy and Economic Research SOCIÉTÉ GÉNÉRALE ASSET MANAGEMENT, PARIS
Hans Genberg	Professor, Economics GRADUATE INSTITUTE OF INTERNATIONAL STUDIES, GENEVA
Yves Genier	Journalist AGEFI, GENEVA
Svein Gjedrem	Governor NORGES BANK, OSLO
Giorgio Gomel	Director for International Relations BANCA D'ITALIA, ROMA
Gerd Haeusler	Counsellor and Director, International Capital Markets IMF, WASHINGTON, DC
C. Randall Henning	Professor AMERICAN UNIVERSITY INSTITUTE FOR INTER- NATIONAL ECONOMICS, WASHINGTON, DC
Eduard H. Hochreiter	Senior Adviser and Head Economic Studies OESTERREICHISCHE NATIONALBANK, VIENNA
Karen Johnson	Director, International Finance FEDERAL RESERVE BOARD, WASHINGTON, DC
Alexander Karrer	Ambassador, International Finance and Monetary Policy Division SWISS FEDERAL DEPARTMENT OF FINANCE, BERN
Pierre Keller	Former Senior Partner LOMBARD ODIER DARIER HENTSCH & CIE, GENEVA
Peter Kenen	Professor PRINCETON UNIVERSITY, PRINCETON, NJ
Ulrich Kohli	Chief Economist SWISS NATIONAL BANK, ZÜRICH
Dino Kos	Executive Vice President, Markets Group FEDERAL RESERVE BANK OF NEW YORK

Alexandre Lamfalussy	Former President EUROPEAN MONETARY INSTITUTE Professor Emeritus UNIVERSITÉ CATHOLIQUE DE LOUVAIN, BELGIUM
Jean-Pierre Landau	Director for France EUROPEAN BANK FOR RECONSTRUCTION AND DEVELOPMENT, LONDON
Frédéric Lelievre	Journalist *LE TEMPS*, GENEVA
Philippe Maystadt	President EUROPEAN INVESTMENT BANK, LUXEMBOURG
Carlo Monticelli	Senior Director, International Financial Relations MINISTRY OF ECONOMY AND FINANCE, ROME
Lars Nyberg	Deputy Governor SVERIGES RIKSBANK, STOCKHOLM
Tommaso Padoa-Schioppa	Member of the Executive Board EUROPEAN CENTRAL BANK, FRANKFURT AM MAIN
Michel Peytrignet	Head of Economics, 1st Department SWISS NATIONAL BANK, ZÜRICH
Christian Pfister	Director Economic Analysis and Research BANQUE DE FRANCE, PARIS
Charles Pictet	Partner PICTET & CIE, GENEVA
Jean Pisani-Ferry	Senior Adviser, French Treasury MINISTRY OF FINANCE, PARIS
Friederike Pohlenz	Head of Section, IMF and International Finance SWISS FEDERAL DEPARTMENT OF FINANCE, BERN
Richard Portes	President CEPR, LONDON
Jan Fredrik Qvigstad	Executive Director and Chief Economist Monetary Policy NORGES BANK, OSLO
Cesare Ravara	Senior Economist CRÉDIT SUISSE, ZÜRICH
Jean-Jacques Rey	Honorary Executive Director NATIONAL BANK OF BELGIUM, BELGIUM
Jean-Pierre Schoder	Head of Monetary, Economic and Statistics Department BANQUE CENTRALE DU LUXEMBOURG, LUXEMBOURG
Claudio Segré	Chairman ARGUS FUND, GENEVA
Jeffrey R. Shafer	Vice Chairman CITIGROUP, NEW YORK
Alexandre Swoboda	Professor, Economics GRADUATE INSTITUTE OF INTERNATIONAL STUDIES, GENEVA

Manijeh Swoboda-Mobasser Investment Adviser
GENEVA

Jens Thomsen Member of the Board of Governors
DANMARKS NATIONALBANK, COPENHAGEN

Gertrude Tumpel-Gugerell Member of the Executive Board
EUROPEAN CENTRAL BANK, FRANKFURT AM
MAIN

Angel Ubide Director, Global Economics
TUDOR INVESTMENT CORPORATION,
WASHINGTON, DC

Ernst-Ludwig Von Thadden Professor, Economics
UNIVERSITY OF LAUSANNE, LAUSANNE

Nigel Wicks Deputy Chairman
EUROCLEAR, LONDON

Bernhard Winkler Counsellor to the Executive Board
EUROPEAN CENTRAL BANK, FRANKFURT AM
MAIN

Ngaire Woods Fellow in Politics and International Relations
UNIVERSITY COLLEGE OXFORD

Pawel Wyczanski Deputy Director
NATIONAL BANK OF POLAND, WARSAW

Charles Wyplosz Professor, International Economics
GRADUATE INSTITUTE OF INTERNATIONAL
STUDIES, GENEVA

Jean Zwahlen Vice-President
UNION BANCAIRE PRIVÉE, GENEVA

List of Tables

List of Figures

List of Boxes

Acknowledgements

We are very grateful for the numerous comments received during the Geneva Conference on the World Economy as well as from Cedric Dupont and Ted Truman. We thank Ghislaine Weder for excellent research assistance.

Foreword

The unexpected volatility and wide swings of exchange rates since 1973 and the debate on the 'international financial architecture' (IFA) launched after the 1994–5 Mexican crisis have generated many official reports, academic articles, and meetings. Yet all the analysis, communication between academics and officials, and negotiations among the latter have not yet brought many substantial changes. For example, an excellent recent survey by the Bank of Spain concludes, '... progress in the reform of IFA since 1998 seems modest... greater in the areas of strengthening the financial sector and transparency, whereas it is significantly less in crisis prevention and especially in crisis resolution.'

Yet there is a widespread perception that the existing institutions are losing effectiveness in the face of globalization and increasing economic and financial interdependence. New major players are emerging, regionalism may be progressing at the expense of multilateralism, and the *ad hoc* responses of recent years seem relatively ineffective.

This sixth publication in the series of *Geneva Reports on the World Economy* offers an assessment by a distinguished team of authors with extensive experience in international economics and international negotiations. They set the stage with a masterly, comprehensive review of the development of international economic cooperation since the creation of the Bretton Woods system in 1944. This will surely become the standard source on the development of the international economy and its institutions over the past 60 years. The report then goes on to propose specific recommendations: a new 'group' of countries/regions with key currencies (dollar, euro, yen, renminbi); a fundamental review of the plethora of existing institutions, organizations and groups; changes to the institutional structure of the IMF; and the creation of a new 'agenda-setting' body for changes in the international financial system.

ICMB and CEPR are delighted to provide a forum for the authors to put forward this framework for improving international economic and financial cooperation. We are confident that it will be widely read and discussed, and we hope it will influence the current wave of reappraisals of the international system.

Tommaso Padoa-Schioppa
Richard Portes

13 August 2004

Executive Summary

This Report looks into existing arrangements that drive international economic and financial cooperation. It argues that the status quo is increasingly untenable and makes a number of proposals to reform the process through which the main economic and financial issues are dealt with.

The status quo needs to be changed because it is losing effectiveness. This loss is the outcome of many changes that have become increasingly obvious over the last two decades. The set of key players has expanded, including several emerging economic and financial giants that have long been sidelined. Not only do these new key players deserve to be involved in the process of international cooperation, but it is also becoming impossible to deal with the world's main challenges without them. The set of issues is also changing. Globalization calls for global answers in areas such as balance-of-payments adjustments, financial regulation and supervision, debt management and debt crisis resolution. Many steps have been taken in these directions lately, largely on an ad hoc basis and without involving all the significant players. More steps are called for, and these steps will have to be designed within a broader framework. Finally, the set of policies has also evolved. We now live in a world of low inflation and integrated financial markets. Monetary policies are mostly dedicated to domestic concerns, and yet are subject to the powerful influences of huge international financial markets. Fiscal policies are constrained by the need for budgetary discipline. Financial regulation and supervision are becoming more sophisticated at a time when markets are developing in places where they were long repressed.

The current system of international economic and financial cooperation owes much to the postwar construction, yet it has considerably evolved since then. This evolution has been driven by two main considerations: pragmatism and effectiveness. The old system has adapted to a succession of events, including the end of the Bretton Woods system of fixed exchange rates, the oil shocks, decolonization, the development of global banking, the end of the cold war and the accumulation of crises in emerging market countries. Pragmatism has meant the creation of various informal groupings, especially the G7, which functioned effectively for many years as a crisis manager and agenda-setter for the international community but cannot be expected to do so for much longer, in light of the changes and challenges arising from globalization. More recently, regional integration has become fashionable, although the record remains modest outside of Europe.

There are good reasons why international coordination is difficult to achieve in a world of sovereign states. Ideally, coordination should be orchestrated by bodies that satisfy four traditional criteria: effectiveness, legitimacy, representativeness and accountability. This is a tall order, and this is why there exist only few formal institutions and many informal arrangements. The IMF and World Bank go a long way to meeting all four criteria, but their effectiveness has been wanting in key areas at crucial times. The need for effectiveness is why the G7 was set up. Its legitimacy has, however, been questioned increasingly. The creation of the G20 was meant to respond to the need for legitimacy, but its role has been limited. Clearly, the challenge remains to be confronted, and it will take time to develop adequate responses.

Unfortunately, problems don't wait. Over the last two decades, episodes of financial stress have regularly appeared, typically leaving a legacy of economic disruption in affected countries and complex debt resolution problems. The international response has typically featured large IMF bailouts, sometimes accompanied by intrusive conditions, rescheduling by the Paris Club, sometimes based on unduly optimistic assumptions, and IMF lending into arrears without commitment to effective action by the debtor. Facing this unsatisfactory state of affairs and the displacement of bank lending by bond issuance, the G7 finance ministers and governors have sought to devise new responses. They encouraged greater IMF transparency and were instrumental in bringing the HIPC initiative to fruition and in creating the Financial Stability Forum to promote international financial stability. The G10 initiated work that eventually led to the adoption of collective action clauses but failed to unite behind the IMF's initiative for a Sovereign Debt Reduction Mechanism (SDRM). The world economic and financial system is not rudderless, but many important issues remain on the agenda, and have been there for a while.

One key challenge is to recognize that the list of key players involved in balance-of-payments adjustments is expanding. A decade ago, many of today's systematically important currencies either did not exist (the euro) or were insignificant (the renminbi and other Asian currencies, soon, maybe, the Brazilian real and the Indian rupee). This evolution is acutely apparent in the IMF and will diminish over time the effectiveness of the G7. Room must be made for these new currencies, but effectiveness must be preserved. One natural solution would be to streamline European representation in existing bodies such as the IMF Executive Board and G7, but political sensitivities stand in the way of a quick resolution. A second proposal is to set up a new grouping, the G4 to bring together the key currency countries (the United States, the euro zone, Japan and China). The G4 can then play the leadership role in dealing with exchange rate adjustments that used to be filled by the G7. For most other global issues, however, the G4 cannot replace the G7. Yet the G7's effectiveness is being undermined by its diminishing legitimacy and representativeness. For these reasons, this Report makes three more recommendations:

1. **A review of existing institutions, organizations, groups and clubs.** The G7 can no longer oversee the plethora of formal and informal bodies, with overlapping tasks. Furthermore, several bodies were created originally to deal with issues that no longer exist. An 'Independent Wise Persons Review Group' should therefore be asked to examine the situation and propose ways to streamline the operations of these bodies, possibly recommending that some be disbanded.

2. **Strengthening the institutional structure of the IMF.** The Fund will undoubtedly continue to play a central role. It has been able to reinvent itself several times – after the end of the Bretton Woods system, for example, and after the Asian crisis. It now needs to go through a new phase of re-engineering. This Report proposes that the role of the Executive Board should be upgraded and the representation of the EU should be rationalized.

   The role of the Executive Board has been slowly undermined by activities elsewhere, including those of the G7. Furthermore, the freedom of action of Executive Directors has declined as a result of new information technologies. One solution is for the senior official dealing with Fund issues in a country's capital to serve as that country's Executive Director. Furthermore, the composition of the Board should be brought into better alignment with the relative economic importance of individual IMF members. The advent of the euro presents an opportunity to rationalize the situation. The aim ought to be to consolidate, perhaps in steps, the representation of the EU into two constituencies: one for the members of the euro area and one for the rest of the EU countries.[1]

3. **Creating a new agenda-setting body for the international financial system.** The G7 does not include some of the key players, but the G20, with 40 ministers and central bank governors around its table, is too large to be effective. A new body, provisionally described as the Council for International Financial and Economic Cooperation (CIFEC), should serve as the agenda-setting body, providing strategic direction for the functioning and development of the international financial system and exercising informal oversight over the various multilateral institutions and forums involved in international economic cooperation. Effectiveness requires that it have few members but include all of the systemically important countries; legitimacy and representativeness require that it be responsive to the needs and concerns of the whole international community. It is suggested that the CIFEC have no more than 15 member countries, represented by their finance ministers. The Secretary General of the UN, the Managing Director of the IMF, the President of the World Bank, and the Director General of the WTO would be invited to its meetings.

Introduction

This Report is a contribution to the debate on the governance of the changing international monetary and financial system. It does not deal with trade issues, focusing instead on monetary and financial cooperation. Trade, of course, is central to world prosperity. The issues raised by cooperation in trade are, however, largely distinct from those raised by cooperation in managing the macroeconomy. Another feature of this Report is that it deals chiefly with process, not substance. It does not aim at providing a reform agenda for each and every international institution in the monetary and financial domain. Instead, the Report should be seen as an attempt to update the current, mostly informal processes for world economic and financial governance.[2] Good outcomes require good processes, and as this Report goes on to argue, good processes need, to the greatest extent possible, to combine effectiveness with legitimacy, representativeness and accountability.

It is commonplace to say, in the words of Bob Dylan, 'the times they are a-changin' and we believe that the time has come to move forward the debate on global political relations that should underpin a changing international monetary and financial system. The emergence of truly global markets makes cooperation both more urgent and more complex. The disastrous effects of financial turmoil on economies around the world have been seen repeatedly over the past 10 years. The economic and the geo-political landscapes have changed radically over the last 15 years as new economic powerhouses have emerged and old political rivalries have receded. Yet the formal institutions through which countries work together on these issues are those established in San Francisco (the UN system) and Bretton Woods (the International Monetary Fund and the World Bank) in the 1940s. The informal structure that gives much of the direction to crisis response and systemic reform (the G7 Summits of heads of state or government, the meetings of G5/7 ministers and governors and the meetings of 'sherpas' and deputies) dates back to the 1970s. Important new bodies were created in the late 1990s (the International Monetary and Financial Committee of the IMF, the G20 and the Financial Stability Forum), but more should be done to meet the demands of today's world and create a structure that is able to adapt to changing requirements in the future. We see a need for more coherence and a sounder basis for legitimacy if the bodies to which the world looks for cooperation among governments are going to be effective. We do not come down on the side of demolition and reconstruction, but favour an accelerated evolution. Our hope is that we succeed in providing a bit of the force of ideas needed to overcome institutional inertia and move forward.

Chapter 1 documents the evolution of the international monetary and financial system, its successes and shortcomings, and how it has adapted to changing circumstances. We then turn to how cooperation can be improved. To begin,

Chapter 2 proposes a number of principles that cooperation ought to meet in order to fulfil reasonable expectations. The following three chapters look at particular features of the international system. Chapter 3 examines the relationship between creditors and debtors, and the role of the major formal and informal international financial institutions. Its main conclusion is that the G7's ability to shape the agenda for debtor and creditor cooperation, including via the IMF, is on the wane. Chapter 4 reviews the evolution of the financial markets, and how they have been dealt with over recent years. It endorses the greater prominence that financial issues have gained in recent years and makes some proposals for strengthening the multilateral response in light of current and likely future challenges in a global financial system. Chapter 5 focuses on payment imbalances among key currency countries. It argues that the emergence of new players calls for the reorganization of economic cooperation in this area. Finally, Chapter 6 brings together the analysis to formulate a number of proposals.

Our study rests on a shared conviction that international economic cooperation is critically important. Indeed, we believe that in a time of an increasingly integrating global economy where the interactions are becoming even more complex, the case for cooperation is even stronger. That case is straightforward; it has been made long ago by Cooper (1968) and Hamada (1976). The need for cooperation stems from economic interdependence and is very general. When two or more countries affect each other, action by any one of them will have an effect on the others. Ignoring interdependence means that each country ignores the others' actions, and will fail to achieve its own objectives. Worse, if one country dislikes the implication for its own economy of others' action and tries to offset them, it may trigger counter-reactions that may leave everyone worse off. The losses incurred when each country optimizes while taking the actions of others as given are not always large. There is considerable research that points to only small gains from cooperation in fiscal stimulus, for example. The failure to cooperate has, however, sometimes been disastrous. A classic example is the use of tariffs. Raising tariffs to protect domestic producers inevitably hurts foreign producers, who will naturally ask for retaliatory tariffs. We have seen how this process destroyed world trade in the 1930s, and this is why GATT was created. The same goes for competitive devaluations, and this is why the IMF was set up.

In practice, things are more complicated, as usual. Cooperation does not come for free and its costs – economic or political – may outweigh its gains. For example, in Chapter 1, we note that the political costs of subjecting a country's fiscal policy to international cooperation are usually so large that we hardly ever see it happening. Coordination may also be harmful. One reason is that governments do not just deal with each other, they also face their own domestic partners, such as trade unions and other organized interest groups. Rogoff (1985) has shown that when governments cooperate with one another, they may invite retaliation from their domestic constituents, which may make the outcome worse than in the absence of international cooperation. Another problem arises when policy-makers have wrong ideas about how their economies work. In that case, Frankel and Rockett (1988) have shown that cooperation may actually hurt everyone. More cases of harmful cooperation can be adduced. In the end, however, it is generally true that some cooperation is better than none, and the right kind of cooperation can make a tremendous contribution to economic well being in today's world of global markets.

So far, we have not been precise at all about the meanings of international economic cooperation. In a widely cited paper, Wallich (1984) distinguishes between four forms of international collaboration:

> 'Coordination, harmonization, cooperation, consultation': these, in descending order, are the terms by which nations recognize – sometimes reluctantly, that they are not alone in the world. … 'Cooperation' falls well short of 'coordination' a concept which implies a significant modification of national policies in recognition of international economic interdependence. It falls short also of 'harmonization,' a polite term indicating a somewhat greater reluctance to limit one's freedom of action. But 'cooperation' is more than 'consultation,' which means little more than that other interested parties will be kept informed.

For Wallich, cooperation encompasses a wide range of activities. At one end, it includes efforts to produce consensus on objectives, like those often reflected in G7 communiqués, without firm operational commitments by the governments involved. At the other end, it includes formal decision-making of the sort that occurs in the Executive Board of the IMF. Furthermore, Wallich's taxonomy does not distinguish between various forms of policy coordination. At times, governments have chosen to pursue a common objective; at other times, they have been obliged to do so, because of the nature of the problem they face. It is also important to distinguish between cases in which they can pursue a common objective by different methods and cases in which they must pursue it by adopting the same methods.

These distinctions are illustrated by two well-known cases, reviewed in Chapter 1: the Bonn Summit of 1978 and the Louvre Agreement of 1987. In Bonn, the G7 governments agreed on the need to stimulate global economic growth and reduce unemployment. To that end, however, each government undertook to adopt measures reflecting its own domestic situation. At the Louvre meeting, the same governments agreed on the need to stabilize dollar exchange rates and adopted a common strategy involving intervention on foreign exchange markets. The difference between the two cases reflects in part the difference between the problems involved. When one country seeks to raise economic growth, it does not necessarily constrain the ability of other countries to pursue that same objective. In fact, it may help them do so. The exchange rate between two currencies, by contrast, is a shared variable; a depreciation of one currency necessarily implies an appreciation of another currency. Similarly, no country can run a current-account surplus unless some other country runs a current-account deficit. There is an adding-up constraint.

The Bonn Summit and the Louvre Agreement are often seen as examples of effective cooperation, and yet they were not fully followed through. Circumstances changed, and so did the incentives to implement what had been agreed upon. There was no further attempt at adapting the agreements and national interests prevailed. That it is hard to identify better examples of G7 cooperation should serve as a sobering reminder of the limits of international cooperation.

Finally, Wallich's taxonomy ranks coordination ahead of harmonization in the severity of the constraints it imposes on national governments. Yet some of the issues discussed in Chapter 4, involving the regulation of the financial sector, accounting standards, and corporate governance, may impose tighter constraints on national autonomy than those imposed by the need for policy coordination in other policy domains. When financial institutions and corporations compete keenly in global markets, there is the risk of a race to the bottom. Each government may be tempted to reduce or relax its regulations to favour its own nationals. It is thus necessary for governments to adopt agreed standards or rules, and the need for harmonization may limit national autonomy more strictly than the need for coordination in macroeconomic matters.

In this Report, the term 'cooperation' is used generically to denote the various efforts of government to collaborate in the management of their affairs and the governance of the global economy. The reader will have little difficulty, however, in identifying instances involving coordination, harmonization, and cooperation as Wallich defined them.

Another important distinction concerns the way coordination is achieved. International institutions are in charge of formal coordination. The IMF, for instance, was created to ensure cooperation in dealing with exchange rates and balance-of-payments adjustments, as discussed in Chapter 5. It was established by an explicit agreement that describes in detail its decision-making process and *modus operandi* as well as the responsibilities of its members. The IMF takes formal decisions, although they are not always followed. The G7, in contrast, only exists *de facto*. It freely develops its own rules and does not have any mandate from outside its restricted membership. The G7 does not make decisions, it only expresses the views or intentions of its members, but these usually lead to action because of the importance that its members attach to ongoing cooperation with their G7 partners.

In practice, as we know, international economic cooperation is carried through a very large number of intergovernmental bodies, some formal, some informal. Some of these bodies have a well-defined task, for example the IMF and the WTO; others define their tasks as they go, for example the G7, G10, etc. Some bodies were set up for a particular purpose which has since disappeared, and yet they have recreated themselves as is the case of the OECD. Chapter 1 presents the scene.

As already noted, a first feature of today's arrangements is that most formal institutions were created in the immediate postwar period. Back then, there were fewer countries, most of which were operating behind high trade barriers and tight capital controls. Globalization was a distant memory of the pre-1914 world. It is, therefore, natural to ask whether the institutions, and the principles that underpin them, are still compatible with current conditions. Have they also managed to adapt their institutional cultures? If we were given a clean slate today, would we reproduce what we have?

A second feature of the current situation is the proliferation of ad hoc informal groupings that seek either to influence the international institutions or work out their own agreements. The most influential of them is the G7. Its creation reflected dissatisfaction with formal international institutions, either because decision-making there is slow and inefficient, or because their original mandates do not allow them to deal with new important issues, or both. For example, the IMF and the World Bank were not well equipped to deal with the indebtedness of the poorest countries; it took a G7 intervention to launch the HIPC initiative. Other informal structures bring together like-minded countries to agree among themselves – i.e. outside the existing formal institutions – on issues of common interest. This has gone furthest with matters pertaining to financial regulation and supervision, with the Basel agreements and the creation of the Financial Stability Forum. Interestingly, these informal but official initiatives involve professional organizations like IOSCO, IAIS and IASB.[3]

In a way, the G7 filled a void, the need for a source of world economic authority. Since a formal authority would, however, have been politically unthinkable when the G7 was established in the 1970s, not even when the G7 developed in the 1980s, the initiative had to be taken informally by the most economically powerful countries of the time. The initiative irked many countries, in both the developed and developing world. Many years later at the end of the 1990s the G7 helped to establish the G20 in an attempt to enlist some important developed and emerging market countries. Another G20, this time bringing together developing countries exclusively, emerged at the Cancun meeting of the WTO to press for more sweeping trade policy concessions from the industrial countries.

The G7's main justification is that it is effective at promoting international economic cooperation. Yet its effectiveness is now declining, partly because its legitimacy is increasingly questioned as new players emerge. The G7 is most visibly active through the annual Summit meetings of the heads of state or government. The evolution of these meetings into an increasingly political body whose agenda keeps expanding (it now deals with trade, the environment, HIV/AIDS, nuclear proliferation, terrorism and more) may in part explain the Summits' declining importance for economic and financial issues. The widening of its agenda further challenges its legitimacy because it now deals extensively with issues of major concern to many other countries. Increasingly, the value of these Summits has been questioned – both objectively in terms of the value of their output and in contrast with the expectations they raise. Less visible, and more productive, are the meetings of G7 finance ministers and central bank governors (and those of their deputies). These meetings do not deal only with 'internal' issues, but they also align national positions on 'external' issues such as emerging-market crisis prevention and crisis management, other matters before the IMF, and development issues.

A third feature is renewed interest in regionalism.[4] The postwar overriding principle was multilateralism, and global institutions fervently defend it, with much justification. The disastrous experience with bilateralism during the inter-war period serves as an important reminder of how quickly the international order can unravel, and how disastrous the consequences can be. On the other hand, regionalism is not necessarily taking us halfway toward bilateralism. Countries that share many common features because of history, geography and stage of development, may make a positive contribution to multilateral liberalization by moving ahead together. This is, after all, what Europe has achieved, with no clear adverse effect on the multilateral order. Regional development banks seem to play a useful role. Other regional arrangements, like Mercosur, NAFTA and the Chiang Mai initiative have received positive, if cautious, support from the multilateral community.

Finally, we observe the emergence of an international civil society. As any civil society, it involves a myriad of organizations, big and small, with all sorts of agendas and modes of operation. They include thousands of NGOs, some of which (e.g. OXFAM) have achieved quasi-official status. It can also take the form of highly visible meetings (the World Economic Forum and its counterpoint, the World Social Forum) and even huge demonstrations that target official meetings (G7, WTO, IMF-World Bank).

These evolutions underlie our belief that the old institutions set up 60 years ago will not be able to deal with the emerging challenges of the world economy. The multiplication of initiatives and proposals, however, reveal the need to revamp some of the existing institutions and to devise an overarching framework. This is the main objective that we pursue in the present study.

1 Economic Cooperation since Bretton Woods: A Changing Agenda, New Players and Evolving Arrangements[5]

1.1 A new beginning

With war raging in Europe and Asia in 1944, representatives of 45 countries gathered in the safety of Bretton Woods, New Hampshire, to establish a postwar financial order. Their work was predicated on two shared premises:

- That the economic calamities of the inter-war period, which were seen to be to an important degree the result of failures in dealing with economic and financial interdependence, or even of governments engaging in mutually destructive policies, should never be allowed to happen again.
- That sovereign nations are ultimately responsible for the economic welfare of their citizens, that they therefore have an obligation to take action to carry out this responsibility and cannot relinquish powers that enable them to do so.

These premises and the tension between sovereign responsibility for economic outcomes and the interdependence of these outcomes across countries have endured and conditioned efforts at international cooperation for the 60 years since. Little else has remained the same, however. Yes, the IMF and World Bank, which were established by the Bretton Woods agreements, remain as the two institutional manifestations of the commitment of governments to cooperate in the monetary and financial domain. Neither institution played the role expected of it initially, however, and both have evolved continuously to adapt to new challenges. The Fund has rarely provided the deliberative and decision-making process that has shaped the financial order.

Direction has come through an alphanumeric panoply of bodies that have arisen from time to time in response to the demands of the day – G5, G7, G10, G20, etc. These demands have been to respond to immediate concerns and to pursue reforms in order to achieve better cooperation into the future. New groups have been formed as officials with the capacity to act have sought to work with others who could either strengthen action or could not be left aside without losing effectiveness. These bodies have often become obsolete, but have rarely been disbanded, sometimes adapting to new roles and sometimes just hanging on. The coming and going of key issues in the agenda, often following watershed events, contrast with the coming and staying of leading bodies dealing with financial issues, as highlighted in Table 1.1. The key groups in the story that follows are listed in Appendix 1.1.

Table 1.1
Economic
cooperation
since Bretton
Woods

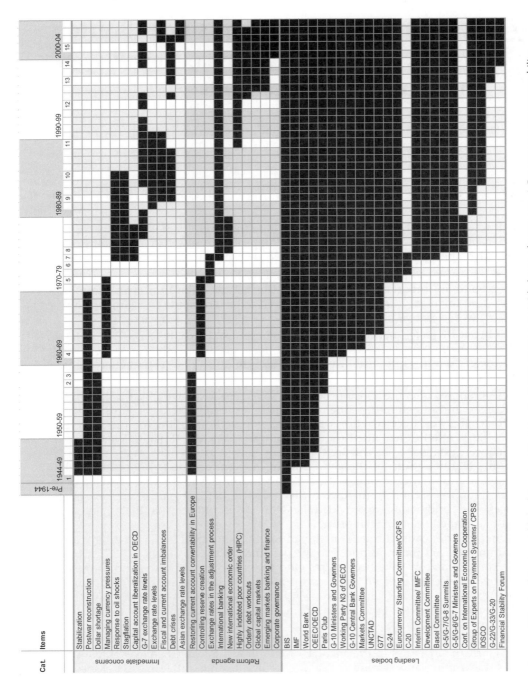

1 Bretton Woods conference. 2 Treaty of Rome established European Community. 3 First pressure on US balance of payments. 4 Current account convertability restored in Europe. 5 Dollar devaluation. 6 First oil shock. 7 Herstatt collapse. 8 Floating exchange rates regularized. 9 Latin American debt crisis. 10 Plaza-accord. 11 Fall of Berlin Wall. 12 Mexico: first crisis of the twenty-first century. 13 Asian financial crisis. 14 Euro established as a wholesale currency. 15 Enron collapse.

<u>1.2</u>   Bretton Woods: the vision and the reality

A consensus that governments were responsible for overall economic performance was new in the 1940s. Marxist thinking – that the state could and should radically restructure society in order to create an economic system that would not be prone to unemployment and poverty – had a strong following and was represented officially by the Soviet Union delegation at Bretton Woods, although it did not play an active role. More powerful was the view that had gained ground in the 1930s and was articulated most prominently by John Maynard Keynes, who did play an active role at Bretton Woods – that governments of countries with capitalist economies could and should respond effectively to unemployment and poverty. This principle of government responsibility for economic outcomes in market economies – the rejection of laissez-faire – was established in the immediate postwar period as the lodestar of economic policy in the United Kingdom by the implementation of the Beveridge Plan, in France by the establishment of the Commissariat du Plan, in West Germany by the introduction of the Social Market Economy of Ludwig Erhard and in the United States by the Employment Act of 1946. The Bretton Woods institutions internationalized the principle.

The Bretton Woods vision (very much a US vision tempered by British wisdom) was that, within a year or so, governments would fix exchange rates and remove restrictions on current account transactions. The Fund and its rules would ensure temporary financing and timely adjustment of balance-of-payments deficits, which would arise mainly from current account imbalances since capital accounts would be closely controlled. The World Bank would ensure the long-term financing of reconstruction in war-ravaged Europe, Japan and China, and (on the insistence of Latin Americans at Bretton Woods) it would foster development in non-industrial countries.

In the event, it proved much more difficult to restore orderly monetary arrangements and to undertake reconstruction. A communist world stretching from the Elbe River in Germany to the 38th parallel in Korea rejected cooperation and challenged the rest of the world with its radically different approach to the organization of economic affairs. It took economic reforms, the US Marshall Plan and the establishment of the OEEC with the role of fostering cooperation among Western European members to get Western Europe firmly on the road to recovery. Even so, macroeconomic imbalances remained huge for years as European countries struggled to acquire dollars. It was not until late 1958 that most European countries undertook to freely convert currency acquired through current account transactions, and not until 1964 that Japan did. These steps were made possible by the growing official reserves of dollars of these countries, which were supplied by a deficit in the US balance of payments on official settlements. Convertibility had no more than been established, when Robert Triffin[6] began calling attention to the emerging strains of the *de facto* dollar reserve standard, which linked the global supply of reserves to US balance-of-payments deficits – strains that became evident in the gold market in 1960 when the election of President Kennedy triggered sales of dollars for gold. Over the ensuing decade, the focus of international monetary discussion was on these strains: how to manage them in the short run and how to reform the system so as to more durably alleviate them over the longer run.

Meanwhile, decolonization was bringing many new participants into the community of nations with needs that were radically different from most of the established members. These needs began to get the attention of the World Bank relatively quickly in keeping with the expanded mandate for the Bank that the Latin Americans had asked for at Bretton Woods. The Bank's reconstruction job was nearing completion and its capacity to support development in poorer countries was broadened by the establishment of the International Development Association (IDA) in 1960, which could make loans that were concessionary and did not expose the parent bank to loss. The needs of these new member countries only moved to the centre of attention in the IMF in the 1970s although a number of developing countries drew on the IMF in the 1960s.

1.3 Fixed exchange rates under pressure: *ad hoc* responses drive institutional change

Balance-of-payments pressures on the United States and the inauguration of President Kennedy in January 1961, which brought a new activist economic policy team to Washington, made 1961 a watershed year in financial diplomacy. The first major undertaking to deal with a potential US need for balance-of-payments financing was the establishment in that year of the General Arrangements to Borrowb (GAB) and of the G10 finance ministers and central bank governors, whose 11 member countries (including Switzerland, which made parallel commitments outside the Fund) were those that had the financial capacity to augment IMF liquidity in the event of a large drawing in the Fund. At roughly the same time, the Organization for European Economic Cooperation (OEEC), having completed its mission to orchestrate European reconstruction, was transformed into the Organization for Economic Cooperation and Development (OECD) with membership extended to the United States and Canada and soon to other industrial countries outside Europe. Working Party 3 (WP-3) of the OECD Economic Policy Committee, comprised of deputy-level finance ministry and central bank officials, was established with a restricted membership of countries essentially the same as the G10. It took on the role of surveillance over participating countries, including passing judgement on the policies of countries whose drawing on the Fund might involve use of GAB resources, much to the distress of non-G10 members of the IMF Executive Board. 1961 also saw the establishment of the London gold pool by eight countries to undertake transactions in the gold market in order to stabilize gold prices, and the beginnings of the swap network among central banks and the Bank for International Settlements (BIS) to expand resources available to counter short-run exchange market pressures. This network developed over the 1960s into a substantial system of reciprocal financing support and led to the establishment of monthly meetings of the G10 central bank governors at the BIS in Basel. Thus, the BIS, which narrowly escaped dissolution at the end of World War II when the Fund was established, found a place in the emerging structure of international financial cooperation.

The US balance of payments remained a preoccupation as fears of a renewed balance-of-payments outflow constrained the US policy response to a slow recovery from the 1960 recession. President Kennedy's economic team chafed under this constraint. Growth in Europe surged onward, increasing self-confidence, bringing inflation concerns to the fore and by 1963 leading to monetary policy tightening that drew funds from the United States to Europe. The US government focused intensely on the balance of payments, seeking ways to squeeze here and there on defence expenditures abroad and, in 1963, introducing an interest equalization tax, the first of an increasingly comprehensive set of controls on capital outflows deployed by the US authorities over the decade. The debate over what economic policy failures lay behind the balance-of-payments pressures raged in WP-3.[7] Very little attention was given, however, to the possibility that exchange rate changes should be part of the adjustment process. In a 1964 report, the deputies of the G10 identified a long list of policies (including trade restrictive measures!) that might be used to correct sustained payments imbalances, emphasizing the obligation to maintain stable exchange rates.

Issues of reserve asset creation became the next focus of study within the G10. The French, under President de Gaulle, were especially critical of a system that they saw as asymmetrical in allowing the United States to escape the disciplines to which others were subjected and lacking an orderly process for providing international reserves. This view led to a French proposal for the creation of a 'collective reserve asset' linked to gold. This asset was to be created and used by the G10 outside the IMF. With the United States distinctly unenthusiastic, but with a gathering interest in reform, the G10 created a Study Group on the Creation of Reserve Assets chaired by Rinaldo Ossola in 1964, which led eventually to the creation of the Special Drawing Right (SDR) within the IMF and without French participation. Non-government economists, led by Fritz Machup, were stimulated by official studies of reform to organize themselves into the Bellagio group, which prepared a report in June 1964. The academics echoed official concern about the reserve creation mechanism, but they also suggested that exchange rates ought to be adjusted more frequently, something that was still unthinkable in official circles. During the long gestation period of the SDR, the issue of international liquidity creation was looked at in a number of forums, including in a series of joint meetings of the Executive Board of the Fund and the deputies of the G10.

In the second half of the 1960s, while systemic discussions remained focused on the provision of international liquidity, immediate pressures arose against European currencies, and especially the UK pound, which was in the process of adjusting to the erosion of its residual reserve currency status. In 1964, an impromptu $3 billion international credit package was arranged for the United Kingdom, and the GAB was activated for the first time in conjunction with a $1 billion drawing on the Fund. Crises erupted again in 1965 and 1966-7, however, culminating in a sterling devaluation from $2.80 to $2.40. After another bout of pressure in 1968, sterling recovered, but the French franc came under intense pressure. Activation of the swap network and an IMF drawing backed by the GAB bought time, but the pressure continued. At a G10 ministers meeting in Bonn in November, revaluation of the German mark and devaluation of the French franc were heatedly discussed, but were in the end rejected by the countries concerned. The following August, however, after Georges Pompidou had replaced Charles de Gaulle as President of France, the franc was devalued by 11.1% without consultation and in the face of relatively mild pressure in the markets. Two months later, following an election in Germany, the mark was revalued by 9.3%. Exchange rate adjustment was no longer unthinkable, at least when elections were not impending.

From 1969 onward, until US President Richard Nixon's announcement of the suspension of gold convertibility, a 10% import surcharge and wage and price controls on 15 August 1971, the untenable value of the dollar became increasingly evident, although there was little agreement on the underlying reasons for this. Nixon blamed speculators and most subsequent writers blame President Johnson's simultaneous pursuit of his 'Great Society' and the Vietnam War. But while budget deficits and inflation generated by the war and expanded social programmes were substantial in the 1965-9 period, this was a time of respite for the dollar as monetary restraint accompanied fiscal expansion. The pressure only became intense in 1971 after interest rates had come down in the recession of 1970 and were kept down by the Federal Reserve.

While the focus of attention of policy-makers was on the problem of reserve provision, which was addressed by the creation of the SDR through amendment of the IMF articles in 1969, and on the question of which country should change monetary or fiscal policy when exchange rate pressures arose, the fatal flaw in the Bretton Woods system proved to be the failure to accept a role for exchange rate changes in the adjustment process, a point made by Solomon.[8] In the light of subsequent trends, it is fair to say that the dollar was fundamentally overvalued against the Japanese yen, the German mark and some other European currencies. The exchange rates that had been set in the early postwar period supported reconstruction in Europe and Japan by allowing for increasing penetration of the slower-growing US market, as US exports to these countries were stimulated by their rapid domestic demand growth. As the reconstruction phase came to an end, the price competitiveness that the United States could once concede inevitably weighed increasingly heavily on US trade performance. Inflation differentials were no longer working in the direction of achieving real exchange rate appreciation for Germany and not working strongly for Japan. In addition, the era of dollar shortage had long passed.

1.4   A new monetary system takes shape

1.4.1   Efforts to re-establish fixed exchange rates fail

Nixon's unilateral action in August 1971 provided a powerful stimulus to multilateral consultation and a proliferation of bodies over the ensuing five years. The immediate focus was on an exchange rate realignment, which was the objective of Nixon's closing of the gold window and temporary import surcharge. The G10 and its deputies met multiple times to debate changes in exchange rates and the price of gold, with deputies putting on their WP-3 hats to examine the size of the underlying imbalances that should be the target of the adjustment. The developing countries, which were excluded from G10 deliberations, found a voice in UNCTAD Secretary General Perez-Guerrero, who expressed concern that poor countries would lose out from a higher gold price since their gold holdings were small. With the French presenting the strongest opposition to a revaluation of their currency and insisting that any adjustment of the dollar take the form of an increase in the dollar price of gold, a *de facto* G2 was born. Nixon and Pompidou met on 13–14 December 1971 in the Azores and agreed on an increase of the gold price from $35 to $38. Two days later there was another meeting of the G10 deputies with the Executive Directors of the Fund where the non-G10 representatives opposed greater exchange rate flexibility, a higher gold price and the taking of such decisions in the restricted setting of the G10. Nevertheless, the following day, the G10 met at the Smithsonian Institution in Washington, and on 18 December the Smithsonian Agreement to realign currencies, raise the dollar price of gold and set wider fluctuation bands was announced in its communiqué. The non-G10 countries had no choice but to accept this *fait accompli*.

US Treasury Undersecretary for Monetary Affairs, Paul Volcker, was a Smithsonian participant who reportedly said at the time that the exchange rate adjustment was not large enough.[9] The new parities came under pressure within six months. By February 1973, market pressures were intense and Volcker undertook a whirlwind trip to consult bilaterally with officials in six countries before US Treasury Secretary George Shultz announced a further 10% dollar devaluation. Pressures on the dollar resumed almost immediately, forcing others to buy dollars in unprecedented amounts. The Europeans agreed among themselves to a joint float against the dollar. This was announced on 10 March 1973, together with the intention of the United States to scrap its capital controls the following year. The announcement was made at a meeting of ministers and governors of the G10 plus other EU members, a constellation that was not seen again. The yen was also set free from its fixed limits. The era of floating exchange rates among the major currencies had commenced.

1.4.2 A comprehensive reform also fails but leaves an institutional legacy

In addition to its immediate actions, the G10 Smithsonian meeting called for the establishment of a Committee of Twenty Members of the IMF Board of Governors (ministers or governors) on Reform of the International Monetary System, which was established in the summer of 1972 and leisurely began to consider the unresolved systemic issues. Unlike the G10, which had been the main centre for deliberation on systemic issues in the previous decade, the C-20 had one member for each IMF Executive Board seat and hence representation from all parts of the world. With the abandonment of fixed parities for exchange rates in the face of market pressure in March 1973, the work of the C-20 became urgent. By the end of 1973 a new system of 'fixed but adjustable' exchange rates was taking shape, but the Arab oil boycott in October, followed by a quadrupling of the oil price by OPEC, created such economic and financial disarray that the effort was abandoned in favour of continued floating and an 'evolutionary approach to reform'.

The C-20 nevertheless left an institutional legacy. The first was its recommendation, quickly adopted by the IMF governors, to create an Interim Committee of Governors with a representative from each Executive Board seat to deal with both immediate and systemic reform issues. This body met twice a year until 1999 when it was reconstituted as the International Monetary and Financial Committee (IMFC). The C-20 also sowed the seeds of the G7 finance ministers and central bank governors when the finance ministers of the United States, France, Germany and the United Kingdom met separately in the library of the White House in March 1973. This group, which soon grew to five members with the inclusion of Japan and brought in central bank governors, became known as the Library Group or the G5. For a number of years its meetings remained discreet and without communiqués.

The abandonment of the C-20 exercise left a number of issues up in the air, including the status of gold and the regularization of floating, which were especially acute issues between the United States and France. Franco-American negotiations took place bilaterally and in G5 meetings into the fall of 1975. A G5 agreement on gold was ratified by the G10 and by the Interim Committee on 31 August, marking the first occasion on which the more restricted group visibly set the course for the global system. The United States and France were not yet reconciled on the exchange rate question, however. The French finance minister at the Library Meeting, Valery Giscard d'Estaing, had meanwhile become President of the Republic and West German finance minister Helmut Schmidt had become Chancellor of the Federal Republic. These two relished monetary issues, and over the next several years pulled up to the level of heads of states and governments issues that had previously been dealt with by finance ministers. Giscard convened a G5 Summit at Rambouillet to pursue a resolution of the unresolved questions in November 1975, at which the last pieces of US–French reconciliation were worked out, paving the way for the second amendment of the IMF Articles to be agreed at an Interim Committee meeting in Jamaica in January 1976. The amendment had the effect of legalizing the move to floating exchange rates and thus put the last nail in the coffin of the postwar exchange-rate regime.[10]

1.5   Impoverished management of a new system

By this time, virtually all of the monetary bodies that played prominent roles through the late 1990s were in place, although the G5 finance ministers and central bank governors became a G7, with the Managing Director of the IMF and the President of the European Central Bank also joining parts of meetings, and the G7 Summits eventually became the G8 with the inclusion of Russia.

The core monetary agenda brought forward from the dissolution of the fixed exchange rate system was two fold: systemic issues of reform, generally approached in an incremental way, and issues of current policies to bring about better economic performance globally. In addition, two structural developments of the 1960s brought new sets of issues into the international financial arena.

1.5.1   Two new institutional realities of the 1970s: new countries and global commercial banks

Between the Bretton Woods conference and the mid-1970s, decolonization greatly expanded the number of sovereign countries. The newly decolonized countries considered themselves marginalized, both in terms of economic performance and in terms of their role in the management of the international financial system. During the 1960s, the developing countries formed their own caucus, the G77, and they used their domination of the UN General Assembly to create UNCTAD as a forum in which to address their concerns. The major financial countries that were members of the G5, G7 and G10 engaged the G77 diplomatically and were somewhat responsive with respect to aid efforts and special trade arrangements, but they resisted any dilution of their control over financial matters. The North/South dialogue became more intense when two developments seemed to shift economic power to the developing world – OPEC's successful drastic increase in oil prices and a temporary increase of other commodity prices. From 1975 to 1979, the Conference on International Economic Cooperation (CIEC) filled Paris hotels with officials engaged in North/South dialogue, with OPEC members lending their support to the South. Little came of these discussions, and most of that which was agreed, like a Common Fund for Commodities and a pledge by the North to provide 0.7% of GDP in development aid, was never followed through. North/South issues were topics of the annual G7 Summits that followed Rambouillet, but finance ministries and central banks stayed on the margins of these discussions. They would take up a central role after the Latin American debt crisis broke out in 1982.

The second development was the growth of the Eurodollar market as a vehicle for global commercial banking, which got a strong boost in the 1960s when US and UK capital controls and other regulatory distortions enabled banks in London to conduct an international business in dollars on more favourable terms than was possible either in New York in dollars or in London in sterling. By the early 1970s, Eurodollar banking in London was at the frontier of finance and growing rapidly. Dollar-based banking in London received a further boost from the placement of huge OPEC receipts beginning in 1974, even though the removal of US measures directed at reducing capital outflows created a more unified dollar market that same year.

As something different and increasingly substantial, the Eurodollar had long been the subject of much alarmist attention and some careful analysis. It was, however, the failure of Bank Herstatt in 1974, and the nearly disastrous way in which it was handled,[11] which showed the need for a coordinated response by the

authorities to the risks forming in international markets. A single national authority could not deal with the safety and soundness of internationally active banks
in isolation. The G10 central bank governors responded by creating the Basel
Committee of Bank Supervisors, which has developed into a major force for establishing global bank regulatory standards, and the Eurocurrency Standing
Committee, which fostered convergence of understanding among central banks
concerning developments in the international banking and finance areas.
International banking issues have generally remained with the technical experts
of these groups, although from time-to-time concern among political leaders has
brought them into G7 Summits. For example, the process of developing minimum
capital standards for banks has gone forward in the Basel Committee with little
attention from more political circles until recently. As we shall see, financial systemic issues took on a much greater prominence from the mid-1990s, and the
original BIS-linked bodies have been elaborated and exposed to greater political
attention as the globalization of financial markets has demanded a coordinated
response to a range of regulatory issues.

1.5.2 The rise and fall of macroeconomic policy coordination

Following agreement on the second amendment of the IMF Articles of Agreement,
international monetary and financial discussions were focused for two decades on
the management of the new system (or 'non-system' as many preferred to call it).
There were a number of proposals for systemic change, some of which were even
discussed informally at G7 Summits, but there were no substantial *global* systemic
changes. (The creation of the EMS in 1979 was a *regional* systemic change of far-
reaching significance.) The main focus of multilateral discussion in the late 1970s
was on policy actions to improve economic performance in the wake of the collapse of fixed exchange rates, high oil prices, high inflation and general stagna-
tion. The United States gave a strong push to the coordination of fiscal policies
after President Jimmy Carter took office in 1977. The Carter economic team had
a strong commitment to multilateralism and a belief in macroeconomic stimulus.
These came together in the 'locomotive' theory, later revamped as the 'convoy'
theory of economic policy, which called for countries in current account surplus
to undertake expansionary fiscal policy. At the 1977 G7 Summit in London, coordinated action was discussed, but the communiqué only highlighted growth
objectives without specifying the means to achieve them. At the Bonn Summit in
1978, policy coordination reached its greatest level of ambition when a deal was
made between the United States, which agreed to lift domestic oil price controls
that were discouraging economization of oil use, and Japan and Germany, which
agreed to undertake specific fiscal expansion. This package continues to be debated, especially in Germany where it was widely seen as the cause of a pickup of
inflation in 1979. A good case can be made that it was a positive step at the time
but was overtaken by the second oil shock in 1979. This was the main impetus for
a revival of inflation in Germany, and it led the Carter administration to shelve
decontrol. Today, however, few would expect substantial results from the fiscal
actions of the sort agreed at Bonn, and there would be greater acceptance of mar-
ket-driven exchange rate adjustments if capital flows did not finance current
account imbalances.

From the beginning, Summit preparation was coordinated by officials who
came to be called 'sherpas', personal representatives of heads of state or government. In the run-up to Bonn, they drew on input from the informal bureau of the
OECD Economic Policy Committee (a group comprised of economics ministry
officials from the G7 countries headed by US Council of Economic Advisers

Chairman, Charlie Schultze). In addition, there were meetings of finance ministry 'sous-sherpas' who also gathered at the OECD in WP-3 along with officials from central banks and from the rest of the G10. Although the post-oil-shock environment of 1979 and the increasing recognition that the United States had a serious inflation problem meant that there was no repeat of the Bonn policy package, macroeconomic policy remained central to summit agendas and the EPC informal bureau continued to prepare a macroeconomic assessment for the Summit until 1981. Economics ministries were not a central part of the Summit process after that.

Since then, the Summit preparation process has been closely held by sherpas and sous-sherpas (from foreign ministries and trade ministries, as well as finance ministries). The focus of multilateral discussion after 1978 was very heavily on the United States where inflation, a current-account deficit, and a weak dollar in 1979-80 had given way to high interest rates, a large budget deficit, a strong dollar and an even larger current account deficit following the implementation of a determined anti-inflationary monetary policy by the Federal Reserve, then led by Paul Volcker, and the enacting of tax cuts proposed by the new US President, Ronald Reagan. The Reagan administration stressed the importance of each country's getting its own house in order and the importance of structural reforms over fiscal policy. This orientation found support, especially with Margaret Thatcher in the United Kingdom and Helmut Kohl in Germany, and international economic policy discussion from working level to the Summit eschewed demand management. With the departure from Summits of Schmidt and Giscard, who as ex-finance ministers had given the early Summits much of their hands-on economic policy focus, the annual gatherings of heads of state or government took on a broader, more political agenda, although political matters had never been entirely absent.

There were strong voices both within and outside of G7 circles who were vociferous in their concerns about the US policy mix of the early 1980s; the combination of tight money and loose fiscal policy produced an environment in which the dollar appreciated strongly. The rising dollar did not create a crisis within the G7 that required emergency meetings and immediate action as had been the case when exchange rates were fixed. The resulting high interest rates and US recession in 1981-2 did, however, bring to a head the financial problems of Latin American governments, which had become deeply indebted to international banks.

1.5.3 The Latin American debt crisis

The Mexican government announced that it could not meet the payments on its debts in August 1982, followed in short order by almost all other Latin American governments and some developing countries in other parts of the world. For the rest of the decade, the Latin American debt crisis was a principal preoccupation of international financial meetings. The response to the crisis brought the IMF and World Bank back into central roles as their lending conditionality and technical assistance combined with continued commercial bank lending kept countries, except Peru, from defaulting on their debts and bought time for banks to rebuild their damaged balance sheets. Collaborating closely with the Managing Director of the Fund, Jacques de Larosière, the G5 and subsequently G7 finance ministers and central bank governors played an active role in charting the policy course. The G7 finance deputies also began to acquire prominence because of their role in the process.

For several years, the debt strategy of the IMF, commercial banks and creditor country governments was to provide additional financing subject to IMF policy conditions in the expectation that the indebted countries could grow out of difficulty. The persistence of the debt problem finally brought finance officials, led by a new US Treasury Secretary, James Baker, to the recognition that indebted countries were not growing out of trouble. The Baker Plan, which called for new lending by banks and the international organizations, was discussed with the G5 ministers and governors and then presented to the Annual Meetings of the Bank and Fund in October 1985. This debt strategy was supported in subsequent Summits, but the reliance on voluntary lending proved a fatal weakness of the Baker Plan. It was again a new US Treasury Secretary, Nicholas Brady, who finally began the process of resolution by putting forward a plan that involved a reduction of debt burdens through restructuring of bank loans into what became known as Brady bonds. Brady put the plan forward in March 1989 after the Mexican finance minister threatened default,[12] and it was supported at the G7 Summit in Paris the following summer after discussion by the finance ministers and central bank governors.

1.5.4 Exchange rate fluctuations: enough is enough!

Even as the debt crisis continued to demand attention, the continued rise of the dollar in the mid 1980s began to concern a US administration that had rejected exchange market intervention, except immediately after an attempted assassination of President Reagan. New Treasury appointees at the beginning of Reagan's second term in 1985 brought less doctrinaire views to the US Treasury against a background of rising protectionist pressure from sectors squeezed by the strong dollar. In September, Secretary Baker convened the finance ministers and governors of the G5 and Canada at the Plaza Hotel in New York, where agreement was reached on policy statements and coordinated exchange market intervention to bring about an orderly decline in the dollar. This initiative was reaffirmed by the G7 Summit in Tokyo the following May. The dollar decline, which had actually begun six months before the Plaza agreement, continued until February 1987 when the finance ministers and central bank governors (now of the G7 with the inclusion of Italy, as well as Canada) met at the Louvre in Paris and signalled that, in their view, exchange rate adjustment had proceeded far enough. They also made new statements of policy intent. Fiscal policy actions promised by the United States and Germany were not implemented, however, and many observers of the Japanese economy have subsequently criticized the Japanese stimulus as having begun the bubble economy. Shortly thereafter, signs of disarray among the G7 were the apparent trigger for the global stock market collapse on 19 October 1987, which was followed by a steep further fall in the dollar. The G7 deputies met frequently in the following months and eventually achieved some success in stabilizing the dollar although the trend continued to be downward. Inconsistency between the policies of central banks, especially of the independent Federal Reserve and Bundesbank, which were focused on achieving and maintaining domestic price stability, and those of finance ministries, which sought exchange rate stability was at times evident to the market. Exchange market intervention was a weak instrument in the face of these inconsistencies, and there was little inclination to alter fiscal policies.

The objective of exchange rate stability declined in importance to the G7 over time as economies were slow to recover from recession in the early 1990s and with the change in US administration in January 1993. Europeans were becoming increasingly focused on the effort to convert the EMS into a system of truly fixed exchange rates as a precursor to monetary union, with a crisis in 1992 setting back UK and Swedish participation for the foreseeable future. The Clinton Treasury continued, except for a much-regretted statement by Secretary Bentsen in the early days of the administration, to favour dollar stability, and it initiated several coordinated intervention forays in the exchange markets in efforts to keep the dollar from depreciating. There was, however, no inclination to dissuade the Fed. from rewarding administration efforts at budget deficit reduction by maintaining low interest rates. The dollar decline continued until the spring of 1995, when the cumulative depreciation had become extreme. This time there was no dramatic conclave like the Plaza, but once the dollar had bounced from its low, a sustained appreciation was supported by coordinated intervention on a limited basis, an increasingly strong US economy and a new Treasury Secretary, Robert Rubin, whose simple, unvarying message was that a strong dollar was in the US interest. Since then, coordinated intervention has been infrequent and modest, although the Japanese ministry of finance has been unilaterally activist at times in selling dollars when the yen reached low levels again in 2000 and especially in buying dollars in unprecedented volume when the yen strengthened in 2003 and early 2004.

Although the limits of official tolerance have occasionally been reached, exchange rate swings that would have been unimaginable in the 1960s have become accepted. G7 Summits have devoted little attention to either exchange rates or macroeconomic policy coordination in recent years. G7 finance ministers and central bank governors communiqués are nevertheless closely parsed by market participants for signs of policy change. Recently, however, the major Asian authorities in addition to Japan, who are not represented in the G7, have been by far the most important official actors in exchange markets.

1.5.5 The 1990s: the transition of the former Soviet bloc and debt redux

Other issues came to dominate the international financial agenda in the 1990s. With movement toward economic and political reform in the Soviet bloc, followed by the dissolution of the bloc and eventually of the Soviet Union itself, the Western response to these developments became a critical issue. Whether to embrace governments that espoused market oriented reforms or to continue to treat the Soviet Union and subsequently Russia as a strategic adversary was the overarching question at first. G7 heads of state or government fairly quickly embraced the reform efforts, although some caution persisted on the political front within the first Bush administration. The initial manifestation of this embrace took place even before the fall of the Berlin Wall in the autumn of 1989. At the Paris Summit in July, a French proposal to create the European Bank for Reconstruction and Development was endorsed and the following year's Summit at Houston called upon the IMF, World Bank, OECD and embryonic EBRD to study the Soviet economy and make recommendations for reform.

The specifics of the Western response to the aspiration for reform in Central and Eastern Europe were much more contentious than the broad principles. They commanded the attention of G7 Summits, meetings of finance ministers and central bank governors, and deputies for a decade. The G7 deputies became hands-on managers of the Western response, dealing with the structure, location and staffing of the EBRD, treatment of bilateral official credits in the Paris Club, IMF and World Bank lending programmes and questions of the structure of reform. The United States became a much more enthusiastic supporter of the Russian government after the arrival of the Clinton administration. The new G7 deputy, Larry Summers, kept that group in the thick of things. A Summit initiative to place a 'Support Implementation Group' in Moscow to oversee the follow-through on commitments at Tokyo in 1993 was brought firmly under the control of finance ministries until it was allowed to lapse a few years later.

Transition economies continued to receive strong political attention from G7 Summits through the decade. Soviet Premier Gorbachev had first been invited to sit in on part of a Summit by the British host, John Major, in London in 1991, and Russian leaders were given increasingly prominent roles in Summits until Boris Yeltsin was made an official member of the G8 at Birmingham in 1998. Summits were, however, less and less focused on economic and financial matters and took place largely without finance ministers.

The leaders of the 1990s did not have the enthusiasm for financial issues that President Giscard d'Estaing and Chancellor Schmidt had brought to their first Summit in 1975. The G7 finance ministries, however, continued to coordinate economic and financial policies towards the former communist countries of Europe. Administration of assistance to Russia was the centre of attention up to and through its default in 1998. The policy orientation subsequently shifted away from large-scale assistance. With the EU increasingly active in accession negotiations with many of the former East-bloc countries and with Russia in a strong balance-of-payments position owing to strong oil markets, the attention of the G7 shifted elsewhere.

Another focus of G7 attention in the 1990s was international indebtedness. This had two aspects. One was the response to the series of financial crises that struck emerging markets beginning with Mexico in December 1994. Participants have different recollections of the extent of consultation among G7 finance ministry and central bank officials as the United States and the IMF prepared loan packages for Mexico. US officials recall extended conversations with G7 counterparts. Others recall being taken by surprise by the size of the IMF support package. A fair view is that there was an effort to consult, but it fell short under time pressures and that the United States was, in any event, firmly committed from the beginning to large-scale support on an accelerated timetable. Once the immediate support had been arranged, however, the US Treasury took the lead through the G7 in addressing a number of weaknesses in the international financial system that were highlighted by the Mexican crisis. These included:

- Lack of transparency concerning government financial positions.
- The need for stronger IMF surveillance.
- The appropriate size of IMF programmes and hence of IMF resources, and the conditionality that ought to apply in the event of a sovereign liquidity crisis.
- The need to strengthen banking systems in emerging markets.
- The need for new workout mechanisms in a world where widely held bonds were rapidly replacing more closely held bank loans in sovereign finance.
- The need to contain moral hazard – that is, the incentives of sovereign borrowers to take on excessive debt and for lenders to provide it when they expect a 'bailout' in the event of a crisis.

The Mexican crisis gave focus to calls for reform of the 'international financial architecture' from Summit participants and their foreign affairs advisers, some of whom dreamed of a new Bretton Woods. The gradualist-minded finance officials fed incremental reforms aimed at the identified problems to the Summits in Halifax in 1995 and Lyon in 1996. The G10 deputies were called upon to study the issues of sovereign debt workouts. They produced proposals that received a cold reception from market participants at the time but were revived and formed the basis for recent initiatives to introduce collective action clauses and related measures to facilitate sovereign debt workouts. Some loosening up of the group structure took place when the G10 deputies also informally invited officials from emerging markets to join in discussions of means to strengthen banking systems. Other industrial countries and some emerging markets were invited to join in the New Arrangements to Borrow (NAB), which supplemented the GAB resources available to the Fund, but the scope for new consultation arrangements proved limited because new lenders were denied membership in the G10 by some of its European members (see Table 1.2).

Table 1.2 Participants in IMF borrowing arrangements[13] (by size of contribution)

GAB, NAB and G10 members	NAB participant only	GAB associate and NAB participant
United States	Australia	Saudi Arabia
Germany (central bank)	Spain	
Japan	Austria	
France	Denmark	
United Kingdom	Kuwait	
Italy	Chile (central bank)	
Switzerland (central bank)	Finland	
Canada	Hong Kong	
Netherlands	Korea	
Belgium	Luxembourg	
Sweden (central bank)	Malaysia	
	Norway	
	Singapore	
	Thailand	

The Asian debt crisis in 1997 demanded emergency coordination. The G7 finance ministers and central bank governors provided the principal venue, and this group played a crucial role in restraining the withdrawal of bank funds from Korea in the last weeks of December 1997. The crisis also gave a new impetus to financial reforms, as have several sovereign debt crises since. The Asian crisis produced a rare public conflict among G7 finance officials when Japan backed the establishment of an Asian Monetary Fund, which the others (most publicly the United States) opposed because of the threat that it posed to the authority of the IMF.

The indebtedness of the poorest countries also became a central concern within the G7. The need for debt reduction for the highly indebted poorest countries (HIPC) was put on the agenda by the British at the Houston Summit in 1990. It was not until the Naples Summit in 1994 that terms for bilateral official debt reduction were agreed, however. By this time, it was evident that bilateral debt reduction would not be enough to bring debt to manageable levels; multilateral debts would have to be reduced. The IMF and World Bank resisted because they wished to maintain the principle that they were always repaid, and they did not want the write-down to come from 'their resources'. The question of how to pay for debt reduction was especially contentious, but the G7 finance ministries fashioned an agreement that was endorsed by the Lyon Summit in 1996. The agreement had some loose ends and other creditors needed to be brought on board. The road proved difficult, and the HIPC initiative has required sustained attention from the G7 to ensure its implementation and get results.

IMF and World Bank policies toward the poorest countries are where differences between the G7 and others have often been most sharp. Since the resources to support these institutions come largely from the G7, they have economic power behind their voting shares. Hence, it is inevitable that they will have dominant voices. It is, however, the poorest countries that stand to benefit or not, and that are asked to meet conditionality. The interests of middle-income countries are also involved. For example, the middle-income countries see the World Bank profits devoted to HIPC debt reduction or to IDA as coming from the interest spreads they pay on their loans from the Bank. At times, the G7 has found that it could not dictate policies in the Fund and Bank. One such occasion was the IMF/World Bank Meetings in Madrid in 1994. The G7 countries reached a fragile agreement among themselves for a new allocation of SDRs and a formula for their distribution which, in the view of non-G7 countries, did not do enough to provide additional resources for middle income and poor countries. The G7 was rebuffed by the Interim Committee and the debate on a new SDR allocation continued.[14]

1.5.6 The rise of global financial market issues

During the 1990s and to the present day, a range of international financial regulatory issues have demanded increasing multilateral attention. There had been antecedents – the attention to gaps in bank supervision that were evident following the Herstatt Bank collapse in 1974, for example, or the increased attention to bank regulation in emerging markets following the Mexico crisis in 1994. Following the Asian crisis in 1997, however, these latter concerns became much sharper and received attention from political circles as well as from financial technocrats. Some officials from Asian countries also railed against the speculators whom they saw behind the crisis, much as Richard Nixon had in August 1971. Subsequent developments have broadened and deepened concerns that problems or potential problems in global financial markets demand global attention. The collapse of Long-Term Capital Management in September 1998, with knock-on effects contained only after a Fed-orchestrated private sector rescue, gave force to concerns that had been voiced by some officials, particularly in continental Europe, about systemic risks posed by largely unregulated financial institutions or even unregulated subsidiaries of regulated institutions, and also the possible risks from the very rapid growth of the use of financial derivatives. Continued financial consolidation has given rise to concerns about the adequacy of supervision of global financial conglomerates. And more recently, corporate scandals from Enron in the United States to Parmalat in Italy have highlighted a range of issues that require a coordinated policy approach across major markets – disclosure standards, accounting and auditing standards and corporate governance requirements. The risks of not coordinating approaches are that gaps will be left to be exploited by the unscrupulous or that conflicting regulatory requirements will damage the functioning of markets. Since innovation in markets is continuous, this is almost certain to be an ongoing area for international cooperation, not just a matter of finding a one-time fix. Finally, the need for cooperative approaches to counter the exploitation of ever more efficient and more global financial markets by criminals, terrorists and (more controversially) tax evaders has brought these issues onto the agenda of G7 Summits, G7 finance ministers and governors, the IMFC and other bodies. And it led to the establishment of the Financial Action Task Force at the OECD to work in these areas.

1.5.7 A new international architecture? Remodelling yes, rebuilding no

The US Treasury responded to the issues identified in the Asian crisis by convening a meeting of G7 finance ministers and central bank governors together with their counterparts from Australia and 14 emerging markets – a G22, which briefly became a G33 – following an announcement by President Clinton at an APEC (Asia Pacific Economic Cooperation) Summit in Vancouver in 1997. This *ad hoc* group established three working groups. These prepared reports on transparency and accountability, strengthening financial systems and international financial crises.

European dissatisfaction with the broad forum that the US Treasury had created to deal with financial issues and the higher political profile that these issues were receiving led to agreement on two initiatives by the G7 finance ministers that were reported to the Cologne Summit of 1999: the creation of the Financial Stability Forum (FSF) and the financial G20 (not to be confused with the G20 of emerging and low income countries that have coordinated their positions in Doha round trade negotiations). The former brings together central banks and financial regulators from eleven countries, including Australia, Hong Kong and Singapore, which were excluded from older groups, and officials from international organizations to deal with a broad range of financial issues. Finance ministry representation in most delegations maintains a link to the G7 finance ministers and Summit processes and, more generally, brings a political perspective into the technical domain of financial supervision and regulation.

The G20 was an effort to initiate a more engaged dialogue across the full range of international economic and financial issues among 'systemically important countries'. Its discussions have ranged widely, even to reach the trade impasse following the Cancun WTO meeting in 2003.

Another institutional evolution of recent years was the creation of the International Monetary and Financial Committee (IMFC) to replace the Interim Committee of the IMF. Although it has brought some flexibility to the formality that marked the Interim Committee by establishing a deputies group to prepare meetings in place of the Executive Board, it has not overcome the problems of the structure of IMF constituencies discussed in Chapter 6.

<u>1.6</u>   The parallel track: regional cooperation

The preceding account has been about cooperation on a global, although usually not universal, scale. In parallel with the events of this account, the transformation of the historical Europe of rivalrous nation-states into the EU of today, with 25 members committed to common or harmonized policies across most areas of economic and financial activity and with 12 members using a common currency regulated by a European Central Bank, is the fruit of a sustained and ever deepening effort of cooperation among its member countries. This ongoing European project is not the subject of this Report, but it has shaped the process of global cooperation in the past and raises important questions about the future.

Disappointment among Europeans with efforts to establish a more stable global monetary system was one very important driver of European monetary integration. Indeed, the maintenance of tighter margins among the six currencies of the European Economic Community than that allowed by the Smithsonian Agreement was a first, tentative step towards what became the euro 27 years later. The European integration process has proceeded with remarkably little tension between participants and their non-European partners, except for the chronically problematic Common Agricultural Policy. A stronger, more stable and somewhat more cohesive Europe has, in turn, facilitated cooperation in a number of areas – notably trade and competition policy. The evolving structure of policy competencies within Europe, however, has outdated some arrangements for cooperation – only the independent European Central Bank can speak to monetary policy in the euro area, and its instruments are, in practice, the main policy levers for influencing the euro's exchange rate, but three national central banks of the euro area sit in key parts of G7 meetings while the ECB is not in the room and five members of the G10 are national European central banks without their own national currencies. This and related issues of the structure for cooperation are taken up in Chapter 6.

Another question raised by the European experience is to what extent regional cooperation might take hold in other parts of the world and whether this would complement or come at the expense of global cooperation. There is clearly some impetus behind regional trade arrangements with overlapping Mercosur, NAFTA, Free Trade Area of the Americas and other agreements or initiatives in the Western Hemisphere and similar developments in Asia. To date, there has been much less development of regional monetary and financial cooperation. Proposals for an Asian Monetary Fund, put forward in the midst of crisis in 1997, were dropped in the face of concerns that the particular proposal would undercut the role of the IMF. There is, however, an ongoing interest in Asian monetary cooperation, and some concrete steps have been taken recently in East Asia – the ASEAN + 3 have established a network of foreign currency reserve swap arrangements and are making efforts to develop an Asian bond market. Some in the region have begun to talk of a regional monetary union as a long-term goal. Regional monetary cooperation is likely to stay on the East Asian agenda and may well be taken up in one part or another of the Western Hemisphere and elsewhere as regional cohesion strengthens in other respects. The European experience shows that regional cooperation need not come at the expense of global cooperation and can be a complement to it. Nevertheless, there may be times when the global compatibility of particular regional initiatives should be questioned, as with the 1997 Asian Monetary Fund proposal.

1.7   The private sector

For the most part, international economic and financial cooperation among governments has been and remains a government to government process, although the Bretton Woods institutions have developed extensive mechanisms to become more transparent and to enable private sector players – NGOs and business – to make their views known before decisions are made. Each government has its own mechanisms for public consultation and accountability that shape its positions in international meetings. And in a few cases, nominally private organizations with public policy mandates have been brought into the framework of cooperation – for example, the International Accounting Standards Board is represented in the Financial Stability Forum.

The lack of formal public/private links in the international groups has not precluded close collaboration when circumstances called for it and the private sector interests were reasonably concentrated, as in the Latin American debt crisis of the 1980s. Cooperation to the same extent has not taken place in the more recent crises centred in capital markets, if for no other reason than the creditors have been more diffuse. It is difficult to imagine institutionalizing public/private partnerships for cooperation at the global level without raising insurmountable issues of legitimacy and representativeness. There may well be occasions again in the future, however, when action to address a problem requires collaboration between governmental representatives in one of the international bodies and the private sector. A flexible approach to cooperation among governments should make it easier to reach out to the relevant parties in the private sector if the situation should arise.

1.8   The situation in 2004

There has been tremendous change over the 60 years since the Bretton Woods conference – in the nature of the manifest problems that called for collective action, in views on what are effective tools of economic management, in the relative capacities of individual states and of the EU, in political and security relationships, in the capacity to meet and exchange information as transportation and communication have become faster and cheaper, and in the groups and networks in which issues are addressed. The weight of concern has oscillated between immediate problems and systemic reforms, but with the idea of a grand rebuilding of the system commanding the energies of officials only once since Bretton Woods (in the failed efforts of the C-20). Gradualism has been the rule, with change driven by immediate problems rather than a comprehensive shared vision of a better world.

Some things have remained the same, however. Economic and financial developments continue to demand that governments work together, arguably now more than ever since both international trade and finance have grown more important. The IMF and World Bank continue to be the key institutions that governments turn to in order to implement policies multilaterally; but governments continue to meet in informal groupings of restricted membership in order to debate and choose a course of action. It has taken leadership, often in the past from the United States, to stimulate action; but the need to gain the acceptance of others, at least in a restricted group, has been important in shaping action. In these groupings, individual representatives continue to be motivated mainly by their responsibilities to deliver good economic performance – growth of output and jobs with low and stable inflation – at home. Thus, cooperation has been forthcoming when benefits could be identified for participants able to block action, and not otherwise. This has not precluded action where the principal benefits went to others: the G7 has supported IMF and World Bank lending to countries with debt problems because of fears about damage to world growth and to their financial institutions. Security concerns have also played a role, but when these have been the dominant consideration, as with aid policies during the cold war, implementation has been taken out of the hands of finance ministers and central bank governors.

Perhaps the most important change over the past 60 years has been an astounding broadening and deepening of financial linkages between countries and their extension from a small group of 10 or 11 financially important countries to a much larger set of actors. With this has come not only greater financial interdependence of the traditional kind but a whole new set of concerns about corporate governance, tax evasion, criminal money laundering and terrorist money flows.

The informal groupings have evolved somewhat in the light of changes in the world, but groups have been easier to form than to dissolve, and membership has been easier to extend than to withdraw. The result is a cluttered calendar of meetings, not all of which are a good use of officials' time. G8 Summits, for their economic contribution in recent years, might well be thought of as one of these. They have evolved, however, to fulfil other useful purposes beyond economic policy. That has left some loss of political focus on economic and financial issues that need attention. Groups of economic and financial officials are nonetheless carrying on with a much broader agenda than one could have imagined 30 years ago.

Many people deplore the relative absence of binding rules on governments' macroeconomic and financial policies and criticize the *ad hoc* nature of consultative arrangements. They long for a lost golden age. The history reviewed in this chapter suggests that there never was such an age. The inter-war period was one of disastrous failure that led to the effort at Bretton Woods to design a system that would support economic growth and stability. Important and durable institutions were created, which have played and continue to play critical roles. But the system of fixed exchange rates envisaged at Bretton Woods was not effective until 1958. It had a brief and turbulent period of operation before it was irreparably damaged in August 1971 and died in March 1973. The efforts at macroeconomic coordination that followed in the late 1970s also failed to show the way to a durable form of cooperation. This does not mean that international cooperation is not important. Even in the macroeconomic sphere, the peer pressure to follow policies that are in both the country's longer-term interest and in the interest of its partner countries continues to be important. Most important, however, are the many and complex ways in which a wide range of policy actions affects the functioning of markets that cross borders. These need to be the main focus of international cooperation going forward.

The practice of responding in an ad hoc fashion to problems as they arise within a sporadically changing framework of formal and informal institutions has been untidy, but often effective. New groups formed in recent years have become more representative and this has given them more legitimacy and more effectiveness in dealing with issues that have come to the fore in recent years. As governments have become more transparent, so has their work in international groups, although officials still find value in off-the-record discussions. The mode of operation has been one of seeking common ground, with accountability still squarely on governments at home for what they agree to and implement.

This leaves us two key questions in 2004, which are addressed in the following chapters: What changes are needed to get the right structure for effective economic cooperation to deal with the most important issues of today? And how can we improve the capacity for change to deal with different problems involving different key actors in the future?

Appendix 1A

Glossary of International Financial and Economic Committees, Groups and Clubs[15]

Committees
C-20
The Committee of Twenty (C-20), officially known as the Committee of the Board of Governors of the Fund on Reform of International Monetary System, was established on 26 July 1972. It had one representative (normally a finance minister or central bank governor) from each IMF Executive Board constituency, and was chaired by Jeremy Morse of the UK Treasury. The Committee and various technical groups met until early 1974, when the effort at comprehensive reform was abandoned. An 'outline of Reform' calling for an evolutionary approach and technical papers were published as it wound up its business.

Interim Committee
The Interim Committee of the IMF was established in 1974 when the C-20 disbanded and continued to meet until 1999. It had a member (normally a finance minister or central bank governor) for each IMF constituency.

IMFC
The International Monetary and Financial Committee (IMFC) was established on 30 September 1999, as a Committee of the Board of Governors of the IMF to replace the Interim Committee. An explicit provision was introduced for preparatory meetings of representatives (deputies) of Committee members. The IMFC has a member for each Executive Board seat, 24 in all, who are normally ministers of finance or central bank governors.

Development Committee
The Joint Ministerial Committee of the Boards of Governors of the Bank and Fund on the Transfer of Real Resources to Developing Countries, better known as the Development Committee, was established in October 1974 to address development issues. Its 24 members (usually ministers of finance or development) represent the constituencies or countries that appoint Executive Directors of the Fund and Bank.

Financial Stability Forum
The G7 finance ministers and central bank governors endorsed the establishment of a Financial Stability Forum in February 1999 to address improvements in the functioning of financial markets and the reduction of systemic risk through enhanced information exchange and international cooperation among the authorities responsible for maintaining financial stability. The FSF meets semi-annually. It has 43 members, consisting of 26 senior representatives of national authorities responsible for financial stability in 11 significant international financial centres; six senior representatives of four international financial institutions; seven senior representatives of three international regulatory and supervisory bodies; a representative each of two committees of central bank experts; a representative of the European Central Bank and the Chairman.

Groups

G5

The Group of Five (G5) finance ministers and central bank governors of major industrial countries was established in the mid-1970s to coordinate the economic policies of France, Germany, Japan, the United Kingdom, and the United States. (These countries' currencies also constituted the SDR.) The G5 was the main policy coordination group among the major industrial countries through the Plaza Agreement of September 1985. It was subsequently superseded by the Group of Seven (G7) finance ministers and central bank governors.

G7

The Group of Seven (G7) major industrial countries have held annual Economic Summits (meetings at the level of head of state or government) since 1975. At the level of finance ministers and central bank governors, the G7 superseded the G5 as the main policy coordination group during 1986-7, when first Canada and then Italy were invited to join. The Managing Director of the IMF usually, by invitation, participates in the surveillance discussions of the G7 finance ministers and central bank governors. Since the establishment of the European Central Bank, its President has taken the place of the governors of the three national central banks of the euro area in the G7 for parts of meetings.

G8

The G8 (first known as the 'Political 8' or 'P8') was conceived when Russia first participated in part of the 1994 Naples Summit of the G7. At the 1998 Birmingham Summit, Russia joined as full participant, which marked the establishment of the Group of Eight (G8). However, the G7 continues to function as a forum for discussion of economic and financial issues, and separate communiqués have continued to be issued by the G7 and G8 Summits.

G10

The Group of Ten (G10) refers to the group of countries that have agreed to participate in the General Arrangements to Borrow (GAB). The GAB was expanded in 1964 by the association of Switzerland, then a non-member of the Fund, but the name of the G10 remained (see Table 1.2 for a list of members).

G20

The Group of 20 (G20), which superseded the Group of 33, was foreshadowed at the Cologne Summit of the G7 in June 1999, but was formally established at the G7 finance ministers' meeting on 26 September 1999. The G20 was formed as a broad group for cooperation and consultation on matters pertaining to the international financial system. (A group of emerging market and developing countries that meets to coordinate positions in WTO negotiations also goes under the name of G20).

G22

The establishment on a temporary basis of the Group of 22 (referred to also as the 'Willard Group') was announced by President Clinton and the other leaders of APEC countries at their meeting in Vancouver in November 1997, when they agreed to organize a gathering of finance ministers and central bank governors to advance the reform of the architecture of the global financial system. It was superseded first by the G33 and then by the G20.

G24

The Group of 24 (G24), a chapter of the G77, was established in 1971 to coordinate the positions of developing countries on international monetary and development finance issues and to ensure that their interests were adequately represented in negotiations on international monetary matters.

G33

The Group of 33 superseded the Group of 22 in early 1999 and was itself superseded by the Group of 20 later in the year.

G77

The G77 was established on 15 June 1964, by the 'Joint Declaration of the Seventy-Seven Countries' issued at the end of the first session of the United Nations Conference on Trade and Development (UNCTAD). It was formed to articulate and promote the collective economic interests of its members and to strengthen their joint negotiating capacity on all major international economic issues in the UN system. The membership of the G77 has expanded to 134 member countries, but the original name has been retained.

Clubs

London Club

The London Club is an informal group of commercial banks that join together to negotiate their claims against a sovereign debtor.

Paris Club

The Paris Club is an informal group of official creditors, industrial countries in most cases, that seek solutions for debtor nations facing payment difficulties. Begun in 1956, its members agree to a set of rules and principles designed to reach a coordinated agreement on debt rescheduling.

2 International Economic Cooperation: Principles for a Changing World

The previous chapter looked at the past, this chapter now looks into the future. It does not intend to guess how international economic and financial cooperation will or should evolve, rather it asks whether the existing system of world governance is outdated and, if so, what principles should be brought to bear. Pressure for change comes from several directions. To start with, the list of issues that require coordination is continuously evolving, mostly expanding. New players, both emerging economic heavyweights and the fledgling international civil society, are knocking at the door, in effect challenging the existing order, while the constellation of older players gradually transforms itself, in particular as Europe's integration deepens. As this process unfolds, the intellectual climate undergoes its own transformation, challenging conventional wisdom. The main message is that merely improving upon past experience will not do, a substantial degree of innovation is clearly required but faces serious hurdles. In particular, everywhere the trend is for policy-making institutions, formal and informal, to pay more attention to 'democratic principles'. Effectiveness has to be balanced by legitimacy and representativeness, and this applies to the international institutions as well.

2.1 A changing set of issues

Success breeds success, but also headaches. One unmistakable sign of success for the world economic order is the process of economic and financial integration. Figure 2.1 tells a familiar story. World trade now stands at nearly 30% of world GDP, a 50% increase over a quarter century. Even more impressive is that gross capital flows rose seven times faster than world GDP over the same period, as did the flow of foreign direct investment. Trade integration picked up speed in the early 1990s, followed by financial integration in the mid-1990s. Financial integration started earlier among the OECD countries, but the major news is that it soon spread to the emerging market countries. A number of financial crises have not lastingly dampened the volume of capital flows. Table 2.1 shows the number of countries where gross private flows exceeded 15% of GDP in 1980 and 2000. The phenomenon is quite widespread, bypassing only South Asia but including a number of African countries. This evolution is well known and sometimes decried. For better or worse, it is reshaping international economic and political relations and deeply transforming the fabric of all societies, in the North – through immigration and outsourcing, for instance – as well as in the South.

Figure 2.1 World trade and capital flows

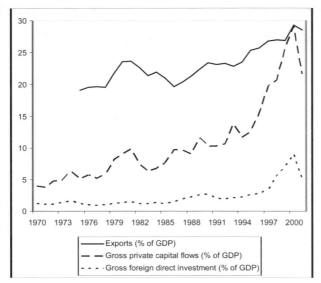

Exports (% of GDP)
— — Gross private capital flows (% of GDP)
- - - Gross foreign direct investment (% of GDP)

Source: World Development Indicators (2004), The World Bank, CD-ROM.

Table 2.1 Number of countries with gross private capital flows exceeding 15% of GDP in 2000

| | 1980 | | 2000 | |
	Above 15%	Observations	Above 15%	Observations
East Asia	1	14	6	17
Europe	4	17	26	33
Latin America	6	32	10	28
North America	0	2	2	2
Middle East and North Africa	4	14	4	14
South Asia	0	5	0	5
Sub-Saharan Africa	2	36	6	21

Source: World Development Indicators (2004), The World Bank, CD-ROM.

2.1.2 Financial integration

Much of the financial integration process is mediated through financial institutions, such as banks or securities and investment houses (henceforth in this chapter termed 'banks' for convenience). Through acquisitions or organic development, a large number of banks operate widespread international networks. International banks are now routinely conducting business in markets half a world away, and are thus exposed to commercial and financial risk far from their headquarters. Similarly, portfolio investors are growing in size and reach. The information technology is here to assure a smooth flow of information; it is much easier for a London bank to keep abreast of the activities of its Hong Kong subsidiary than it was to monitor its Newcastle branch a few decades ago. Technology has its devilish side too, however. Ever more sophisticated financial instruments constantly challenge internal controls over far-flung activities. The case of Barings in Singapore immediately comes to mind.

The interlocking of bank activities naturally raises the question of who regulates and supervises international firms. Long gone is the time when international cooperation could be achieved by timely exchange of information among national authorities. For good and bad reasons alike, banks have seized on existing differences in regulations and the severity of supervision to optimize their activities. The BCCI case served as a wake-up call that a much more coordinated approach to supervision was needed. The result has been a vigorous effort to agree on supervision practices and instruments and, more recently, accounting standards, for example the setting up of the Financial Stability Forum. Furthermore, the authorities must be ready to intervene simultaneously and trust each other to undertake adequate and prompt corrective action. The LTCM case, which prompted monetary authorities to share information in a timely way, provides a good example.

A characteristic feature of the responses to this set of challenges is that they rely on voluntary cooperation. This form of cooperation reflects the current lack of appetite for giving up sovereignty and for building new international institutions with supranational power. Yet, the limits of voluntary compliance are plain to see. Given the substantial amount of value added and jobs created by the finance industry in all continents, a number of small countries have proceeded to become world-scale financial centres. Table 2.2 provides measures of the size of the 20 largest financial centres reporting to the BIS; it lists the assets of reporting banks *vis-à-vis* the rest of the world and the stocks of international bonds and notes issued. The list includes very large countries but also very small ones. With much prosperity at stake, many of these small countries are understandably reluctant to adopt international arrangements agreed by the large powers. Typically, these agreements are reached for countering tax in the OECD and for money laundering in the Financial Action Task Force, which was established following the 1989 G7 Summit. While combating tax evasion and money laundering are legitimate aims of international cooperation, the legal basis for imposing these rules on sovereign countries is lacking.

Table 2.2 International asset positions of financial intermediaries: the top countries (US$ billions – end 2003)

	Bank assets		International bonds and notes
United Kingdom	2888.2	United States	3064.3
Germany	1639.6	Germany	1254.3
United States	1433.1	United Kingdom	1161.9
Japan	1294.2	Netherlands	904.5
Cayman Islands	1002.4	France	723.6
France	971.7	Cayman Islands	451.2
Switzerland	819.2	Italy	386.1
Luxembourg	630.0	Canada	286.6
Netherlands	526.7	Spain	231.3
Belgium	476.9	Australia	177.2
Singapore	427.6	Austria	173.9
Hong Kong	409.3	Ireland	166.8
Jersey	279.6	Luxembourg	158.4
Ireland	246.2	Japan	119.9
Italy	274.9	Sweden	117.5
Bahamas	252.4	Netherlands Antilles	98.6
Spain	230.1	Argentina	90.2
Austria	147.8	Belgium	85.9
Canada	131.8	Finland	71.7
Guernsey	112.0	Brazil	71.6

Source: BIS (2004), *Quarterly Review,* March.

2.2 Players and rules of the game

2.2.1 The players

It is sometimes argued that the collectivity of the G7 no longer includes the current global key players and that the G7 reflects a world that is no more. As Chapter 5 of this Report shows, such arguments have some validity in respect of balance-of-payments adjustment among the key currency countries. In other respects, however, as Table 2.3 shows by using GDP measured in current US dollars to compute each country's economic weight, the G7 countries are, by and large, the world's biggest economies. Over the last 40 years, the list of the economically largest seven countries has not changed, even though the ranking within this group has been slightly modified. Back in 1965, China could not be a member of the G7, for obvious political reasons. On the basis of GDP size, it would have been replaced by India whose eighth rank is now occupied by Canada.

It was these economic rankings, together with the fact that they were all industrialized democracies, which provided the rationale for the membership of the G5 and later the G7 Summits of heads of state or government.[16] Their original motivation in the turbulent global economy of the 1970s was largely economic, though the problems of global politics always featured to some extent on their agenda. For one reason or another, however, their subsequent agendas have increasingly tilted towards politics and diplomacy, and this has further complicated the issue of which countries should be members.

The focus of the other emanation of the G7 , the group of G7 finance ministers and central bank governors, has remained naturally focused on economic and financial issues. The finance ministers provide the Summits with much, if not all, of their economic conclusions and it is doubtful whether the Summits add most value, other than perhaps to convey a broad political endorsement to the finance ministers' work. Stability in the economic top league may suggest that governance of the formal institutions of cooperation – IMF, World Bank, WTO – is not in need of reconsideration. Indeed, with six exceptions, each country listed in Table 2.3, has, *de jure* or *de facto*, its own permanent Executive Director at the IMF. The exceptions are Mexico, Spain, Brazil, Sweden, South Korea and Argentina. Of the eight single-country seats on the IMF Board, six are filled by the countries in the top of the list in Table 2.3, suggesting two anomalies, Russia (ranked 16th) and Saudi Arabia (ranked 22nd).[17] Nor are countries' IMF quotas seriously at variance from what their GDP and trade weights would predict.[18]

Table 2.3 Ranking by GDP weights: 1965 and 2001

2001 ranking	Country	GDP weight	1965 ranking	2001 ranking	Country	GDP weight	1965 ranking
1	United States	33.8	1	11	Brazil	1.7	15
2	Japan	13.9	5	12	India	1.6	8
3	Germany	6.2	2	13	South Korea	1.4	41
4	United Kingdom	4.8	4	14	Netherlands	1.4	16
5	France	4.4	3	15	Australia	1.2	11
6	China	3.9	6	16	Russia	1.0	NA
7	Italy	3.7	7	17	Argentina	0.9	10
8	Canada	2.3	9	18	Switzerland	0.8	18
9	Mexico	2.1	14	19	Belgium	0.8	17
10	Spain	2.0	12	20	Sweden	0.7	13

Source: World Development Indicators (2004), The World Bank, CD-ROM.
Note: GDP converted at market exchange rates

Yet, two important changes have occurred. First, the deep political divide that prevailed two decades ago has given way to a more subtle situation. The end of the Soviet bloc has brought Russia into the group of market economies, even if much more remains to be done there to complete the transition. Russia's seat at the IMF and its admission to the G8 are not fully justified by its economic weight. Of greater significance is the fact that the Socialist model, which used to rule a majority of the world's population, has been discredited enough to prompt nearly every country in the world to seek to integrate itself into the world economy. This is the case of China, of course, but it is also true to various degrees of many other countries like India, as well as the former European satellites of the Soviet Union. China and India, whose combined population amounts to almost 40% of the world's total, seem likely to continue to grow at a fast pace. Their 2001 GDP rankings at market exchange rates have not yet changed much from 40 years ago, but current trends predict the emergence of a new world deeply at variance with that of the twentieth century. Brazil too could well assume much greater economic importance. This evolution in the making must surely influence the way economic cooperation is conducted in the future.

The other major change is Europe's gradual economic and political integration. The original Common Market has just expanded, with 10 new countries. The creation of the euro adds a further dimension of integration to the continent. This evolution raises a number of questions about the way Europe should be represented in international forums. The IMF, for instance, exerts surveillance on fiscal policy and on monetary and exchange rate policies. Yet for fiscal policy each EU country is regarded as a separate entity, but monetary policy is now the responsibility of the Euro system, consisting of the ECB and the national central banks, while competence for exchange rate policy is shared in a somewhat unclear way between the EU Council of Ministers and the ECB. Four European countries are G7 members and are accompanied to G7 Summits by the President of the European Council (if he or she is not already a Summit participant) and by the President of the European Commission.

EU representation at G7 meetings of finance ministers and central bank governors is complicated and depends on the subject under discussion. For discussions relating to monetary and exchange rate policy the President of the ECB and the President of the EU Finance Ministers Council (ECOFIN) attend (unless the President comes from a non-euro member state, in which case the last ECOFIN President from the euro area attends) and the four central bank governors from the euro area leave the room. For all other business, the EU representatives do not attend, but the four central bank governors do. The Commission has usually attended only when issues relating to Russia and former Soviet Union states have been discussed (in view of the Commission's substantial programmes of financial aid for those states). Because of its collegial nature, the President of the ECB cannot commit his institution unless he has a prior mandate, a position which he shared to a large extent with the President of the Bundesbank in pre-euro days.[19] These complexities reveal the difficulties posed by the development of a large bloc that is not a country, yet is more than 25 disparate units. Chapter 5 further examines this question and suggests ways to tackle it.

2.2.2 Rules of the game

Like any system that exercises collective responsibilities, the governance of the international financial system ought to comply with the widely accepted principles of effectiveness, legitimacy, accountability and representativeness. Given the special nature of this system – in particular the absence of any democratic world authority and the mix of formal and informal bodies – not all principles can be adhered to. Yet, there should be at least some acknowledgement of their force.

Effectiveness
Effectiveness requires the ability to react adequately and in time. To be adequate, a response must not be driven by too many extraneous considerations, or constrained by too many contradictory pressures. A timely response may be difficult when the problem at issue can be addressed only after consultation with many stakeholders, including in some instances international institutions, interest groups, and the private. Effective negotiations require a thorough analysis of the issues that require collective treatment and the ability to develop, often promptly, a common position. Obviously, discussions must be limited to a reasonably small number of countries and their representatives must have the capacity to make commitments to action.

Legitimacy
The second consideration is legitimacy. Decisions ought to be taken by people who have been given an explicit mandate to that effect. In world affairs, characterized by the absence of any supra-national authority, legitimacy rests with individual countries in the exercise of their sovereignty. If, however, decisions by a group of countries impinge on the welfare of other countries, countries outside the group will tend to question the legitimacy of the group's decisions.

Accountability
Accountability has several levels of meaning. At the most basic level, it can signify the provision of an account and explanation of the actions taken ('reporting accountability'). At a deeper level, accountability can signify a willingness of those who render an account to be ready to modify future action in response to the reactions of those to whom the account is made ('response accountability'). At its deepest level, accountability can signify the ability of those to whom an account is made to determine the future actions of those who give the account ('control accountability').

Representativeness
The previous sentence, however, leaves open two questions: Can international bodies be held accountable in any way to the governments of countries that are members of the body and can they also be held accountable to the governments of countries that are not members but are affected importantly by those bodies' actions? The answer to the first question – when the relevant constituency includes only the member countries – is not easy as it could lead to ineffectiveness if it gives explicit or implicit veto rights to a large number of countries. The answer to the second question – when the relevant constituency includes all countries – is 'no' in most cases, so ways must be found to represent their interests. In other words, international bodies may not always be sensitive to all the countries affected by their actions. At the very least, their membership should be sufficiently representative and their accountability should be such that those countries' needs and interests are taken into account. If they are not representative in this sense, their legitimacy may be called into question.

These attributes are clearly not independent of each other. For instance, insufficient legitimacy or representativeness may have the effect of preventing decisions from being accepted by all parties concerned, making them ultimately ineffective even though they are well and promptly thought through. Legitimacy may be conferred by a formal delegation of power and yet challenged because important stakeholders are left out the process. Legitimacy also stands to be undermined by a lack of accountability. On the other hand, representativeness may enhance legitimacy and thereby contribute to effectiveness, but it may also impair effectiveness by increasing the size and heterogeneity of a particular body.

One way of approaching the inter-relations between these four criteria is to ask, for each body, what is the 'minimum winning coalition', i.e. which countries' support is needed to reach and implement a decision. If effectiveness is considered the only criterion, a very small number of countries, possibly just one, should be involved, and the G7 could already be seen as over-sized. Giving weight to the other criteria necessarily involves trade-offs. More representativeness – transferring voice from outside to inside – means a larger coalition which may undercut effectiveness. Legitimacy requires an explicit mandate which may reduce the domain of possible actions but, on the other hand, it should ease compliance with decisions. Accountability may have good effects in reining in the behaviour of members of the coalition, but it may also have perverse effects if some members left out of the winning coalition exercise their right of appeal without restraint. And inasmuch as accountability calls for transparency, it may seriously unravel the willingness of states to be truthful.

2.2.3 How do current arrangements measure up to the four principles?

The G7, at least at the level of finance ministers and central bank governors, has been effective in a number of important instances, as illustrated in Chapters 1 and 3. The Bretton Woods institutions also display effectiveness in being able to act in a timely manner in agreed ways, even though there have always been questions about the value of some of their actions and their ability to reform themselves. The G7 is a group of 'major industrialized democracies'. As such, its members presumably share the general aspirations and interests of other industrialized democracies. It would be difficult, however, to claim that the G7 group is legitimate in that it has a mandate from these countries or that it represents other countries. In contrast, the IMF is legitimate as, upon joining it, all member countries accept its authority. The IMF also goes a long way towards representativeness since every country is represented on the Executive Board by an Executive Director, whether individually or as part of a multi-country constituency.

The G7 is an informal forum where a self-selected group of national states concert action in a world of independent states. The G7 process meets the first basic test of reporting accountability. The Summit meetings of heads of state or government meet amidst enormous publicity, statements and reports are published, and the participants give press conferences, make speeches and are interviewed after each Summit meeting. The same broadly applies to the meetings of finance ministers and governors, though statements on some aspects of their business, notably exchange rate policy, are often opaque. At the level of response accountability, however, the position is less clear cut. There is no formal process whereby the G7 modifies its future actions in response to feedback from those affected by its previous actions. To succeed in achieving consensus in the wider forums of the international financial community, however, the G7 has perforce had to be ready to shape its approaches to the views of other countries. Otherwise, there would be deadlock and stalemate. The G7 has been most successful when it has recognized this constraint. At the deepest level of accountability, control accountability, the G7 inevitably fails the test, although its members are individually accountable to their electorates. Control accountability has no applicability to a world of independent states. In the modern world of international financial cooperation, there is no international body, nor likely to be one, which could seek to determine the actions of a group of national states, such as the G7. The problem, of course, is that effectiveness and the three other considerations often clash. This is a thorny issue. Without effectiveness, the most legitimate process loses much of its value.

Without the three other attributes, however, especially legitimacy, the G7 is likely to face increasing opposition from other countries affected by its decisions as its relative economic weight in the global economy declines. So whatever the G7's effectiveness, its legitimacy is at best very limited since it is a self-appointed directorate. Moreover, by definition, seven governments that make decisions of worldwide importance cannot be credited with accountability and representativeness.

Even if it is judged that the G7 has functioned for a quarter of a century with some effectiveness, it is difficult to escape the conclusion that the G7 process is now coming under some pressure, and not only in the streets of the cities where its heads of states or governments meet. Its partial transformation into a G8 and the invitations issued to twelve other heads of states and governments to join their eight peers for parts of their discussion, as happened at the Evian Summit in 2003, are telling signals that even the G7/8, is concerned that it cannot by itself 'carry the world on its shoulders'. In short, the legitimacy of the G7, to the extent it has it, is beginning to come under question and, if it remains in its present format, this in due course will begin to erode its effectiveness.[20]

The examples of the IMF and the World Bank show how it is possible to combine at least limited effectiveness and legitimacy. In their cases, the relevant Executive Boards and the International Monetary and Financial and Development Committees, respectively, operate through the indirect representation of all member countries. Even though the effective degree of control of these boards is open to debate, the setup provides some legitimacy, while their sizes are small enough for thoughtful yet timely deliberation; the constituency system also allows for some degree of representativeness. The disadvantage of a constituency system is the tendency, which in some cases may become a requirement, to seek consensus within individual constituencies, as it can inhibit creativity and innovation. In addition, Board members are typically quite isolated from their capitals, which both limit their influence and reduce their accountability. Intermediate solutions do not come for free, though. We argue in Chapter 3 that, in many instances, the IMF, if left on its own, would not have made progress without prior agreement among the G7 countries and the influence they then exerted on others.

2.3   A changing environment

While today the players have changed and the game must be played differently, perhaps the most significant challenges to economic cooperation come from the changing political and intellectual environment. This sort of change is not new, of course. The world that invented Bretton Woods profoundly differed from the world that had created the League of Nations less than three decades beforehand. During the 60 years since the Bretton Woods agreements, the evolution has been as significant, if not more so. The difference, of course, is that the evolution has been more gradual, fortunately avoiding the tragedy of a world war, so it may be less visible, and there is no green field site on which to start anew. Yet, the differences are striking.

2.3.1 Politics and economics interactions in the post-cold war world

The end of the cold war has, and still is, fundamentally transforming Europe. It is also deeply affecting relationships among the countries that used to be aligned against the perceived Soviet threat. The willingness to accept the US leadership in economic matters has declined along with the need for US military protection. This sentiment is perceptible among many European countries, but also among emerging market countries. Conversely, the US administration appears to lose patience with allies who take a political distance in world affairs. The challenge is to shield economic cooperation, which typically benefits all countries, from fall-out from political conflicts. The G7, at least at the finance ministers levels, seems to have succeeded in the recently troubled climate.

2.3.2 New monetary policies

In most countries for almost four decades after the Second World War, central banks pursued unspecified and wide objectives, including high employment, low inflation, and balance of payments and exchange rate targets. Moreover, few central banks were distinct independent branches of the state; rather they were under the direct control of their treasuries. Over the last two decades, the situation has been radically transformed, in response to an evolving academic consensus supported by empirical evidence that independent central banks are more successful in controlling inflation.[21] One way or another, with few notable exceptions, central banks have been granted independence and most are now focused on price stability, several of them having adopted formal inflation targeting.

The independence of central banks means that it is no longer possible for treasuries to agree among themselves on package deals that include commitments that imply monetary policy actions, as was attempted in the Louvre agreement. Central banks can agree among themselves, if they so wish, but their agreements are likely to be based on narrower objectives, and certainly not to facilitate agreements among national treasuries. This makes cooperation significantly more complex.[22]

Indeed, the explicit identification of price stability as an overriding monetary policy objective, with or without the adoption of the inflation targeting strategy, implies that central banks are concentrated on domestic conditions. External conditions still matter, of course, but only inasmuch as they affect domestic inflation: the effects of external conditions – chiefly the exchange rate, but also foreign asset prices and payment imbalances – are relatively small in large countries and the euro area. As a result, the main potential players harbour limited interest in monetary cooperation.

This attitude is further reinforced by the sharply increased size of world financial and foreign exchange markets. The conventional wisdom among central bankers, backed by academic research, is that the markets have become overwhelmingly large.[23] Therefore, official intervention on foreign exchange markets, a traditional area of coordination, can have no long-lasting effects. And the same may be true of policies aimed at combating asset price bubbles, which central banks are loath to deal with or even appear to do so, individually and collectively.[24]

2.3.3 Scepticism about fiscal policies

Much as central banks, now highly sceptical of their own ability to affect economic conditions, have adopted a limited view of their mandate, most governments have given up the kind of fiscal policy activism still in vogue in the 1980s. Here again, the change of heart is based on academic research, as well as on a legacy of high public debts.[25] In addition, we can no longer claim to know very much about the effects of one country's fiscal policy actions on other countries or on the exchange rate. Old certainties have been disproved and few definitive results survive scrutiny.

It is not just that we know better our limits. Economic and financial integration has also changed the role that fiscal policy can play. In small open economies, much of the effect of an expansionary fiscal policy dissipates into increased imports, providing limited stimulus at home and a negligible impulse abroad. Large economies, typically much less open, may capture more of the impact of their fiscal policy actions, but opinions about what can be achieved vary a great deal. Japan has conducted aggressive policies for most of the decade when its economy was stagnant, with little result beyond a mammoth public debt. The EU does not have a fiscal policy of its own, each country retaining sovereignty within the eroding constraints of the Stability and Growth Pact. Some countries would be willing to use the fiscal policy instrument, but this would require coordination, especially among the largest euro area member countries, and Germany is traditionally opposed to activism in this area.[26] In addition, the Stability and Growth Pact aims at limiting the use of this instrument too passively, allowing the automatic stabilizers to run its course. In the end, the only country that has recently used fiscal stimulus actively on a large scale is the United States, though it is unclear whether its motivation is governed by cyclical or structural or political considerations. At any rate, being relatively closed, the large countries have little to benefit from coordination in this area, and much to lose when subjecting a highly political instrument to external constraints.

It is understandable, therefore, that the willingness to cooperate on fiscal policies, never strong to start with, is currently particularly weak. At most, it comes in through the back door of current account imbalances. Since one country's current deficit is the rest of the world's surplus, current accounts are an issue of common concern. *Ceteris paribus*, a change in the budget balance generates an equal change in the current account. The much discussed, and often confirmed, twin deficits phenomenon in the United States (Figure 2.2) is a good example of this link. The EU and Japanese cases serve, however, as important reminders that budget and current balances can even have opposite signs for long periods. Current accounts react to changes in private investment and saving, as well as changes in the fiscal stance.

This observation explains the current stalemate. A common, and probably valid, view is that closing the US current account deficit requires closing its budget deficit as a necessary, although very likely not a sufficient, condition. The US administration's view seems to be that a fiscal retrenchment on their side is bound to exercise a contractionary effect on the world economy unless countervailing action is taken. For this reason, they call for countervailing action elsewhere. There is an element of truth in this analysis, and policy cooperation may be desirable on both the fiscal and monetary (exchange rate) sides. With a gross public debt in excess of 150% of GDP, Japan is hardly motivated to play the role of a locomotive pulling the world, while the larger euro area countries have violated, or are close to violating the Stability and Growth Pact.

Figure 2.2 Budget balances and current accounts

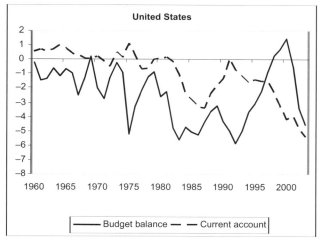

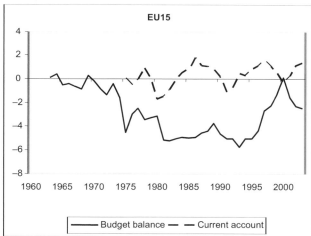

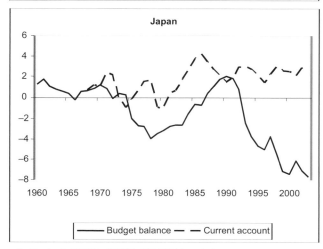

Source: Economic Outlook (2003), OECD, CD-ROM, vol. 2.

<u>2.4</u>   Legitimacy under stress and the anti-globalization backlash

Section 2.2 above argued that for cooperation to be durably effective, it must be legitimate. It further observed that G7 leadership finds its justification in its expected effectiveness, but legitimacy, accountability and representation are also important. The international financial institutions have legitimacy, since all member countries are represented in their key decision-making bodies, but because each country's influence is tied to its voting weight, power is firmly held by a small number of countries, mostly those that belong to the G7. There is, however, little prospect of change in the systems for weighted voting which rule in the international financial institutions. The countries that place their taxpayers' money in the international financial institutions or stand behind them would not do so without a proportionate means to control their activities and so safeguard their taxpayers' commitment. That proportionate means is a system of voting where votes are broadly weighted to the financial exposure of taxpayers.

It was only a matter of time, therefore, until the legitimacy of the international financial architecture would be questioned by those who lack influence. Of course, from the beginning, there were many critics, but these were mostly expert observers and academics. Vibrant, occasionally violent, demonstrations have also long been a familiar sight in countries subject to tough IMF programmes, but those sporadic reactions were quickly dismissed. Inept or corrupt governments were to be blamed, so went the argument, and had they heeded the advice that they had long been given, they would not have had to call upon the IMF for emergency support and face the associated conditionality. In addition, as was often pointed out, the IMF was used as a convenient scapegoat to impose unpopular but needed policies at reduced political cost.

As described in Chapter 1 and further analysed in Chapter 3, the situation changed in the wake of the Latin American and Asian crises of the 1990s. Criticism has moved beyond the narrow circles where it had long been confined. Some Asian governments that had previously been praised for conducting prudent policies felt more coerced than helped when they unexpectedly found themselves in need of emergency assistance. When they asked for urgent short-term loans to prevent a catastrophic collapse of their exchange rates, they were handed a long series of structural conditions that it would take months or years to fulfil. In addition, as noted by Feldstein (1998) among others, many of these structural conditions were intrusive, implying significant wealth redistribution and reaching deep into national sovereignty. The fallout has been wide, leading the IMF to pull back more closely to its core business of macroeconomic management.

The US Congress, often not supportive of the international financial institutions, expressed outrage at the Mexican rescue in 1995. The D'Amato amendment followed, temporarily barring the US treasury from providing bilateral financing to crisis-stricken countries. The Asian crisis triggered a new round of criticism and led to the commissioning of a report from a Committee chaired by Allan Meltzer, a long-time critic of the IMF known for having proposed its dismemberment. The Meltzer report did not go to that extreme, but it urged a severe scaling down of the role and resources of the international financial institutions. Many other reports were produced as part of a widespread debate on the 'international architecture', another sign of generalized concern.[27]

This is also when the anti-globalization movement appeared on the horizon. It erupted on the scene when protesters managed to block the WTO meetings in Seattle in 1998. Since then, from Washington, DC to Prague, from Geneva to Trieste, WTO, IMF, World Bank, and G7 meetings have been disrupted or threatened with disruption. Crowds that had not assembled in large numbers since the Vietnam War era took again to the streets. The Davos World Economic Forum, seen as a symbol of globalization insensitive to social needs, had to be moved to New York. The anti-Davos World Social Forum, launched in Porto Allegre, has become a focal point criticism; it always draws influential politicians – including ministers – from both the developed and the developing countries. The actual level of support for this 'politics of the street' varies from country to country, but such issues as the environment, debt and trade are now widely discussed.

Of course, the diverse movements involved in these demonstrations harbour ambiguous and sometimes conflicting agendas, which run from outright rejection of capitalism to a more limited criticism of current *de facto* world governance. Symptomatically, they tend to target the key institutions of international economic cooperation. Influential economists provide intellectual backing for the criticism, and they raise questions about legitimacy and world governance (Rodrik, 2000; Stiglitz, 2002).

These questions will not go away, if only because there are no easy answers. The anti-globalization movement is in flux, but it has already achieved some success. It has encouraged a rapid rise in the number and variety of NGOs and given them increasing prominence. Several NGOs have become part of the international cooperation system itself. The international financial organizations have not only formally acknowledged their existence but have also involved them in their own work. While the NGOs can be thought of as elements of an emerging civil society, their growing influence is raising new legitimacy issues. Some of them now exercise a significant influence, but who do they represent and who decides which ones should be embraced by the official community? The NGOs still have to work out their own governance and legitimacy if they are to claim to represent various segments of the world population.

2.5   Challenges ahead

This chapter has documented the many factors that call for a rethink about how international economic cooperation functions. It is not only that many new countries have appeared on the scene, but the menu of issues has changed too. The emphasis today is that less is needed at the macroeconomic level and more at the microeconomic level, for example in areas of regulation, supervision and standards. At the same time, existing arrangements show signs of ageing. The debate on the global architecture has produced a long list of old and new grievances and an equally long list of conflicting remedies. How to turn all this ferment in a force for rational change? This section responds briefly to that question, and the following chapters respond in more detail.

2.5.1 Effectiveness and legitimacy

The examples presented in Section 2.4 suggest four useful principles. In the present situation where the nation state is the main, in fact only, source of legitimacy, not all four of them are likely to be met by any international body. Since this calls for trade-offs, some hierarchy is useful to keep in mind. Above all, effectiveness is the precious and essential attribute of international cooperation. Any suggestion for change must pass the effectiveness test. Yet effectiveness is a necessary condition, but not a sufficient one. It must be associated with as much legitimacy, accountability and representativeness as possible, probably in that order.

Legitimacy comes next, because bodies with insufficient legitimacy run the risk of seeing their decisions increasingly challenged, thereby reducing their effectiveness. Full legitimacy – defined as allowing all citizens of the world to be involved in delegating power – is clearly not achievable, at least in the foreseeable future, because there is not, and probably cannot be in foreseeable world circumstances, any universally accepted process for bestowing legitimacy. Legitimacy can only be achieved by asking countries to delegate power, already a formidable challenge. *Representativeness* is already difficult to achieve at the national level, and it is clearly much more challenging in a world of states with different levels of involvement in the world economy and dependence on it. The problem lies partly in the heterogeneity of needs and views. It also lies in the fact that not all countries allow for adequate representativeness in their own modes of governance. Yet, overlooking the interests of particular groups or countries stands to sap legitimacy, and ultimately effectiveness. *Accountability* is exercised *ex post*. It is a fundamental requirement in national democracies. It works mostly through elections, but it is often exercised through public opinion pressure. In international cooperation, accountability is an elusive concept, since there is no international democracy and no international public opinion. *De facto*, it must take the form of accountability to governments, but which ones? Obviously, representativeness becomes entangled with accountability. In short, the basis for judging any new proposal for improving international cooperation is to secure effectiveness with as much legitimacy, accountability and representativeness as possible.

The overriding importance of effectiveness suggests that only a limited number of national states should be involved. Too many players 'around the table' complicate dialogue, make reaching consensus difficult if not impossible, and may result in inconsistent decisions. Legitimacy, on the other hand, calls for the presence of the main players, and representativeness requires taking into account the interests of tens of smaller players. Clearly, no arrangement can square that circle. There is no magic number. The G7's success partly lies in its size, but also in the relative economic and political similarity of its members. Bringing in new players will not only enlarge the size of the group but also make it less homogeneous; the key challenge is to ensure that effectiveness is preserved.

Another issue is whether any new arrangement also needs administrative support. If so, should this support be formally dedicated to international cooperation or, instead, be informally drawn from national bureaucracies on a case by case basis, as is currently the case within the G7 with its system of 'sherpas' and 'deputies'? Setting up a (small) international bureaucracy sharpens the need for legitimacy. It also raises the question of accountability. Moving in that direction would require evidence of a strong need.

These conflicting requirements require a pragmatic approach. It is unlikely that a single all-encompassing body would provide the answer. The experience surveyed in Chapter 1 clearly suggests that the economic role of the G7 Summits is nearing its decline, while the meetings of G7 finance ministers and central bank governors are effective but lack legitimacy, accountability and representativeness. We will suggest a combination of new bodies with different assignments and degrees of formality, each of which would provide a degree of effectiveness and/or legitimacy to the overall network. The downside of this approach is that it operates against the perceived need to limit the number of informal groupings. One solution is to introduce an informal hierarchy of groupings and to assign tasks. The challenge here, however, is to identify a body with the effectiveness and the legitimacy to implement such a solution.

2.5.2 More issues, more institutions?

One of the major implications of economic integration is that the list of issues of collective interest is expanding. From tax competition to mutually recognized standards, the list has become wide, and it is still growing. For a long time, the tradition has been to deal with each new issue by setting up a new international organization. Walking through Geneva is testimony to this approach: the Universal Postal Union (created in 1874) deals with (written) mail, ILO (1919) with labour issues, ITU (1865) with telecommunications, WIPO (1967) with patents, WTO (1995, the successor to GATT created in 1947) with trade, and many more, in addition to the Bretton Woods institutions, the regional development banks and a host of UN institutions (UNCTAD, UNDP, ECLAC, UNECE, etc.) with less specific mandates.[28] The tradition of dealing with each issue by setting up an institution seems to have come to an end, the creation of the European Bank for Reconstruction and Development (EBRD) being an exception. Although international financial stability has emerged as a major international concern, no new institution has been created; the Financial Stability Forum remains an informal network, as is the Basel process. Maybe the closest concession to tradition has been the creation of a new department (Capital Markets) within the IMF.

The resistance to creating new institutions as new issues arise is apparently a response to several concerns, some positive and some negative. The strong opposition to a proliferation of international bureaucracies is fairly general and is shared by many governments and legislatures. It reflects a feeling that there are already enough bureaucracies, that new tasks should be taken up by existing institutions rather than by creating new ones, and that rivalries between institutions ('turf fights') is what prevents this from happening. It reflects, too, a feeling that the staffs of the international institutions are overpaid, compared to pay in national governments. It is, in part, an acknowledgement that once an institution is established, it is very difficult to change its direction, let alone to wind it up. Some governments may fear that the establishment of any new institution will reduce their power since the institution will have sufficient independence to encroach upon the sovereignty of the national states. Whatever the reasons, however, there is a strong antipathy to the creation of new institutions. As the G7 Heads stated at the Cologne Summit, 'This [Strengthening and reforming the International Financial Institutions (IFIs) and arrangements] does not require new institutions, but the existing institutions to adapt to meet the demands of today's global financial system'.

Yet new issues continually arise in international financial cooperation and present the international financial community with the challenge of devising ways of dealing with them which are above all effective, but to the fullest extent possible, legitimate, accountable and representative. Therefore, the international community has followed one of two approaches in recent years. The first approach is to delegate a new task to one or more of the existing formal institutions. The second is to set up an informal structure. One example of the first approach is the IMF's acceptance of the task of ensuring adherence to various codes and standards of good practice. An example of the second is the establishment of the Financial Stability Forum with the task of seeking to secure coordination among those concerned with stability in major financial markets.

2.5.3 Speed of change

The current challenge is not just to deal with a proliferation of new issues, but to adapt existing institutions, most of which were set up decades ago when many now independent countries were parts of vast empires and economic integration was limited. Olson (1965) has suggested that long periods without upheavals allow interest groups and bureaucracies to become entrenched and able to block reforms that threaten them. This may well apply to the existing pattern of international economic cooperation. Back in 1944, when much of the current system was conceived, an old order was dead and discredited. It was then possible to start from near zero and dream up the best possible response to the needs as they were perceived at the time. Sixty years later, deep reforms on the 1944 model are not conceivable.

For this reason, the theme of this Report is that some changes are in order and can be implemented, mostly in an incremental fashion. The founding fathers of the 1944 Bretton Woods order were right to be bold visionaries, and they have left a lasting legacy even if they failed to envisage the world that would quickly emerge. Today is a time for patience and ingenuity to build on and modify an existing structure on an ongoing basis. Even that, in our world of competing interests and enormous complexity, will require statesmanship of the highest order.

3 Cross-border Debt – Managing the Challenges

3.1 Introduction

This chapter characterizes the international financial system as a system that facilitates exchanges of resources from creditors in return for claims from debtors. To illustrate the working of the system, the chapter focuses on three episodes of financial stress in the last 25 years when tensions have arisen between debtors and creditors. It describes some of the techniques devised by the international community aimed at bringing some degree of harmony into the divergent interests of debtors and creditors. Although it identifies the IMF as the principal instrument used for this task, it argues that, in practice, the G7 has, with some success, set the strategy and policy direction for this work. It concludes with the prognosis that the G7's ability to shape the agenda for debtor and creditor cooperation will wane.

3.2 The need for an international system

3.2.1 Transfers of resources in exchange for claims

At its most basic the purpose of the international financial system is to assist in the efficient allocation of capital across borders, a task that is crucial for the successful development of the global economy. It does this by providing a mechanism for the cross-border transfer, in accordance with agreed contractual terms, of financial resources in exchange for claims, and so establishes the claims of creditors on debtors. Financial resources are usually cash, or near cash. Claims can take a great number of forms, for example equity, securities and loans of varying terms and maturity. Participants on either side of the transaction can be, for example, governments (sovereigns) and their various agencies, the international financial institutions such as the IMF and World Bank, financial market companies such as banks, securities houses and institutional investors, and other companies and private individuals. They may deal as principals on their own account or as agents on behalf of someone else. Intermediaries and infrastructure companies of various kinds – such as custodians, exchanges and settlement and clearing houses – provide services to support this business.

Whatever the nature of the claims and however complex the transactions, the ultimate participants in the international financial system – those who own the resources transferred across borders and those who issue the claims – fall into one of two classes. They are either debtors or creditors, including, in each case, intermediaries working on behalf of their respective class. A participant can be both debtor and creditor, depending on the transaction. In net terms, however, a participant will fall into one of the two classes. A participant's position may differ too according to asset class, country and nature of the counterparties, for example, banks, bondholders and equity shareholders.

Stated in such basic terms, the international financial system might be viewed as a complex payments and settlement system – a system where payment is delivered in return for a promise of servicing the claim at some specified time. Certainly an international financial system requires efficient and safe systems for cross-border payments and settlement. But an efficient and stable international financial system requires much more than safe and efficient 'pipework' connecting debtors and creditors. Even if the pipework is safe and efficient, the behaviour of transactions flowing through the system can stress the system so that it becomes unstable and inefficient, to the detriment of the interests of both debtors and creditors.

3.2.2 A complex system subject to stress and crisis

This brief description of the modern international financial system demonstrates its enormous complexity. Like most complex systems, it can become subject to stress and to crisis with resultant damage to the economies of states and to the global economy generally. Financial stress can arise when the interests of debtors and creditors conflict or when there is an expectation in the financial markets that their interests might conflict. In the normal course of business, such conflicts are unusual. It is in debtors' interests to service creditors' claims so as to maintain their creditworthiness and put themselves in a position to receive further resource flows and issue further claims. But the interests of debtors and creditors can, and probably will, diverge if the debtor is, or is expected to be, unable or unwilling to honour contractually agreed terms. Financial stress can then follow, especially if the change in the debtor's prospects or intentions is a surprise.

Surprises can happen for several reasons. There may be a change in the state of the market in which the transaction takes place; liquidity may dry up or legal uncertainty may arise about the ownership of assets because of threats of nationalization or doubts about the reliability of collateral and court processes. Perceived prospects of one group of debtors or of a particular country may deteriorate. This deterioration may, through the process of contagion, affect other debtors and other countries. Such events can lead to a loss of confidence that contracts will be honoured. The more this loss of confidence is generalized beyond the individual debtor or country or asset class to other debtors, countries or assets, the greater is the risk to the international financial system.

In times of financial stress, a debtor's first instinct might well be to seek to retain control over the assets, if any remain, out of which the claim might be paid. The creditor's first instinct might be to secure whatever assets are accessible in settlement of his claim. If the debtor is in the private sector, the foreign claimant can seek recourse in local bankruptcy courts, though this may take much time, and legislation might block it in times of acute financial stress. If the debtor is a government or a government agency, the route via bankruptcy courts is unlikely to be available.

If the creditor is lucky, determined or strong, he may succeed in securing his claim, but only at the expense of the creditor class as a whole. This clash of interests within the creditor class is illustrated by the intervention in 2000 of Elliott Associates in the rescheduling of Peru's Brady bonds. Peru had to settle with the company because the company had managed to obtain an order in a Brussels court that would have stopped Peru from paying interest on its Brady bonds and thereby push it into a costly default.

Well-managed cooperation between creditors and debtors to manage and resolve financial crises can in such times of financial stress go some way to reconcile the conflicting interests within and between debtor and creditor classes. Even with such well-managed cooperation, however, it might prove impossible to deliver an outcome where no creditor is unduly favoured or penalized. A disorderly scramble for assets can easily impose avoidable losses on the creditor class as a whole and at the same time darken the debtor's prospects of early return to the capital markets.

3.2.3   The response of the international financial community

The international financial community has long recognized the risks to the international financial system implicit in such situations. (The international financial community is defined here as the governments of creditor and debtor countries, their respective private sectors and the international financial institutions, principally the IMF, the World Bank, the regional development banks and institutions such as the BIS and OECD.) Led by the major creditor countries, it has devised instruments and approaches designed to prevent financial stress and to manage and resolve the consequences in the event of its occurrence. Such developments for the prevention, management and resolution of financial crises have almost always been developed ad hoc in response to crises.

Typically, the instruments and approaches have focused on the provision of information to markets (transparency); the reduction of incentives for creditors and debtors to act imprudently (moral hazard); the provision of liquidity to tide debtor countries through times of difficulty; and the establishment of creditor/debtor forums to resolve outstanding debt problems (debt restructuring).

For many years, these instruments and approaches have focused on the resolution of crises in debtor and creditor relationships, rather than on their prevention or management. In the years before the Second World War, various debt conferences were convened, often with the tacit encouragement of the United States and the United Kingdom governments, in attempts to resolve strained relationships between creditors, often bondholders, and debtors who had ceased to service their debt. For some three decades after the Second World War, the issue did not figure prominently on the agenda of the international financial community. Systems of exchange controls severely constrained the ability of private creditors and debtors to engage in cross-border transactions, other than for the purposes of trade finance. In these years, the agenda of the IMF, the international institution with the task of maintaining the international financial system, was dominated by problems of balance-of-payments adjustment. The Fund's central task was seen as the maintenance of a system whereby most developed countries' exchange rates remained pegged against the dollar. The main risks to the system were viewed as the shortage of the dollar, the currency which financed trade and on which many countries' growth depended; the intensification of trade and exchange controls; and the risk of the introduction of 'beggar my neighbour exchange rate policies'. Strained relationships between debtors and creditors were not regarded as posing major risks to the system.

The last 25 years have seen a fundamental change in the agenda for international financial cooperation. Issues of debtor and creditor cooperation have come to share the agenda with the more traditional items, such as the promotion of growth and orderly exchange rate adjustment. The reasons for this change in the agenda are well documented.

The liberalization of capital markets, developments in information technology which facilitate the cheap transfer of information, the development of innovative lending techniques together with new approaches to development, all have played a role. In the 1990s, syndicated bank credits were increasingly replaced by securitized loans – in the form of marketable securities, typically bonds – as the main lending instrument. Neither governments, nor the international financial institutions, planned in any systematic way the development of these changes. Initially, in the 1980s the emphasis was on measures to manage and resolve financial crises. In the 1990s attention focused too on measures to prevent crises. Moreover, new institutional arrangements, albeit of an informal nature, emerged to provide some oversight of these developments and to organize the response by the international financial community. Principal among the new arrangements was the emergence of the G7 finance ministers' and governors' group.

3.3   Three episodes of stress in debtor and creditor relationships

The international financial community's response to the changing international financial scene was shaped by three major episodes. They were the Latin American debt crisis of the early 1980s; the programme for granting debt relief to the Highly Indebted Poor Countries (HIPCs); and latterly the series of financial crises of important emerging market countries from Mexico, through Asia to Russia, Turkey, Brazil and Argentina. These episodes shared a common characteristic: a conflict between the interests of debtors and creditors, which required management and resolution as well as measures to prevent their recurrence.

3.3.1   The Latin American debt crisis

In the early 1980s, the inability or unwillingness of some major Latin American countries to service their debts posed an immediate threat to the solvency of major creditor banks in the United States and, to a lesser degree, creditor banks in other countries. If major banks had been allowed to fail, the international financial system as it existed at the time would have been put under great stress. The crisis led to grave social and economic distress for the affected economies in what came to be called their 'lost decade'. Less skilful handling of the aftermath, by the IMF and the governments principally involved, could have precipitated an even more severe crisis in the international financial system as well as in the affected countries.

3.3.2   The HIPC initiative

The debt problems of the poorest countries were of a different nature. Much of their excessive borrowing had been financed by official and officially guaranteed credits and by the multilateral financial institutions. As countries went into default, unpaid interest accrued, sometimes to very high levels. The scale of these countries' defaults was never large enough to endanger the stability of the international financial system. Their debts were, however, a burden to the countries and stood little chance of repayment. There was no financial reason for the creditor countries to sustain evidently uncollectable claims against some of the world's poorest countries. From the viewpoint of the creditor, the more sensible course was to reduce debt. This would put the debtor in a position where at least some part of the original debt could be repaid or, if that was not possible, where its economy could be developed as a source of imports from, and exports to, creditor countries. This led to a series of initiatives starting with the bilateral creditors in the Paris Club and eventually including the multilaterals in the HIPC initiative. The HIPC initiative also included in its most developed form a series of measures aimed at ensuring that a country was capable of sustaining new debt and intended to provide assurance that it would use new resources for development and growth.

3.3.3 The emerging market crises

The emerging market crises of the 1990s (which in fact spilled over into the next decade as is evidenced by the crisis in Argentina and near crises in Turkey and Brazil) shared some of the features of the Latin American debt crisis of the 1980s. Some of the countries involved were the same; Mexico was the first participant in both crises. In both cases, moreover, the crises were precipitated by a sudden reversal of capital inflows.

In the 1980s, however, the inflows had been used to finance large current account deficits that then had to be reduced sharply, and this involved a large, long-lasting reduction of economic growth. In the more recent crises, by contrast, especially in the Asian countries, the growth depressing effects were severe but did not last as long. They were due largely to the exposure of unsound private sector lending aggravated by the adverse effects of large currency depreciations on the balance sheets of financial and non-financial firms, rather than the need to reduce unsustainable current account deficits. In these capital account induced crises, diversity within the class of creditors was much wider than it had been in the crisis of the 1980s. In the 1980s, a small number of commercial banks were the main private sector creditors, and their claims took the form of syndicated loans. In the 1990s, the creditor class included both banks and holders of securities, including bonds, equities and other instruments.

<u>3.4</u>   The need for new techniques, instruments and approaches

These three episodes of stress between the interests of creditors and debtors stimulated the international financial community to devise new techniques, instruments and approaches in an attempt to reduce the vulnerability of countries to crises. They have also sought to find responses when crises nonetheless occur, which provide support to the debtor country while encouraging debtor and creditor responses that avoid undue economic hardship.

3.4.1 Liquidity

Section 3.3 outlines some typical consequences of stress in relationships between debtors and creditors. A perennial feature of such stress has been a run on the debtor's currency. Creditors 'rush for the exit' in an attempt to liquidate their claims on the debtor before foreign reserves are exhausted or exchange controls are introduced or private sector debtors seek the protection afforded by bankruptcy proceedings. Such episodes can be immensely destabilizing, both to the country concerned and, through contagion, to the international financial system more generally, as was the case in the Russian crisis of 1998. So the top priority of the international financial community has been to act to restore confidence in the debtor's ability to service creditors' claims.

In such circumstances the international financial community has invariably resorted to two actions. It has required the debtor country to accept an IMF sponsored adjustment programme and it has sought to assemble a lending package intended to persuade creditors that they need not rush to redeem their claims on debtors. Because of the links with the Fund sponsored adjustment programme, the IMF has often played the central role in coordinating the necessary actions to assemble the lending packages. It has involved, as need be, other international financial institutions, creditor governments and the private sector. In the crises of the 1980s, the Fund's task was to put together sufficient resources to cover 'the financing gap'. This was in effect the amount needed to ensure the financing of current account outflows foreseen in the Fund programme for the country concerned. The Fund faced essentially the same task in the crises of the 1990s, but the size of the financing packages were often much larger in that episode, since capital accounts, not current accounts, provided the source of financial stress.

The core of Fund lending packages has been the contribution made from its own resources. Even in the 1980s, however, the magnitudes of financing gaps were often too big for the Fund's capacious purse, even when it was supported, sometimes reluctantly, by lending from the World Bank and the regional development banks, notably the Inter-American Development Bank and the Asian Development Bank. Much ingenuity and political pressure was therefore devoted to mobilizing additional funding from the public and private sectors. Typically, in the 1980s, the export credit agencies of the G10 countries were tapped for credit to finance essential imports. At the same time, private sector banks were asked, with varying degrees of pressure, to roll over existing credits and to provide new money. Similar techniques were used in the crises of the 1990s, though the capital account origin of the crises rendered the magnitude of the fund raising task much greater. Some creditor governments had resort to lending from their exchange reserves, though in the wake of the Mexican crisis of 1994-5 the freedom of action of the major lender, the United States, was inhibited temporarily by the US Congress. The BIS coordinated short-term lending by its member central banks, often acting under a government guarantee.

Such techniques succeeded, at least on paper, in mobilizing apparently enormous sums from creditor country governments and their private sectors to support debtor countries in times of stress. Table 3.1 sets out the financial packages for three Asian countries.

Table 3.1 Financial packages for three Asian countries (billions of US dollars)

	Thailand	Indonesia	Korea
IMF	4.0	10.1	21.1
World Bank and ADB	2.7	8.0	14.2
Other (mainly bilateral)	10.5	18.0	23.1

Note: The bilateral funding in the Korean case was the 'second line of defence' that was never disbursed.
Source: Kenen (1991).

Yet significant proportions of some financial packages amounted to mere window dressing as they were not readily available for use. The use of such window dressing devices led the IMF's Independent Evaluation Office in its evaluation of the Fund's involvement in the capital account crises of the 1990s of Indonesia, Korea and Brazil to make the following stern, but totally justified, comment:

> Since restoration of confidence is the central goal, the IMF should ensure that the financing package, including all components, should be sufficient to generate confidence and also of credible quality. Financing packages prepared by

the IMF should not rely on parallel official financing, unless the terms of access are clear and transparently linked to the IMF-supported strategy. Attempts to inflate the total amount of financing by including commitments made under uncertain terms would risk undermining the credibility of the rescue effort. This implies that if the IMF is to play an effective role as crisis coordinator, either it must have adequate financial resources of its own or the availability of additional official financing should be made subject to a single, predictable framework of conditionality.

The high level of Fund lending has been maintained in recent years in response to successive crises. In 2003 the Fund provided $30 billion financial assistance to Brazil in an apparently successful attempt to restore market confidence. Indeed, IMF credit outstanding has tended to rise in recent years, despite a fall in the number of country programmes.

Some critics have characterized these large financing packages as bailouts that created moral hazard and encouraged excessive risk taking. The critics go on to argue that while such bailouts may in the short term alleviate tensions between debtors and creditors, they create further tensions in the longer term as creditors and debtors are given incentives to undertake imprudent transactions and thereby contribute to further instability in the international financial system. This topic was examined in depth in Eichengreen (2000) whose main conclusions are summarized in Box 3.1.

BOX 3.1 Eichengreen (2000): A summary

Some wishful thinking:
- IMF policy should be changed to prohibit rescues of countries with lax policies. But the costs of inaction are too painful for the official community to bear.

- IMF disbursements should be conditioned on commitments by private investors to agree to restructuring, new money or rollovers. But often the investors cannot be identified in sufficient time and cannot be compelled to act collectively. In the end, the perceived costs of inaction would force the Fund to back down.

Institutional reforms should reflect the causes of financial crisis:
- Investor panics are best dealt with by payments' standstills, either IMF imposed or endorsed.

- Crises reflecting inconsistent policies and disappointing economic performance require debt restructuring, whichcollective action clauses (CACs) could make easier.

Reforms should:
- be prioritized
- be feasible
- rely on market forces
- limit reliance on IMF resources.

Such judgements point to the conclusion that CACs, not international standstills, should be the priority in the strengthening of the international financial architecture.

Source: Eichengreen (2000).

3.4.2 Restructuring public sector debt – the role of the Paris Club

The Paris Club plays a key role in the management of creditor and debtor relationships relating to public sector debt. It describes itself as '... an informal group of official creditors whose role is to find co-ordinated and sustainable solutions to the payment difficulties experienced by debtor nations. Paris Club creditors agree to rescheduling debts due to them... It is the voluntary gathering of creditor countries willing to treat in a co-ordinated way the debt due to them by the developing countries.' Since 1983, the total amount of debt covered by agreements between the official creditors and debtor nations has been $416 billion. For the emerging market countries, a standard procedure was to reschedule debt payments, often over several years, rather than provide debt reduction. But the Club's agreement to reschedule was usually, but not invariably, made conditional on the debtor having a current programme of some sort with the IMF. For the poorest countries, the Paris Club was initially the principal instrument for settling outstanding differences between debtors and creditors – latterly by agreeing to a substantial write-off of debts.

Discussions in the Club have often been tense, whatever the status of the debtor. Its members sometimes reached different judgements about the political and economic needs of debtors and some were less willing than others to concede their claims as creditors. Debtors too were often unwilling to accede to the Club's requirements, though usually their bargaining power in the room was limited. In most cases, however, sometimes after long bargaining extending into the early hours, agreements were reached. All too often, however, the debtor would return for a new rescheduling, backed by the reality that it had the power simply not to pay.

3.4.3 Restructuring private sector debt – the role of the London Club

Discussions between private sector creditors and sovereign debtors have traditionally taken place in the so-called London Club.[29] They could be as fraught as those that took place in the Paris Club. Where parallel discussions took place in the Paris Club, there were attempts to maintain comparability of treatment between private and public sector creditors. Differences in lending instruments and terms often rendered judgements about comparability contentious, however, and much suspicion was engendered between the two sectors. Yet again in the end, agreements were reached. It remains to be seen whether that same result will be obtained in the case of the current negotiations with Argentina.

The increasing substitution of bond finance for bank finance and the consequent increase in the number and classes of creditors have made it much more difficult to coordinate the interest of creditors. Various *ad hoc* committees of bond holders have been established on a case by case basis, but their membership is often not comprehensive and their mandates have been challenged. The issue of creditor coordination is further explored in Section 3.4.5 below.

3.4.4 Lending into arrears

The development of the IMF's policy of 'lending into arrears' has provided another source of acrimony between the public sector and private sector creditors. During the 1980s debt crisis the Fund made it a condition of its programmes that a member country's arrears, including to commercial banks, should be eliminated during the programme period and that new arrears should not be accumulated. This enabled the Fund to link the availability of Fund resources, and Paris Club rescheduling, with the agreement of bank creditors to restructure arrears and to provide new money. The banks' precarious financial positions gave them little option but to acquiesce in this strategy.

By the end of the 1980s, however, their stronger financial positions and the growth of a secondary market in banks' claims much reduced the banks' incentive to provide new money and reschedule old debt. In these circumstances the Fund's refusal to lend when the debtor country had arrears gave the creditor banks the power to block Fund negotiations with that country merely by refusing to restructure arrears. So in 1989 the Fund began, subject to strict conditions, to lend to countries even when they had arrears to private bank creditors. In 1998-9 the Fund extended the policy to arrears on payments to bond holders, as bonds had replaced syndicated bank credits as the main source of emerging market finance from the private sector. The Fund will, however, lend into arrears only when a debtor country is deemed to be making a good faith effort to reach a collaborative agreement with its creditors. The interpretation of this condition became particularly tortured in the negotiations with Argentina in 2004.

3.4.5   Bond financing: new techniques for managing relationships between debtors and creditors

The increasing replacement of bank credits by bond finance during the 1990s had other significant consequences for the management of debtor and creditor relationships in times of financial stress. This development has enormously increased the number of investors with a direct stake in the outcome of debt rescheduling and reduction. Issues of intercreditor equity have therefore jumped to the top of the agenda.

Because of their number and the diversity of their interests, creditors in this new world were not willing to have their interests bargained about in 'clubby' smoke-filled (no doubt nowadays metaphorical) rooms. The restructuring of some outstanding bonds of Pakistan and Ukraine in 1999 and Ecuador in 2000 concentrated minds. Appendix 3.1, drawn from an IMF paper, gives some details of bond restructurings. Fortunately, the countries involved were not significant players in international financial markets and the financial disturbance was limited. These episodes, however, prompted further thinking in the financial community about new ways to resolve stresses in debtor and creditor relationships. Following much discussion in the IMF Board, in the G7 and G10 and in private sector and academic circles, two proposals for improving cooperation between debtors and creditors eventually emerged: the inclusion of collective action clauses (CACs) in bond contracts and a treaty based sovereign debt restructuring mechanism (SDRM). The proposal for an SDRM is the more radical and comprehensive approach and one that the IMF management saw as possibly complementing CACs. Box 3.2 and Box 3.3 outline the main features of CACs and the SDRM respectively.

The discussion of CACs revived an idea that had been floated unsuccessfully by the G10 in the mid-1990s. The idea had made little progress at that point. The international private financial community was hostile to the concept for fear that it would make it easier for countries not to pay their debts when they could do so. Emerging market countries that did not include CACs in their bond contracts (mainly those that issued bonds under US law) feared that the inclusion of such clauses would raise market suspicions that they contemplated default. They made too the reasonable debating point that the debt contracts of many developed countries omitted such clauses. The subsequent experience, however, with restructurings by Pakistan, Ukraine and especially Ecuador, along with the fear that if they continued to oppose CACs they would engender more support for the SDRM,

---

BOX 3.2 Collective action clauses[30]

- In 1980, bonds comprised only 2% of external countries' external debt of $600 billion; by 1999, 19% of $2.6 trillion.
- CACs are of four types.

  1. Collective representation clauses set out mechanisms for coordinating discussions and possible action between the issuer and bondholders.

  2. Majority action clauses allow a qualified majority of creditors to agree to a change in the terms of a debt contract, which is binding, on any dissenting bondholders.

  3. Sharing clauses ensure that all payments from the debtor are distributed between creditors on a pro-rated basis.

  4. Non-acceleration clauses require a minimum threshold of bondholders to demand immediate repayment of principal following default.

- Provision for bondholders' meetings and majority action clauses are (in 2000) routinely included in bonds governed by English and Luxembourg law, but not in bonds governed by New York or German law.
- Of the 625 emerging market bond issues between 1990-2000, 31% were governed by English law, 28% by New York law, 19% by German law, 2% by Luxembourg law and the remainder by the law of other jurisdictions.

Source: Dixon and Wall (2000).

BOX 3.3 A Sovereign Debt Restructuring Mechanism (SDRM)[31]

The purpose of an SDRM is to provide a legal framework for the restructuring of foreign debt.

An SDRM would typically include some or all of the following elements:

- Majority restructuring: allowing, through the establishment of a universal statutory framework (a treaty), a super majority of creditors to reach an agreement binding on all creditors subject to the restructuring.
- Deter disruptive litigation: discouraging creditors from seeking to enhance their position through litigation during the restructuring process, sometimes, but not necessarily, through automatic stays on enforcement.
- Protecting creditor interests: safeguarding creditors through transparency of operations and adequate assurances that their interests are being protected during the restructuring process.
- Priority financing: inducing new financing by excluding a specified amount of new financing ('seniority') from the restructuring, if such exclusion were supported by a qualified majority of creditors.
- Dispute resolution forums: resolving disputes during the voting process or when claims are being verified.

Source: http://www.imf.org/external/np/exr/facts/sdrm.htm

led leading emerging market countries to introduce CACs into their borrowing contracts. Mexico led the way in February 2003 and was rewarded by an approving G7 statement while paying no discernibly higher interest rate. A few months later, at its meeting in April 2003 the International Monetary and Financial Committee, after acknowledging the progress made in developing model CACs, concluded that:

> In view of the experience gained through the implementation of CACs and the interest in a code of conduct, and recognizing that it is not feasible now to implement the SDRM [sovereign debt restructuring mechanism] proposal, work should continue on issues raised in the SDRM discussions, such as [...] inter-creditor equity that are of general relevance to the orderly resolution of financial crises.

Section 3.5 below reviews the role played by the G7 in the progress made with CACs and in the failure of the SDRM. It has sometimes been suggested that an obscure subsection of the Fund's Articles, Article VIII Section 2 (b), could be invoked to block creditor litigation if a debtor country suspended its debt payments or those of its residents. This provides that: 'Exchange contracts which involve the currency of any member and which are contrary to the exchange control regulations of that member maintained or imposed consistently with this Agreement shall be unenforceable in the territories of any member.'

Yet this Article has remained very much a dead letter, despite an apparently strong Executive Board interpretation of 1949, making clear that private sector parties will not receive the assistance of the judicial or administrative authorities of other Fund members in obtaining the performance of such contracts. Whatever the previous interpretation of Article VIII(2)b, however, its significance today for the management of debtor and creditor relationships is most unclear. For example, an expansive interpretation, bringing debt contracts within the meaning of 'exchange contracts' is highly controversial. It is, however, certain that in the modern world the use of the subsection to block litigation against a defaulting debtor is not practical politics. Extraterritoriality has its limits.

There, the debate between debtors and creditors rests. All parties, public and private, presumably share the same objective, namely '...to make the restructuring of unsustainable debt more orderly, predictable and rapid'.[32] It is no longer possible for the Managing Director of the IMF to marshal 'financing packages' by dealing with a handful of major export credit agencies and G7 governments in the Paris Club and a committee of commercial banks in the London Club. Yet crisis, or the prospect of crisis, has always been the mother of invention in the international financial system. It was a crisis that persuaded a handful of major banks to help in dealing with the LTCM crisis in 1998, in line with the wishes of the Federal Reserve. Maybe CACs will provide mechanisms for orderly workouts. Maybe a financial crisis will force some version of the SDRM back on to the agenda, despite the strong antipathy to this approach evinced by private creditors and some major debtors.

3.4.6 New measures to prevent crises in debtor and creditor relationships

In part, the need for future action will depend on the success of the measures introduced by the IMF in the late 1990s, aimed at preventing crises in debtor and creditor relationships. The Fund's measures to strengthen the architecture of the international financial system has covered five areas:

- **Transparency and openness:** by making timely, reliable data, as well as information about economic and financial policies, practices, and decision-making, readily available to financial markets and the public.

- **Developing and assessing adherence to internationally accepted standards:** by securing adherence to international standards and codes of good practice, covering, for example, the transparency of fiscal, monetary and financial policies as well as the quality of accounting and auditing practices, bankruptcy regimes, corporate governance, banking and securities market regulation, and social policy.

- **Strengthening financial sectors:** by improving supervision and regulation of the financial sector through stronger assessments of countries' financial systems under the Financial Sector Assessment Programme jointly administered by the IMF and the World Bank.

- **Enlisting the private sector:** by the stronger involvement of the private sector in crisis prevention and resolution, for example by establishing channels of communication and relationships during periods of relative tranquility, which can be called upon in periods of stress.

- **Extending IMF financial facilities:** by the creation of a new IMF instrument of crisis prevention, the Contingent Credit Line (CCL). The CCL is a precautionary line of defence available to member countries with strong economic policies designed to prevent future balance-of-payments problems that might arise from international financial contagion. (In fact, no member state proved willing to apply for a CCL.)

Some believe that these measures will significantly mitigate the incidence of financial crises and facilitate their management and resolution. Others argue that, while these measures are useful, they do not deal with the fundamental issues affecting debtor and creditor relationships which, in their view, could be addressed only by an SDRM.

3.5 The role of the fund and of the G7 finance ministers and governors

3.5.1 G7 methods and methodology

The brief description of the various measures for bridging the interests of creditors and debtors shows that the IMF has provided the linchpin for virtually all the initiatives described. The World Bank has played an important role too, especially with the HIPCs. The Bank's mandate and activities have not, however, given it the same central role that the Fund has played in the management of creditor and debtor relations. Its functioning is not therefore examined in this Report. The Bank and the several regional development banks are, however, significant creditors in their own right, and questions have been raised about their role in a world when many of their borrowers have access to global capital markets. Such issues also go beyond the scope of this Report.

The IMF has undoubtedly played a crucial and fruitful role, but its seemingly central role only partly reflects the reality. Certainly, when the 1982 Mexican debt crisis erupted, in mid-August, the Managing Director of the IMF effectively took the leadership role, supported by central bankers and ministers from some creditor countries. Thereafter, however, the leadership role was increasingly assumed by the G7 Group, and especially the G7 finance ministers and governors. It was they who identified the need for, specified the broad working outlines of and provided the political drive for most of the initiatives carried forward by the Fund. Since the middle of the 1980s very few, if any, initiatives have succeeded without G7 support.

The G7 was not the first 'Group' to become involved in major international monetary issues. Back in the 1960s, the G10 elaborated the General Arrangements to Borrow (GAB). In the 1970s the Board of Governors of the IMF established a Committee on the Reform of the International Monetary System, otherwise known as the Committee of 20. In 1978 the Committee's recommendations were implemented in somewhat cut down form in the Second Amendment of the Fund's Articles of Agreement, which established the right of members to adopt exchange rate arrangements of their choice. This work of the G10 and the Committee of 20 was effectively carried out under the aegis of the IMF and was concerned, broadly, with the grand architecture of the international monetary system.

The G7 involvement was different, especially from the end of the 1980s. The G7 had no formal or informal connection with the IMF, other than that provided by the Managing Director's attendance at a limited part of the meetings of the G7 finance ministers and governors. The Group involved itself in most issues relating to the functioning and performance of the international monetary system and to some involving individual country matters, many of which went well beyond the immediate purview of the IMF. Their statements became full of prescription, guidance and encouragement to various bodies, notably the IMF and World Bank, on all the issues of the day. The pattern was set by their statement of September 1988, which stated, 'The Ministers and Governors confirmed their support for the work of the IMF and the World Bank. They will cooperate closely within the framework of both institutions with all member countries, especially the developing countries, to cope with the problems of the world economy.'

This statement ushered in a period, which extends until the present day, in which the G7, principally in the form of the G7 finance ministers' and governors' group, sought to provide strategic direction and management to creditor and debtor relationships and to the prevention, management and resolution of financial crises. As an informal group, the G7 had perforce to work informally. Their technique was to hammer out a common position among themselves, promulgate it in a declaration or statement and then work in the many international forums, particularly the Executive Boards of the IMF and World Bank, for its implementation. The finance ministers' and governors' declaration of 30 October 1998 is a classic example of their technique of operation and is, in many ways, the high point of their work in the 1990s. The Declaration set out a comprehensive work programme, summarized in Box 3.4, which sought to remedy the weaknesses in the international financial system exposed by the financial problems that had emerged in Asia.

On the same day as the finance ministers and governors issued this comprehensive Declaration, the heads of state or government of the G7 countries issued a supportive parallel statement. The Leaders agreed that the Declaration's proposals should be implemented promptly and called for the finance ministers to extend their work and to present a report to the next year's Economic Summit at Cologne, Germany. To round-off the day's action, the IMF Executive Directors of the G7 countries submitted a memorandum to the Fund's Managing Director and its Executive Board outlining a work programme to put into effect the finance ministers and governors proposals. In February 1999, moreover, the G7 finance ministers' and governors' issued a document entitled 'Global Financial

---

BOX 3.4 G7 finance ministers and governors' Declaration of 30 October 1998

In their Declaration of 30 October 1998, the G7 finance ministers and governors:

- Called for the creation of a new IMF facility to help deal with contagion.
- Pledged bilateral support in appropriate cases.
- Committed their governments' and private sectors' with compliance with various procedures and IMF sponsored codes to increase transparency of certain public and private financial transactions.
- Called upon the OECD to complete its work on a corporate governance code, asked the IASC to finalize by early 1999 its proposal for internationally agreed accounting standards.
- Called upon other countries participating in international markets to observe the codes and standards, asked the IMF to check that observance as part of its regular Article IV surveillance and to publish the results and upon the IMF, World Bank, OECD and regulatory organizations to assist countries to meet the codes and standards.
- Agreed to work together to strengthen financial market surveillance.
- Called upon the private sector to facilitate 'collective action clauses'.
- Reaffirmed the IMF's policy of lending into arrears.
- Agreed to support a broad range of reforms to improve the transparency of the IMF.
- Set in hand work to strengthen the international financial architecture.

Architecture: A Plan for Implementation as Presented to the Heads in December 1998'. And some two months later, the substance and much of the detail of this G7 programme was reflected in the April communiqué of the Interim Committee. The IMF Executive Board then implemented the plan through the programme of measures described in Section 3.5 above. Finally, at the Cologne Summit in June 1999, the Heads duly received the finance ministers' report that they had requested eight months earlier, and their own Communiqué set out in definitive terms the G7's views on a range of issues. These are summarized in Box 3.5.

BOX 3.5 The Cologne measures to strengthen the international financial architecture

Rejection of the need to create new institutions but a call on the existing institutions to adapt to meet the demands of today's global financial system.

Reaffirmation of the central role of the IMF and the World Bank in the international financial system. Strengthening and reforming the international financial institutions including through:

- the establishment of the Financial Stability Forum;
- the creation of the International Monetary and the Financial Committee;
- the commitment to establish 'an informal mechanism for dialogue', which was to become the G20.

The enhancement of measures to increase transparency, including through codes and standards.

Strengthening financial regulation in industrialized countries.

Strengthening macroeconomic policies and financial systems in emerging markets.

Improving crisis prevention and management, and involving the private sector.

Promoting social policies to protect the poor and vulnerable.

The eight months of intense activity between November 1998 and June 1999 showed the effectiveness of G7 leadership. The finance ministers and governors promulgated a plan; it was followed up at the IMF Board; endorsed by the IMFC; and then given the highest political backing by the heads of state or government.

This intense activity is perhaps the most fully developed case of the G7 providing a leadership role. The Group did not, however, invent that role in 1998. Almost a decade earlier the finance ministers and governors had set out their views in highly prescriptive terms (which are in part replicated in Box 3.6). They listed the actions required by the major participants engaged in international debt issues; namely the IMF, the World Bank, the commercial banks and the governments' export credit agencies in the Paris Club.

Eighteen months later, in another intervention into debtor and creditor relationships, the finance ministers and governors said, 'They … expect commercial banks to move forward expeditiously with other countries which have opened negotiations on new financial packages.' In November 1991, moreover, they concluded difficult negotiations with eight of the former Soviet Republics about outstanding debt owed to their export credit agencies. And two years later, the Paris Club followed the G7's lead by signing an agreement with the Russian Federation.

BOX 3.6 Extract from the G7 finance ministers and governors' Statement, April 1989

They [the finance ministers and governors] also encouraged the IMF and World Bank to take, in accordance with their established principles, appropriate steps to support efforts to reduce the debt burdens of countries which are committed to substantial economic reforms. This support should be accomplished by setting aside a portion of policy-based loans to facilitate debt reduction transactions…They further concurred that diversified financial support from the banks is needed to support sound economic reform programmes through a broad array of new lending and debt/debt service reduction mechanisms…The ministers and governors also encouraged the IMF to continue to collaborate actively with the Paris Club.

The G7 were active too during Mexico's financial crisis in 1994-5. At their meeting in February 1995 they '…expressed their total satisfaction with international efforts to assist Mexico that would help ease its financial crisis'. The next major financial crisis involved South Korea and likewise led to a strong response by the G7 ministers and governors. On the day before Christmas in 1997, the Canadian Minister of Finance published a statement on their behalf. It expressed G7 support for bringing forward the disbursement of IMF commitments and of part of the financial package put together by the G7 countries and six other countries. Typically, these G7 statements were followed up, in greater or lesser detail, by action in the relevant international forums and bodies.

The role of the G7 is less clear in the discussions of CACs and the SDRM. The G10, of which the G7 comprised seven of its 11 (*sic*) members, was the forum in which the discussion of CACs had originally begun in 1995. This early work was not embraced by private creditors or by sovereign debtors, despite supportive statements from the G7 in 1998. It was not until February 2003 that it was given practical effect, when Mexico included CACs in an international bond issue, a development that was promptly welcomed by a supportive statement from the G7. The SDRM, by contrast, was an initiative of the IMF management. It received cautious support from the G7 finance ministers and governors at their meeting in September 2002, but it was effectively killed at their meeting in April 2003, as it had by then become apparent that there was strident private sector opposition and that the need for treaty change made adoption of the SDRM politically impossible.

The G7's interest in debt went beyond debt of the emerging countries. Debt of the poorest countries has been an enduring subject of discussion in the ministers' and governors' meetings. In September 1988 the ministers and governors welcomed 'with great satisfaction the fact that the necessary arrangements have now been worked out by the Paris Club to implement the new Toronto [Economic Summit] approach [to rescheduling] as regards the debt of the poorest countries'. The Toronto terms were subsequently improved at a series of G7 Economic Summits, culminating in the Cologne Summit of 1999. The decisions of the Summit Heads were usually preceded by intense discussion among G7 finance ministers and then subsequently translated into operational practice and detail in the Paris Club. The ten or more members of the Paris Club not members of the G7 were often extremely frustrated at being asked to rubber stamp what they regarded as a series of G7 *fait accomplis* on HIPC and other Paris Club business. Yet without this G7 leadership it is difficult to see how the international creditor community would have made any progress in resolving this complex and contentious issue.

An extension of the G7's interest in the poorest countries was their work in leading support for countries hit by chronic political instability, war or other catastrophe. The Group had taken the lead in the first half of the 1990s in encouraging the Soviet Union/Russia to take the first steps to integrate into the global economy. More recently, at their meetings in September 2003 and February 2004, the Group took the lead in signifying their support for the reconstruction of Afghanistan and Iraq. At their September 2003 meeting the finance ministers undertook to '...work together with the Palestinian authorities, the IFIs and other institutions to contribute to the design of a Comprehensive Plan for the revitalization and reconstruction of the Palestinian economy and to implement it in the context of the peace process along the Road Map. We have instructed our Deputies to report by the Spring meetings.' This interest in what have come to be known as 'failed states' was not new. In the autumn of 1995, the parlous condition of Bosnia became a matter of high concern in G7 capitals. So in October, the ministers and governors '...urged the IMF and World Bank to conduct expeditiously a thorough needs assessment [of Bosnia] so that the international community can respond quickly, flexibly, and on suitable terms as soon as conditions warrant.'

These references to G7 interest in the Palestinian Authority and in Bosnia indicate the Group's methodology in tackling such problems. With the backing of the polictical support in the G7 statements, the members of the Group took the lead in the various international forums, notably the IMF and the World Bank, in enlisting the expertise and, on some occasions, the financial support of those institutions. The emphasis of much of the work of the Fund and the Bank in such 'failed states' was on capacity building – helping to lay the basis for functioning institutions and providing technical expertise and assistance. The G7 members have also worked bilaterally, with ad hoc coalitions and in quasi-consultative groups of aid donors, to achieve similar ends. It is difficult to avoid the conclusion that the world community will continue to have a need for some instrument, akin to the G7, to provide the political momentum required to coordinate and drive forward work on the difficult problems of preventing the emergence of and coping with the difficulties of failed states.

3.5.2 An assessment

This brief history illustrates how the G7 has sought to shape creditor and debtor relationships during the last two decades. The Group's stance has been mainly reactive, responding to events and crises. That was perhaps inevitable and wise in a world where the power of governments to manage the vastly increased international capital flows was limited, compared to the two previous decades. If the Group has had 'a philosophy', it has been to protect and to promote a stable and open global financial system, to encourage emerging market countries, including the former Communist states, to participate in that system and help alleviate the lot of the very poorest countries with a view to their eventual participation. The Group has not escaped criticism, and four areas of its activities are briefly discussed below.

In the early 1980s the attention of the G5/7 countries was, understandably, focused on restoring the health of the major banks which had been gravely imperilled by bad debts incurred by Latin American governments (and to a lesser extent governments elsewhere). It took a long time, however, for attention to be focused on the need to create the conditions required for sustainable growth in the debtor countries. Two plans, named after successive US Secretaries of the Treasury, the Baker Plan and the Brady Plan, sought to do this. The Baker Plan sought to stimulate growth in the debtor countries and the Brady Plan to facilitate the write down of private sector claims by providing official finance. Both plans sought to lay the basis for renewed growth in the debtor economies, but the initiatives would have been of even greater value if they had been launched a year or so earlier. Yet such delays should not be regarded as an intrinsic fault in the informal process which the G7 has epitomized. They are symptomatic of the difficulties in the way of assembling a consensus for action in matters relating to international financial cooperation. There is no reason to believe that more formal institutional machinery with correspondingly formal procedures and processes would have been more expeditious.

The G7's campaign to alleviate the debt burden of the poorest countries has been slow and, in the case of some countries, grudging. It began in 1988 at the Toronto Economic Summit when the G7 heads of state or government agreed the so-called Toronto terms. Those terms were gradually improved at a succession of Economic Summits – London in 1991, Naples in 1994, Lyon in 1996 and Cologne in 1999. In retrospect, it is disappointing that the wider, deeper and faster relief available under the Cologne terms was not available earlier. Indeed there is reason to question whether they went far enough. Certainly, the costs of the initiative are great: the cost under the latest framework may come to exceed $29 billion, divided more or less equally between bilateral and multilateral creditors. It is important too to ensure to the extent possible that the HIPCs make good use of the debt relief and remain in a sustainable debt position. Yet progress has often been painfully slow. Even today, there are still disputes among the creditor countries about the sharing of the financing burden.

As regards the G7's work on Russia, history has still to give its verdict on whether G7 efforts have helped or hindered that country to deal with its post-Soviet problems. The G7's efforts in the failed states suggest that the haul is a very long one indeed and that without the rudiments of viable political governance, the prospects of success are poor. Yet despite the as yet unproven outcome, the leadership of the G7 finance ministers helped to focus the attention of the international financial community on the economic problems of countries that have great political importance to the world community.

As for the financial crises of the 1990s, these were crises that few, if any, policy-makers, including in the G7, foresaw. It is possible, with the benefit of hindsight, to discern signs of the build up of unsustainable short-term liabilities, for example in Mexico, Thailand and Korea. If the measures in the G7 Action Plan, described in Box 3.4 and Box 3.5, had already been effective, the Asian financial crisis of 1997–98 might well have been mitigated. The IMF's own Independent Evaluation Office (IEO) carried out an extensive and thorough analysis of the Fund's role in the capital account crises in Indonesia (1997–8), Korea (1997–8) and Brazil (1998–9). The IEO concluded that the initial programmes for all three countries failed to achieve their stated objectives, but subsequent experience under the revised programmes was very different. The IEO also found that IMF surveillance was more successful in identifying macroeconomic vulnerabilities than in recognizing the risks posed by balance sheet and corporate governance related weaknesses. Such weaknesses are at the core of debtor and creditor relationships. The IEO report concluded with the six recommendations that are summarized in Box 3.7.

BOX 3.7 Independent Evaluations Office's recommendations: The IMF and recent capital account crises – Indonesia, Korea and Brazil

- To increase the effectiveness of surveillance, Article IV consultations should take a 'stress testing' approach to the analysis of a country's potential exposure to a capital account crisis.

- Management and Executive Board should increase the impact of surveillance, for example through greater candour and accessibility to the public.

- The IMF should carry out a comprehensive review of programme design in capital account crises.

- Financing packages should be sufficient to generate confidence and be of adequate quality.

- The IMF should be proactive in its role as crisis coordinator.

- Better resource management in the Fund to promote country expertise and to create 'centres of experience' on crisis management.

Yet despite the criticisms levelled against G7 stewardship during the last 20 years, the global economy has undoubtedly seen great progress in that period. G7 leadership can claim some, but not all, of the credit for that progress. Many minds outside the G7 – from the international institutions, from academia, from many countries in different stages of development and from the private sector – have contributed to establishing the conditions for the recent economic progress. G7 promotion and sponsorship of a framework for economic and financial cooperation has, however, helped to provide strategic leadership which has worked in the direction of an open, stable and balanced world economy. Without the G7, it is difficult to see from where that leadership would have come.

3.5.3 The future of G7 leadership

Such a conclusion will not be happily received everywhere. Many countries understandably chafe under, and some understandably resent, G7 leadership. A country with an economy that has a significant impact on, or is significantly impacted by, developments in the world economy does not appreciate a self-selected group of countries taking decisions that affect it. Nor does a country that has seen a decline in its relative importance or influence. Sometimes too the G7 has acted insensitively, for example at the 1994 Madrid meetings when it kept the Interim Committee waiting, only then to present it with a take it or leave it proposition on an important matter of business. The Interim Committee understandably 'left it'. In short, legitimacy is an issue of increasing importance for the G7. In the end, moreover, effectiveness is diminished when legitimacy is called into question.

There is already evidence of stirrings against the legitimacy of G7 leadership. As early as November 1997 senior officials from a group of Pacific countries met in Manila, in what was to be called 'the Manila framework,' to develop a concerted approach to restoring financial stability in the region. Representatives of the IMF and the World Bank attended. Representatives from Europe were not invited, though two effectively gate crashed some of the proceedings. Around the same time President Clinton and the other leaders of APEC countries announced the establishment on a temporary basis of the Group of 22. This group of finance ministers and central bank governors had the task of advancing the reform of the architecture of the global financial system. Membership of the Group of 22 comprised finance ministers and central bank governors from the G7 industrial countries and 15 other countries from the larger emerging market and transition economies.

At the Cologne Summit in June 1999 the G7 finance ministers sought to seize back the initiative in the efforts to shape the structure of global governance. Their report to the G7 heads called for '...an informal mechanism for dialogue among systemically important countries within the framework of the Bretton Woods institutional system.' Accordingly, in September 1999 the G7 finance ministers and governors announced the establishment of the G20. Its membership is composed of the finance ministers and central bank governors from G7 countries and 12 other countries significant for the global economy, together with the Presidency of the EU. The European Central Bank, the Managing Director of the IMF, the Chairman of the IMFC, the President of the World Bank, and the Chairman of the Development Committee also attend. The G7 declared that the G20 would be 'a new mechanism for informal dialogue in the framework of the Bretton Woods institutional system, to broaden the dialogue on key economic and financial policy issues among systemically significant economies and promote cooperation to achieve stable and sustainable world economic growth that benefits all.' The declaration predicted that 'discussions held in this group will prove useful to complement and reinforce the role of the governing bodies of the Bretton Woods institutions.' Since then, the G20 has met five times.

There are signs too of restlessness about the balance of power in the IMF. The International Monetary and Financial Committee at its April 2003 meeting considered '...it important that, as pointed out in the Monterrey Consensus, all members should have an adequate voice and representation in the institution.' At its September meeting the Committee stressed '... that the IMF's effectiveness as a cooperative institution depends on all members having an appropriate voice and representation. The Committee welcomes the measures being taken to improve the capacity of developing and transition member countries to participate more effectively in IMF policy formulation and decision-making.'

This restlessness reflects in part the normal tensions that exist between debtors and creditors. Debtors understandably feel, especially in times of financial stress, that it is the creditors who make the rules. Yet an examination of the events of the last two decades does not suggest that creditor governments have irresponsibly abused their creditor positions. Creditor governments have provided very large sums of money in times of financial stress to help smooth debtor and creditor relationships. They have supported the Fund's policy of lending into arrears and have urged their private sectors to cooperate in alleviating debtors' distress. They have written off substantial amounts of export credit.

Even so, the experiments with G22, G33 and G20 and the grumbles about IMF quotas suggest that some debtor countries are becoming increasingly unhappy with present arrangements and that the G7 countries have started to recognize that their power to shape the development of debtor and creditor relations may be waning.

The tectonic plates look to be shifting. Chapter 6 considers some possible consequences and proposes a remedy.

Appendix 3A[33]

Recent Sovereign Debt Restructurings

There have been at least five sovereign debt restructuring cases since the late 1990s. Russia and Ecuador restructured most of their debt following a formal default, while Ukraine and Pakistan restructured their debts in the shadow of default. Argentina, which initially planned a voluntary debt exchange, was forced to default following the first leg of its debt exchange. Moldova completed the restructuring of its sovereign debt very recently and it is not covered in this appendix.

Russia (1998–2000)
In response to a rapidly deteriorating economic situation, resulting mainly from the government's inability to implement important fiscal reforms, on 19 August 1998 the authorities announced a devaluation of the ruble, a suspension of payments on the sovereign's domestic debt, and a unilateral moratorium on private sector payments on external liabilities enforced through extensive capital and exchange controls (debt held by households and the central bank was excluded from the exchange restrictions). These announcements, and the subsequent dissolution of the government, triggered a banking crisis . There was no overall coordinating framework for the restructuring of Russia's various classes of debt. Domestic debt, London Club debt, and Paris Club debt were restructured in separate processes. Eurobonds were excluded from the restructuring altogether. Domestic ruble debt, amounting to 10.8% of GDP (of which 7.8% of GDP was held by domestic banks and the remainder by non-residents) was restructured first. An initial restructuring offer for London Club debt in September 1998 failed, triggering protracted negotiations. Eventually, on 11 February 2000, a restructuring agreement was announced by the London Club's Bank Advisory Committee, under which US$31.8 billion in Soviet-era debt was exchanged for US$21.8 billion in new bonds (completed by August 2000). Private creditors pushed for a new Paris Club rescheduling on similar terms but the notion of 'reverse comparability' was rejected. The improvement in oil prices took pressure off Russia's debt service profile. The Paris Club (with exposure of roughly US$37.5 billion) ultimately agreed to a rescheduling but not to a debt reduction.

Ukraine (1998–2000)
While Ukraine's overall stock of external debt was not particularly large (public external debt stood at roughly 39% of GDP in 1999), low levels of reserves and a spike in debt-service payments through 2001 made a debt restructuring unavoidable. A selective restructuring of domestic debt held by banks in August 1998 was followed by the restructuring of two bond-like instruments held by non-residents in September and October 1998, and a further restructuring in June 1999. After these piecemeal arrangements, the debt exchange in April 2000 tried to deal more comprehensively with the short maturity of Ukraine's bonded debt.

In total, the restructuring covered US$2.5 billion of external (Eurobond) debt and US$0.3 billion of domestic debt, representing about 9% of GDP. Of this amount, about 1.3% of GDP was held by domestic banks. A large part (roughly 50–60%) of the Eurobonds was held by retail investors. To limit the outflow of capital, exchange controls were imposed in September 1998, with no deposit freeze.

Pakistan (1999)

Sanctions imposed by bilateral official creditors following Pakistan's nuclear tests in May 1998 exacerbated the fragile external position, and triggered a debt crisis that had been looming during much of the 1990s. The financial instability that followed led the authorities to impose a deposit freeze on most foreign currency deposits (amounting to roughly US$7 billion). In January 1999, Pakistan concluded an agreement with the Paris Club, reducing debt service by US$3.3 billion, or 5% of GDP, in the period up to end-2000. Following an agreement with London Club creditors in June 1999, with a credible threat of default, Pakistan launched an exchange of Eurobonds in November in order to fulfil the comparability of treatment clause included in the Paris Club agreement. The Eurobonds had a face value of US$608 million (about 1% of GDP), of which one-third is estimated to have been held by residents (11% by domestic banks) and the remainder by financial institutions and retail investors in the Middle East. In addition, Pakistan was able to reschedule US$512 million of short-term trade credits and US$415 million of medium-term commercial credits. Domestic debt remained unaffected. Provisions to tighten capital controls further were introduced in June and October 1999.

Ecuador (1999–2000)

When a protracted banking crisis ultimately evolved into a bank run in March 1999, the government declared a bank holiday, deposits were frozen and the exchange rate was floated as pressures on the sucre mounted (no capital controls were imposed.) In September 1999, under continuous financial pressure, the government defaulted on its Discount Brady bonds while staying current on its other bonds. Holders of the Discount Brady bonds voted to accelerate their claims, however, forcing Ecuador to default on the other Brady bonds and its Eurobonds. In January 2000, amid political turbulence that resulted in a new government, a new economic plan was announced based on full dollarization of the economy. On 27 July 2000, almost 11 months following the initial default, Ecuador announced a comprehensive exchange offer for its external debt (with a face value of US$6.5 billion). Domestic public debt maturing between September 1999 and end-2000 (both in domestic and foreign currencies) was restructured separately (with a face value of US$346 million), as were external credit lines to closed banks (US$80 million). The total debt restructured was equivalent to about 50% of GDP, of which roughly one tenth was held by residents and the bulk by institutional investors in London and New York. In September 2000, Ecuador reached a rescheduling agreement with the Paris Club.

Argentina (2001–2)

With very high and rising spreads making it increasingly difficult to meet debt-service payments on rolled over debt, Argentina announced a two-phase approach in late October 2001 to restructure its roughly US$100 billion of domestic and external debt owed to private creditors. Phase 1 was aimed at domestic resident investors and involved the exchange of US dollar and Argentine peso bonds into new government-guaranteed loans (limiting the attractiveness to foreign creditors who have a preference for more marketable securities). The exchange, carried out in December 2001, involved approximately US$42 billion in sovereign debt and US$16 billion in provincial debt. Of the exchanged federal bonds, US$13 billion came from domestic banks' own accounts, US$11 billion from their clients, and US$17 billion from pension funds. By end-December, before Phase 2 could be initiated to restructure the remainder of mainly foreign-held sovereign debt, the financial and political situation had deteriorated considerably, and Argentina announced a moratorium on debt not included in Phase 1. While debt service was to be maintained on the loans issued in Phase 1, the general pesoization of domestic contracts in March 2002 included the loans of Phase 1. Several domestic debt operations were conducted between May and September 2002 (including deposit exchange schemes and bonds issued to banks to compensate them for the asymmetric pesoization of assets and liabilities) but little progress has been made in restructuring foreign-held sovereign debt. On 14 November 2002 the World Bank announced that Argentina failed to make an amortization payment of around US$715 million. In the event, the payment was made in January 2003, which enabled the World Bank to reactivate its lending operations to Argentina. A comprehensive solution to Argentina's debt problems is still pending.[34]

4 Enhancing Cooperation to Keep Up with Global Financial Markets

Micro issues in the financial markets, as contrasted with the macro issues of exchange rate systems and balance-of-payments adjustment, have played a larger and larger role in the agenda for international cooperation over recent years. These issues have included the supervision and regulation of banks and other financial service companies, the fight against money laundering and tax evasion, the convergence of accounting practices and the promulgation of codes of good practice and standards for various players in the markets. Some issues have been driven by systemic considerations such as the need to mitigate the threat to global financial stability that could be posed by the failure of a major private sector counterparty to honour its obligations. Some have been driven by the need to strengthen financial systems in emerging markets – a need underscored by the Asian financial crisis of 1997–8. Other issues have been driven by what is increasingly seen as a security imperative – preventing the open international financial system from being abused by criminal and terrorist elements. There has been substantial evolution over recent years in the multilateral network of institutions and groups charged with meeting the growing and changing requirements in this area. This chapter reviews issues in financial markets that have come to the fore in the past and how they have been dealt with. It then makes some proposals for strengthening the multilateral response in light of current and likely future challenges in a global financial system.

4.1 The emergence of financial issues on the international agenda

4.1.1 Forces for change in financial markets

Since the late 1950s, innovations in financial markets have repeatedly challenged regulators and other sectoral policy-makers to identify and deal with the consequences for their responsibilities of growth and innovation in cross-border financial activity. Growth and innovation have been driven by five fundamental forces:

1. **The search for ways around capital controls, reserve requirements and other regulatory constraints.** These create profitable arbitrage opportunities for those ingenious enough to exploit them. The Eurodollar market developed in the 1960s and early 1970s as a response to US capital controls and reserve requirements. It ultimately transformed international banking and, along the way, posed a series of challenges for banking officials that crossed national borders: maintaining the integrity of clearing and settlement sys-

tems; allocating supervisory responsibilities; and discharging lender of last resort responsibilities. The most fundamental question was whether the regulatory distortions that gave rise to the market should be reinforced to contain its growth or be dismantled. The answer that emerged over the 1970s and early 1980s was to dismantle the regulatory distortions and that was done gradually. More recently, the major examples of regulatory arbitrage have involved emerging markets, where many constraints are still imposed on international capital flows as well as in domestic markets. As examples, non-deliverable forward markets in non-convertible currencies such as the Chinese renminbi have developed in Hong Kong and elsewhere, and the resourcefulness of arbitrageurs was vividly illustrated at the time of the Asian financial crisis when a foreign credit of more than $100 million dollars to a Korean corporation was structured as sale/repurchase agreements for golf course memberships since these were not covered by capital control regulations.

2. **Advances in finance theory and information technology.** These have interacted to create an explosion in the choices available to fund managers and corporate treasurers for managing risk and liquidity. Derivatives and structured financial products have brought those managing large portfolios remarkably close to the idealized Arrow-Debreu world of complete markets. This would not have been possible without the computing power that allows traders to evaluate complex transactions nearly instantaneously. And without low cost, high volume communications channels it would not be possible to conduct a large volume of transactions at the speed required to profit from them. All of the computing power available today, however, would be worth little or nothing without the fundamental developments in finance theory that have occurred over the past 25 years.

3. **A global shift from indirect (bank or deposit based) finance to direct (securities based) finance.** This has been partly driven by finance theory and information technology, but also reflects a long-term evolution in the structure of finance. The growing role of securities markets has been associated with a rise to prominence of new or previously marginal institutions in international finance, a field that was once dominated by banks, and by the emergence of financial conglomerates. The shift from bank to securities-based finance also reflects in part the banks' experience in the 1980s, when the forced rescheduling of their syndicated sovereign credits made this form of lending less attractive and brought new investors into the market who used instruments thought not to be so readily susceptible to rescheduling. The creation of Brady bonds in the process of cleaning up the debt problems of the 1980s gave emerging market bond finance a big boost because it gave birth to a trading and research infrastructure that could be used to support new issues.

4. **Pursuit of the gains from diversification.** As regulatory and technological impediments to cross-border financial activity have come down, those with money to invest have sought to diversify risks internationally. Similarly, many financial institutions and corporations have sought to diversify their sources of funding. The result has been a strong growth of cross-border portfolio investment in developed countries and, when permitted, in emerging markets.

5. **The exploitation of financial systems by criminals and terrorists.** The creation and rapid growth of multiple channels for moving and investing money around the world opened up opportunities for criminals and terrorists to use the international payments system for laundering or otherwise transferring illegally gained proceeds. While accounting for a tiny part of cross-border financial activity, these activities pose large challenges to policy-makers. Concern about these problems increased gradually, with the United States first raising concerns about the use of financial institutions by drug traffickers. Continental European concerns were sharpened by the commitment to full liberalization of capital flows by European Community countries in 1988. At the following G7 Summit, the heads of states and government agreed on a course that led to the establishment of the Financial Action Task Force. Initially, attention was focused on the abuse of the payments system by illegal drug traffickers. Terrorist money flows received some attention from the beginning, however, and have become much more the focus in recent years.

4.1.2 The changing financial landscape

These forces have given rise to growth in international financial activity, which has far outstripped the growth of trade and has altered the composition of financial activity (see Table 4.1). From 1977 to 1987 cross-border bank liabilities grew at nearly 20%, despite the Latin American debt crisis during that period. Since then, international banking growth has slowed to less than 10% per year. By contrast, international bonds outstanding grew by 14.2% from 1987 to 1998 and then accelerated to an average growth rate of 22.7% from 1998 to 2003. International equity issuance grew at an average rate of 21.3% from 1987 to 1998 and maintained a strong 19.5% growth rate from 1998 to 2003 despite poor market conditions over most of the latter half of that period. Thus, securities markets gained relative to banking from 1987 when data were first collected. While available data do not allow a separation of derivatives activity of an international nature from domestic derivatives activity, the global growth of derivatives of all kinds, both over-the-counter and on exchanges, has been strong.

Table 4.1 Growth and changes in international finance

	1977:Q4–1987:Q1	1987:Q1–1998:Q2	1998:Q2–2003:Q3
	(compounded annual growth rates of dollar amounts, %)		
Cross-border bank liabilities	19.1	9.5	9.8
International bonds outstanding	–	14.2	22.7
New international equity issues*	–	21.33**	19.5
OTC derivatives (notional value)	–	–	18.7
Exchange traded derivatives (open interest)	–	30.1	71.1
World trade value***	8.5	7.3	4.1

Notes: *Growth measured using 4 quarter averages ending with the start and finish dates.
   **From 1986:Q4.
   ***To nearest available year.
Source: BIS

4.2 The present state of financial cooperation

4.2.1 The objectives

The growing scale and complexity of international finance have posed a continually expanding set of issues that demand cooperation among the national authorities charged with the oversight, supervision and regulation of their own financial markets. There is broad international agreement on the fundamental objectives:

- reduction of systemic risk;
- prevention of problems building up in financial systems – for example, an accumulation of unsound credit – that could have damaging macroeconomic effects;
- consumer protection;
- fostering the effective functioning of financial markets to produce an efficient allocation of savings to investments; and
- prevention of abuse of the system by criminals and terrorists.

Although these objectives are broadly shared across countries, they are not always shared by all of the regulators within individual countries that have multiple regulators. In the United States, for example, the Federal Reserve has historically emphasized the first two objectives – reducing systemic risk and adverse macroeconomic impacts. By contrast, the Securities and Exchange Commission (SEC) has focused on the third – consumer protection. This difference can be traced to the problems that prompted the establishment of the two organizations and to the legislation governing them. Differences have persisted because the distinct problems on which each organization concentrates have continued to be the most common failures in the markets for which each is responsible.

4.2.2 Impediments to cooperation

As financial markets and institutions have broken down old boundaries domestically, attempts have been made to reorganize financial supervision and regulation. In the United Kingdom, for example, a single institution, the Financial Services Authority, has been charged with supervising the whole financial system – a challenging task in a country with highly developed financial markets but one that can surely minimize domestic frictions. More recently, three financial market regulators in France were combined to form a new Autorité de Marchés Financier, but banking and insurance supervision remain separate. Despite these steps, the regulatory environment in many important countries is fragmented and populated by often rival financial regulators. The United States, for example, has three national banking regulators and 50 state regulators, separate national securities and futures markets regulators and 50 state securities regulators, as well as 50 state insurance regulators with no national regulator. The EU is rapidly becoming as complex. It has established a Committee of European Securities Regulators (CESR) and more recently a Committee of European Banking Supervisors (CEBS) and a Committee of European Insurance and Occupational Pensions Supervisors (CEIOPS) to improve cooperation among relevant European regulators and supervisors, but there are still 60 bodies involved in a four-level process for the securities markets alone. Similar situations arise in the European banking and insurance sectors.

Sectoral regulators have tended to seek their own kind when they go abroad for meetings. Issues often cross traditional lines of responsibility, however, as well as international borders. The supervision of financial conglomerates is an especially important example. Consolidation of financial supervision and regulation within countries, wholly or substantially, will greatly facilitate international cooperation. In the absence of this, however, it is already apparent that international cooperation requires that disparate regulators be brought together internationally. Regulation of activities that are increasingly done under one roof cannot be done in clubs of national regulators having limited, different jurisdictions. The creation of the Financial Stability Forum (FSF), discussed below, reflects recognition of this fact, yet the day-to-day conduct of international cooperation still resides, in the main, with several separate clubs, each with its own mandate and jurisdiction.

International cooperation is also hindered when national regulators see themselves as the protectors of those they regulate. This often occurs within a country but also arises when interests differ across countries. The negotiation of Basel I, the first international accord on bank capital requirements, was complicated by the efforts of national regulators to set the rules in ways that would be more favourable to their countries' banks given the structure of their business, and similar problems have afflicted the effort to design Basel II, the proposed successor to the present accord.

In short, despite widespread agreement on the fundamental objectives of international cooperation as it relates to the functioning of the financial system, differences in national systems of regulation and differences in national interests as they relate to particular financial-sector firms make multilateral efforts at policy cooperation in this area very difficult. The political reality described in Chapter 6 of this Report is especially true for financial markets. Power for political decision-making still ultimately resides in states, or to a limited extent in the case of the EU in a grouping of states, while the process of globalization has increased integration and interdependence. In the financial area, consumer interests intrude strongly and pervasively, and these are accepted national policy concerns even as the internet opens up cross-border provision of services. When banks operate in several countries, it is not always clear who should serve as lender of last resort – a matter in which legislatures, as national fiscal authorities, are much interested. Supervisory law is often deeply embedded in other national laws, such as the law relating to corporate bankruptcy. Action against money laundering involves national criminal law. Accordingly, the creation of supra-national authorities is not now conceivable in this area, whatever the advantages might be from the standpoint of the efficiency and stability of the financial system, nor is it likely to be for the foreseeable future. Progress depends on national actions, concerted in multinational bodies that have the properties stressed in this Report: they must be effective, legitimate, representative and accountable.

4.2.3 The roles of international organizations

During the past several years, some leading international organizations, notably the IMF, the World Bank, the BIS and the OECD, have become increasingly active in helping their members meet the five fundamental objectives described in Section 4.2.1 above. With the assistance of other public and private-sector bodies, they have developed a great many standards and codes for judging the quality of national statistics, the transparency of fiscal and monetary policies and, most importantly for this chapter, the quality of the financial infrastructure in individual countries. Codes have been written dealing with bank supervision, regulating securities markets and the insurance industry, as well as for judging the quality of the payments system, accounting standards, corporate governance, and insolvency regimes. Compliance with these codes is voluntary, as is participation in the Financial Sector Assessment Programme (FSAP) run jointly by the IMF and World Bank. Nevertheless, the Fund compiles and publishes assessments of compliance with a subset of standards and codes, and it also appraises its members' progress in meeting certain standards and codes during its annual consultation with each member country. Furthermore, a majority of its members now consent to the publication of the staff reports resulting from those consultations. Thus, there is pressure on governments to adhere to these codes.

4.2.4   The organization of the present structure of cooperation

The collapse of the Herrstatt Bank in Germany in 1974 concentrated the minds of G10 central banks on the risks in the emerging Eurodollar market. There had long been diffuse and often misplaced concerns about the risks in that market, but the collapse of the Herrstatt Bank highlighted two concrete problems. One was in the functioning of the payments systems for international transactions, which was disrupted when Herrstatt was closed in the middle of the day, before interbank settlements had been completed. The second was the recognition of potential gaps and overlaps in supervisory responsibility for banks. The G10 central bank governors launched work in both of these areas and instituted a broad collective overview of international markets. These three strands of work became institutionalized over time and continue today in the Committee on Payments and Settlement, the Basel Committee on Banking Supervision and the Committee on the Global Financial System, all of which function under the auspices of the Bank for International Settlements (BIS).

Thus the central banks were the first members of the regulatory community to be pulled together to address transnational problems. The approach they adopted was to convene experts to deal with often extremely technical matters. These early responses shaped ensuing developments: central banks have remained at the centre of the process even as the net has been thrown wider to encompass securities and insurance regulators, and the work has remained largely in the hands of technical experts insulated from both domestic and international politics.

Over the years, the multilateral financial agenda has become vast (see Box 4.1). One result has been that groups have proliferated. The Basel Committee alone currently has about 30 technical working groups and task forces. Some groups completed their assigned tasks and closed down. Other committees have continued in existence to deal with issues as they have come along in their areas of competence. Regulators other than those dealing with banks have also become more active internationally – at times joining broad-based groups (a Joint Forum of Banking, Securities and Insurance regulators has been meeting since 1995) and also forming their own groups. (The International Organization of Securities Commissions (IOSCO) was formed by 11 securities regulators in 1983. It has grown into a standards setting body of 181 members.)

4.2.5   The role of politics in financial cooperation

The high degree of independence from direct political control enjoyed by many financial supervisors has given rise to international groups that are technically anchored and relatively politically insulated. This approach has had advantages. When there has been a clearly identified problem that fell neatly into the existing structure, it has been possible to bring experts together to deal with it with little political involvement. For example, bank supervisors could gather in Basel in 1975

BOX 4.1 The multilateral financial agenda

The breadth of the financial agenda is shown by the recently completed and ongoing work relevant to sound financial systems reported by the Financial Stability Forum Secretariat in September 2003.

Macroeconomic management, surveillance and transparency
- The IMF/World Bank Financial Sector Assessment Programme.
- Foreign exchange management.
- External vulnerability.
- Portfolio investment data.
- Transparency of IMF policies.

Market infrastructure
- Role of central banks in payments systems.
- Combating money laundering.
- International financial reporting standards.
- Auditing standards.
- The accounting profession.
- Corporate governance principles.
- Systems for insolvency and creditor rights.
- Legal underpinnings of global markets.
- Sovereign workouts.
- Information exchange among securities regulators.
- Oversight of payments and settlement systems.
- Implications for developing countries.
- Relevance for debt management.
- Security of information.
- Insurance on the internet.

Financial system strengths and weaknesses
- Observance of standards and codes.
- Financial soundness indicators.
- Global financial stability.
- Foreign direct investment in the financial sector.

Market functioning
- Risk transfer.
- Ratings agencies.
- Credit default swaps.
- Transparency and disclosure in reinsurance.
- Stock repurchase programmes.

Prudential regulations and supervision
- Bank capital adequacy.
- Risk assessment and management.
- Electronic banking.
- Internet securities activity.
- 'Know-your-customer' risk management.
- Short-selling transparency.
- Insider trading.
- Money laundering and financing of terrorism.
- Insurance sector principles for regulation and supervision.
- Conflicts of interest in securities research.
- Private pensions.   (contd.)

BOX 4.1 (contd.)

Combating terrorist financing
- Implementation of agreed measures.
- Terrorism insurance.

Offshore financial centres
- Assessment of supervision and regulations.
- Statistics collection.

Highly leveraged institutions
- Disclosure.

E-finance
- Implications for developing countries.
- E-finance and debt management.
- Outsourcing and security.
- Insurance on the internet.

---

and agree on the Concordat that allocated supervisory responsibilities among them. The political interests of the participants sometimes cropped up at their meetings, where participants were sensitive to the interests of the institutions that they supervised, but the meetings were relatively free of the broader clash of interests that typically characterize both national and international politics.

Yet this insulation from politics also had a downside when it came to setting the agenda for international cooperation. Expert groups tend to interpret their mandates narrowly and resist taking up questions beyond their customary purview. This tendency has been exacerbated by the leading role of the G10 central bank governors in the banking area, which, like the G7, represents only the most developed countries. The members of the Basel Committee of Bank Supervisors, for example, declined initially to take on the problem of bank supervision in emerging markets, although poor supervision had been identified following the Mexican crisis of late 1994 as posing broader risks. They did respond, however, to pressure from the more political G7, which was faced with defects in financial structure that were at the centre of the Asian crisis (and to the threat of a competing initiative by the IMF and World Bank). Once engaged, the Basel Committee has done excellent work to set standards that respond to the circumstances of banks in emerging markets as well as those of global financial institutions. And they have brought emerging market supervisors into some of their work, if not into full membership.

There is more reason to insulate from undue political influence the process of coming to agreement on specific measures to deal with rules for effective market functioning. When stakes are high for particular groups, however, it becomes unrealistic to seek technocratic solutions without political input. The current efforts to establish a new global standard for bank capital requirements – Basel II – illustrate this. The regulators who laboured for years to reach agreement on Basel II felt they had produced a more efficient system that would be readily embraced. The changes had implications, however, for the relative competitive positions of banks and for the cost, and possibly for the availability, of funds to various classes of borrowers. This made the exercise inherently political, and the ultimate adoption of Basel II or some variant of it was thrown into doubt late in the day by the intervention of elected officials. Accounting standards have also become political issues, both in Europe with respect to the proposed treatment of derivatives in the proposals of the International Accounting Standards Board and in the United

States regarding the proposed treatment of employee stock options by the Financial Accounting Standards Board.

Politicians have brought more passion than wisdom to both of these issues, but it is clear that the political process cannot be ignored. This political dimension to the work of the Basel Committee and the accounting bodies suggests that both should perhaps be subject to some political input. This is hardly the case now. The G7 have made some cursory references to their work. It seems unlikely, however, that such references denote considered reflection by the ministers or their supporting senior officials. It is difficult to get timely focus on what are very technical issues. At the same time, there are, as noted earlier, dangers in bringing such work under political oversight. There is a risk that important issues, which while technical, will become the subject of political horse-trading. There is a more serious risk that politically powerful institutions will obtain relief from needed prudential measures by going over the heads of the regulator or standard setter. At minimum, however, there is clearly a need for more transparency in the processes by which agreements are reached and for broader efforts to seek a consensus among all concerned. Beyond this, there should be an ongoing effort to strike an appropriate balance between the technical and the political.

4.2.6   The creation of the Financial Stability Forum

The establishment of the Financial Stability Forum (FSF) in 1999 went a long way toward bringing some political input into the setting of the agenda for international cooperation in the financial area. The initiative for the Forum did not come from either the central banking or regulatory community. It followed an initiative of the G7 finance ministers and governors at their meeting in October 1998 when they asked one of their members, the then Chairman of the G10 central bank governors, Dr Hans Tietmeyer, to:

> ... consider with them [i.e., the appropriate bodies] the arrangements for cooperation and coordination between the various international financial regulatory and supervisory bodies and the international financial institutions interested in such matters, and to put to us expeditiously recommendations for any new structures and arrangements that may be required.

The remit of the FSF is broader than banking, and its membership is broader than the G10 (see Box 4.2). Its country membership arguably includes all of the important financial centres and none that are unimportant, although one could always debate about individual cases at the margins. National delegations vary in composition but include the central banks (usually at the level of deputy governors), other important financial regulators in most cases, and 'deputies' (senior officials) of Finance or Economy Ministries in many cases. This provides both the relevant competencies and some measure of political connection through the cabinet departments. The Forum also includes major relevant international organizations and standards-setting bodies. The pragmatic decision was made to include a representative from the International Accounting Standards Board (IASB), although it is a private sector body, because it is playing a critical role in seeking to establish a high level global standard for accounting.

4.3   Improving the process

4.3.1 Change will continue

One can be confident that financial markets will continue to be a centre of innovation and produce surprises that require an internationally coordinated policy
response. Fifteen years or so ago there was a widespread expectation that, after a
period of adjustment to more liberal regulatory approaches, the markets would
settle down into a steady state. This has not happened because innovation is in
the nature of competitive markets. Thus the FSF is likely to be continually challenged to organize work on new issues.

BOX 4.2 The membership of the Financial Stability Forum

National Authorities (26)

Australia
Reserve Bank of Australia

Canada
Department of Finance
Bank of Canada
Office of the Superintendent of Financial Institutions

France
Ministry of the Economy
Autorité des Marchés Financiers
Banque de France

Germany
Ministry of Finance
Bundesanstalt für Finanzdienstleistungsaufsicht
Deutsche Bundesbank

Hong Kong
SAR
Hong Kong Monetary Authority

Italy
Ministry of the Economy and Finance
Banca d'Italia
CONSOB

Japan
Ministry of Finance
Financial Services Agency
Bank of Japan

Netherlands
De Nederlandsche Bank

Singapore
Monetary Authority of Singapore

United Kingdom
Bank of England
Financial Services Authority
HM Treasury   (contd.)

BOX 4.2 (contd.)

United States

Department of the Treasury
Securities & Exchange Commission
Board of Governors of the Federal Reserve System

International Financial Institutions (6)

International Monetary Fund (IMF) (2)
World Bank (2)
Bank for International Settlements (BIS)
Organization for Economic Co-operation and Development (OECD)

International Standard Setting, Regulatory and Supervisory Groupings (7)

Basel Committee on Banking Supervision (BCBS) (2)
International Accounting Standards Board (IASB)
International Association of Insurance Supervisors (IAIS)(2)
International Organization of Securities Commissions (IOSCO) (2)

Committees of Central Bank Experts (2)

Committee on Payment and Settlement System (CPSS)
Committee on the Global Financial System (CGFS)

European Central Bank

Note: Numbers in brackets show number of representatives per member or category of members

---

4.3.2   Six proposals to strengthen the current structure

The creation of the Financial Stability Forum was a tremendous step forward in the multilateral arrangements to deal with financial issues. There are nevertheless anomalies and deficiencies that should be addressed. Within the context of the creation of a Council for International Financial and Economic Cooperation (CIFEC) as envisaged in Chapter 6, we propose six steps that could build on the creation of the FSF to establish a stronger infrastructure for cooperation on financial issues.

1. The FSF should receive a renewed mandate from the CIFEC. Although the FSF has interpreted its mandate flexibly and its membership has gone far beyond the G10 or central banks, it is still a creation of the G7 rather than of a broader and more politically accountable group.

2. The FSF should meet at the level of principals – ministers, governors and heads of organizations – perhaps once a year. At present, the FSF is essentially a deputies-level body. It can seek to influence the work of various groups but has little or no authority to direct their work.

3. The FSF deputies should report to the new principals group, which would be in a stronger position to give direction to the organizations and working groups that carry out the actual work in the financial area. The current FSF takes note of the work of others, but it does not formally direct it. The current FSF practice of providing reports to the IMFC should also be continued, but the IMFC is an IMF organ and is not the right body either constitutionally or in composition to direct the FSF and the groups that do the work in the financial sector. The FSF chairman should likewise provide reports to

the CIFEC and take part in relevant parts of its meetings. This would open up a channel for political priorities to shape the agenda for the FSF. The composition of the FSF will ensure, however, that its work does not become unduly political.

4. The responsibility to the FSF of the many working groups and other bodies should be made explicit. For example, groups like the Basel Supervisors should receive new mandates from the FSF Principals to replace those that they now have from the G10 central bank governors. New bodies should be convened by the FSF as the need arises. The G10 governors played a critical role in taking action to ensure that important issues were addressed. Its composition has, however, long been anomalous for this role. The issues are not only or often even mainly those involving central banks. The G10 governors group has become even more anomalous with the creation of the European Central Bank, which has assumed many of the responsibilities of national central banks in the euro area.

5. Representation on the FSF needs to be flexible so that it can accommodate future changes in the financial landscape, although its present membership seems about right. The CIFEC will provide the mandate and should therefore agree to any membership changes, but new members ought not to be admitted without the consent of the FSF Principals. Otherwise there is a risk that the CIFEC will too easily agree to additional membership in political deals involving unrelated matters. The FSF could become unwieldy and ineffective if this happened.

6. The small Secretariat of the FSF should be maintained. It plays an important role in collecting and organizing information on what is going on in all of the organizations and bodies. The FSF's secretariat should not, however, undertake the analysis of issues or draft substantive reports. That work should continue to be done in sub-groups that use national resources and those of the standing international organizations such as the IMF, the BIS, the World Bank and the OECD.

4.3.3 Continued flexibility and pragmatism will be required

The FSF should be flexible in directing work to standing committees and ad hoc groups. The lengthy list of recent and current work in Box 4.1 shows that international cooperation in the financial sector is far from finished business. Some of the unfinished work – for example, the development of a new approach to sovereign debt workouts – can be completed and left to the side for a long time. This work is currently being done in the G10, which has taken up a series of issues over the years; these issues, which have not been closely related and could have been assigned to an ad hoc group commissioned by the FSF or the G20 if these bodies had been in existence earlier. It is not clear that the G10 needs to be continued as an active body although it will need to remain in formal existence until the borrowing arrangements in the IMF are revamped. Much of the financial agenda will, however, require ongoing consultation on implementation and periodic review to keep up with evolving markets. This will require continuing bodies. The updating of bank capital standards is a good example. No sunset clause should be imposed on the Basel Committee.

National (and EU) authorities should remain the regulators and supervisors of the financial markets. Currently international cooperation is ambitious, but the authorities involved have rejected approaches that would involve supra-national authorities. National authorities enact the rules, enforce them and do the supervision. We endorse this approach and believe that it has been shown to be effective. It does, however, involve close cooperation going beyond Wallich's definition recalled in Chapter 1. For example, the establishment of bank capital adequacy standards has been an intense exercise in harmonization within the Basel Committee. Harmonization may also be needed to reconcile the differing specific measure that have been taken in the United States and the EU to strengthen corporate governance in the wake of recent scandals, as conflicting requirements have created problems for the functioning of markets. Coordination involving trades among countries has been used in the process of allocating supervisory responsibilities for institutions operating across national or sectoral borders. And consultation has made a contribution to better policies across a broad range of financial issues where the transnational element is secondary. The development of bankruptcy practices and procedures in emerging markets is a good example. It will continue to be important to select the appropriate approach on a case-by-case basis as new issues emerge.

As said earlier, the FSF has done a tremendous job since its establishment five years ago in bringing focus and coherence to multilateral work on financial issues. There is no pressing need to fix something that is not broken. But creating a Principals Forum, correcting some anomalies and embedding the FSF in the proposed new structure overseen by CIFEC will help to ensure its continued effectiveness.

<u>5</u> Balance-of-payments Adjustment among Key Currency Countries

Previous chapters of this Report described the evolution of economic cooperation among the major industrial countries and drew attention to new needs – those posed by closer economic integration and those posed by the emergence of new players, ranging from China on the one hand to the 12-country euro group on the other. This chapter deals with one of those new needs. It argues that the emergence of new players calls for the reorganization of economic cooperation in one of its principal forms – managing balance-of-payments adjustment among countries with systemically important currencies. These countries are described hereafter as key currency countries, although one systemically important currency, the renminbi, lacks some of the attributes usually used to identify a key currency.[35]

<u>5.1</u> Economic interdependence and policy interdependence

Most of the world's many countries can achieve and maintain a viable balance in their external payments without other countries' acquiescence or involvement. They may at times require financial assistance from the IMF to buy enough time to deal with their problems. The effects of their national policies do not, however, impinge importantly on the generality of other countries' situations, and their governments can therefore modify their policies without having to anticipate policy responses by other countries' governments.

This was once true for all but one country – the United States. In the first two decades following World War II, the United States had the dominant economy and currency, and the policy adjustments of other countries had very little impact on them. In subsequent decades, however, the economies and currencies of Western Europe and Japan took on more importance for the United States. The situation was not yet symmetrical. On the one hand, the role of the dollar as a reserve currency – the one that other countries held and used to manage their exchange rates – conferred an extra degree of freedom on the United States. It was indeed the only country that could use its own currency to finance imbalances in its external payments. On the other hand, the use of the dollar by other countries to define and adjust the external values of their currencies constrained the United States, as it could not readily alter its own exchange rate.

Yet economic interdependence had become a fact of life, and economic interdependence gave rise to policy interdependence. None of the major industrial countries, not even the United States, could continue to ignore the impact of other countries' policies or the impact of changes in the values of their currencies on the value of its own national currency. By the mid-1980s, then, governments had begun to think in terms of policy coordination – adopting 'packages' of policy changes that could be mutually beneficial.

5.1.1 Forms of policy coordination

The history of policy coordination and of the organizational framework for it was reviewed in Chapter 1, and there is no need to review it here. It is important, however, to recall a point made in the Introduction to this Report, which distinguished between various forms of policy coordination.

At times, policy coordination has focused on achieving a common objective, such as faster economic growth or reduced inflation, in the belief that the objective could be achieved more effectively, without introducing tensions or imbalances, if the objectives were pursued collectively. That was the strategy adopted by the G7 countries at the Bonn Summit of 1978. The declaration issued at that Summit began with the statement in Box 5.1, which focused on the need for faster economic growth. The same statement also acknowledged, however, the need for the second type of policy coordination – one aimed at reconciling conflicting objectives or, in different terms, coming to terms with constraints, such as the balance-of-payments constraint.

It is virtually impossible for all large countries to run current account surpluses at the same time. It is likewise impossible for one large country to achieve a depreciation of its currency unless some other countries are willing to countenance a corresponding appreciation of their currencies. And another important policy constraint lurks behind these simple arithmetic constraints. A large appreciation of a country's currency is apt to generate protectionist pressures, especially in periods of slow growth and high unemployment, and it will then test the strength of its government's commitment to the multilateral trading system. Hence, the way that a government seeks to achieve a viable balance in its external payments is not a matter of indifference to its trading partners.

BOX 5.1 Extract from the Declaration of the 1978 Bonn Summit

We are concerned, above all, about worldwide unemployment, because it has been at too high a level for many years, because it hits hard at the most vulnerable sections of the population, because its economic cost is high and its human cost is higher still. We will act, through measures to assure growth and develop needed skills, to increase employment. In doing this, we will build on the progress that has already been made in the fight against inflation and will seek new successes in that fight. But we need an improvement in growth where that can be achieved without rekindling inflation in order to reduce extremes of balances of payments surpluses and deficits. This will reduce destabilizing exchange rate movements. Improved growth will help to reduce protectionist pressures. We need it also to encourage the flow of private investment, on which economic progress depends.

A programme of different actions by countries that face different conditions is needed to assure steady non-inflationary growth. In countries whose balance-of-payments situation and inflation rate do not impose special restrictions, this requires a faster rise in domestic demand. In countries where rising prices and costs and creating strong pressures, this means taking new measures against inflation.

The declaration then goes on to list the specific policy commitments of each G7 country.

5.1.2 Policy coordination and balance-of-payments adjustment

The history of balance-of-payments adjustment among the major industrial countries speaks to the practical importance of these basic propositions. In the early 1980s, for example, the United States attracted large capital inflows, the dollar appreciated hugely, and the current account balance swung sharply into deficit. Protectionist pressures built up strongly, and they were not quelled until the appreciation was reversed. The reversal itself can be ascribed in part to the Plaza Agreement of September 1985, in which the major industrial countries (the G5 in this instance) declared that an exchange rate realignment was required and that they were ready to cooperate closely in achieving that result, and the G5 then backed their words by intervention on the foreign exchange markets.

Critics of the Plaza Agreement note correctly that the dollar had ceased to appreciate before the agreement and had indeed started to depreciate. In the run-up to the G5 meeting, however, there were signs that the dollar was turning around again. Theory and experience both suggest, moreover, that intervention is not likely to have long-lasting effects on exchange rates unless it affects the money supplies of the relevant countries – that the 'sterilization' of its monetary consequences can deprive it of any permanent influence. By intervening continuously, of course, a country can fix the value of its currency vis-à-vis some foreign currency, and it can go on doing that for as long as it is able and willing to build up or run down its foreign exchange reserves. Yet episodic intervention, even if sterilized, can sometimes affect exchange rates temporarily, especially when currency traders have taken on large long or short positions in a particular currency, and it is more likely to be effective if it is coordinated – conducted by all of the relevant countries together, not by one country alone. Its impact is difficult to measure, is uncertain in duration, and may vary from case to case.

5.2 The role of exchange rate changes

How do exchange rates contribute to balance-of-payments adjustment? Consider a large country with a current account deficit that it cannot expect to finance for long by piling up external debt. It could, of course, reduce its current account deficit by tightening its fiscal or monetary policies, so as to reduce aggregate expenditure and thus reduce its imports. If it did nothing else, however, it might have to induce a deep domestic recession to effect a significant improvement in its current account balance. It would therefore do better to combine a reduction of aggregate expenditure with a depreciation of its country's currency. By reducing the foreign-currency prices of a country's exports and raising the home-currency prices of its imports, a depreciation serves to switch global expenditure toward domestic output. It can therefore offset the output-depressing effect of a reduction in aggregate expenditure while further improving the current account balance. When a country is large, however, some other large countries must be willing to accept currency appreciation and must also adopt expenditure-raising policies in order to avoid the output-depressing effect of the switch in global expenditure away from their economies. In other words, they must adopt the obverse of the policy mix pursued by the country having the current-account deficit.

Note further that the argument of the previous paragraph holds symmetrically. A country seeking to reduce a current account deficit cannot rely exclusively on a depreciation of its country's currency to achieve that aim. Unless fiscal or monetary policy is tightened too, the expenditure-switching effect of a depreciation will put upward pressure on domestic prices, reducing the effectiveness of the depreciation. Adopting language usually used to describe the problem facing the United States, dollar depreciation, by itself, is not the safest or most efficient way to reduce the US deficit. It must be combined with domestic policies to stimulate saving by the private sector or reduce dissaving by the public sector.

When exchange rates float more or less freely, of course, the timing and size of exchange rate changes necessarily depend on the activities of market participants, which will in turn reflect their views about future policies, including the likelihood of official intervention. Furthermore, exchange rate changes affect trade flows with lags and may indeed affect them perversely in the very short run. These qualifications do not, however, call into question three fundamental propositions:

1. Balance-of-payments adjustment typically requires a combination of remedies – changes in aggregate domestic spending and exchange rate changes.

2. Large countries cannot undertake balance-of-payments adjustment unless some of the other large countries take part in the process – and the incidence of the process will depend on the number of countries that participate, as well as the way in which they participate.

3. The incidence of the adjustment process will also be affected by market participants, because of the role they play in deciding how the depreciation of one large country's currency will manifest itself in appreciations of other countries' currencies.

5.3 Principles and practice

5.3.1 The rules of the Bretton Woods System

The Bretton Woods Conference of 1944 sought to put in place a rule-based monetary system to regulate balance-of-payments adjustment. Under the original Articles of Agreement of the IMF, no government could change the exchange rate for its currency, defined for all practical purposes in terms of the US dollar, without IMF approval, and that approval would not be forthcoming unless the IMF found that the country faced a fundamental disequilibrium. That critical condition was never defined clearly, however, and though the major industrial countries did not change their exchange rates frequently, they rarely gave the IMF much notice of an impending change. Furthermore, one of those countries, Canada, set its currency free to float without suffering any significant penalty. There were rules of the game, but the IMF could not enforce them strictly.

5.3.2 The rules of the present system

When the Bretton Woods System collapsed completely in 1973, it took some years to replace it, and the new rules of the game were less restrictive in principle. In fact, it proved very hard to describe the game itself, let alone constrain the options available to individual countries.

Box 5.2 reproduces the language used to describe those options in the amended Articles of Agreement of the IMF. Under Section 1 of Article IV, members are committed to promote a 'stable system of exchange rates', which is not quite the same as exchange rate stability, but under Section 2, individual countries may choose and change their exchange rate arrangements. Nevertheless, Article IV draws an important distinction between a country's exchange rate regime and the

---

BOX 5.2 Extract from the Articles of Agreement of the IMF

Article IV Obligations Regarding Exchange Arrangements

Section 1. General obligations of members

Recognizing that the essential purpose of the international monetary system is to provide a framework that facilitates the exchange of goods, services, and capital among countries, and that sustains sound economic growth, and that a principal objective is the continuing development of the orderly underlying conditions that are necessary for financial and economic stability, each member undertakes to collaborate with the Fund and other members to assure orderly exchange arrangements and promote a stable system of exchange rates. In particular, each member shall:

(i) endeavor to direct its economic and financial policies toward the objective of fostering orderly economic growth with reasonable price stability, with due regard to its circumstances;

(ii) seek to promote stability by fostering orderly underlying economic and financial conditions and a monetary system that does not tend to produce erratic disruptions.

(iii) avoid manipulating exchange rates or the international monetary system in order to prevent effective balance-of-payments adjustment or to gain an unfair competitive advantage over other members; and

(iv) follow exchange policies compatible with the undertakings under this Section.

Section 2. General exchange arrangements

(a) Each member shall notify the Fund ... of the exchange arrangements it intends to apply in fulfilment of its obligations under Section 1 of this Article, and shall notify the Fund promptly of any changes in its exchange arrangements.

(b) Under an international monetary system of the kind prevailing on January 1, 1976, exchange arrangements may include (i) the maintenance by a member of a value of its currency in terms of the special drawing right or another denominator, other than gold, selected by the member, or (ii) cooperative arrangements by which members maintain the value of their currencies in relation to the currency or currencies of other members, or (iii) other exchange arrangements of a member's choice.

Section 3. Surveillance over exchange arrangements

(a) The Fund shall oversee the international monetary system in order to ensure its effective operation, and shall oversee the compliance of each member with its obligations under Section 1

(b) In order to fulfill its functions under (a) above, the Fund shall exercise firm surveillance over the exchange rate policies of its members, and shall adopt specific principles for the guidance of all members with respect to those policies. Each member shall provide the Fund with the information necessary for such surveillance, and, when requested by the Fund, shall consult with it on the member's exchange rate policies.

---

country's exchange rate policies. Under Section 1, each country must refrain from manipulating its exchange rate to block balance-of-payments adjustment or gain an unfair competitive advantage, and under Section 3, the IMF is supposed to exercise firm surveillance over its members' exchange rate policies. The IMF devotes a lot of staff time to this task. Every year, staff missions visit most of the Fund's member countries, engage in extensive consultations about the countries' policies, prospects and problems, and prepare comprehensive reports, which are then discussed by the Executive Board. With the member's consent, moreover, a summary of the Board's discussion is made public, and many members also permit the publication of the staff reports.

This process is useful in many ways. In recent years, for example, surveillance has identified structural vulnerabilities, especially in countries' financial systems, that need to be addressed in order to reduce the risk of currency and banking crises. Surveillance has also been used to assess debt sustainability. But this broadening of surveillance has come at a cost. The Fund would find it hard to claim that it exercises firm surveillance over its members' exchange rate policies in the light of specific principles. Box 5.3 reproduces the published summary of the Executive Board's views about China's exchange rate. It can hardly be deemed to constitute a firm assessment. Like much of the debate about the renminbi, moreover, it blurs the distinction between regime choice and policy choice.

BOX 5.3 Extract from the IMF Public Information Notice on the 2003 Article IV Consultation with the People's Republic of China

Most Directors noted that there is no clear evidence that the renminbi is substantially undervalued at this juncture. Directors also felt that a currency revaluation would not by itself have a major impact on global current account imbalances – particularly given China's relatively small share in world trade. Nevertheless, Directors considered that the rapid build-up of foreign exchange reserves indicates some pressure on the exchange rate and imposes costs on the Chinese economy, especially difficulties in preventing excessive monetary expansion. In this context, Directors observed that increased flexibility of the exchange rate over time would be in the best interest of China. In particular, it would allow more room to pursue an independent monetary policy, help cushion China's economy against adverse shocks, and facilitate adjustment to the major structural reforms that are underway. Directors considered that China could, in a phased manner, introduce more flexibility to its exchange rate without causing major disruptions to its economy. Most Directors stressed that a move toward flexibility should be carefully planned and sequenced with ongoing structural reforms that are crucial to its success, and emphasized the need to move speedily with these reforms. They felt that the timing of a shift toward greater exchange rate flexibility should be left to the authorities to decide. A number of Directors felt, however, that the authorities should take advantage of the present circumstances to take quickly an initial step toward greater exchange rate flexibility. Directors underscored the need to improve the functioning of the foreign exchange market by eliminating trading restrictions and surrender requirements, widening the base of participants, and developing instruments for foreign exchange risk management.

5.3.3   The rules and the renminbi

The Chinese authorities have blurred that distinction when they have insisted that the renminbi is *their* currency – that they alone have the right to make decisions about it. No exchange rate is the property of a single country. The dollar value of the renminbi is also the renminbi value of the dollar. And the 'shared' nature of an exchange rate takes on particular salience when the two countries involved are large, and even greater salience when, as in China's case, the exchange rate affects third countries strongly and appears to influence their exchange rate policies. The case for a revaluation of the renminbi derives in part from the expectation that it will induce other Asian countries to let their currencies appreciate against the dollar instead of continuing to accumulate large stocks of reserves.[36]

The US authorities have also confused regime choice and policy choice when they have focused on the need for greater exchange rate flexibility rather than the level of the renminbi itself. A single significant revaluation of the renminbi and of other Asian currencies could make a larger, more immediate contribution to the global adjustment process than a modest widening of the band within which the renminbi can fluctuate freely. The statement made in Box 5.3, that China's share in world trade is too small for a revaluation of the renminbi to have a major impact on the adjustment process, is flatly contradicted by Table 5.1. There, China is shown to have the fourth largest level of foreign trade – smaller than that of the United States, the euro area, or Japan, but larger than that of any other country – yet has thus far opted out of the ongoing realignment of key currency exchange rates.

Table 5.1 The world's main trading countries and recent changes in their dollar exchange rates

Country or country group	Total trade (2002) in US$ billion*	GDP 2002 in US$ billion	Percentage appreciation (+) of currency against US dollar	
			2002–4**	2003–4**
United States	1,896	10,446	–	–
Euro area	1,907	6,648	36.4	14.6
Japan	754	3,992	17.0	6.3
China	621	1,237	Nil	Nil
United Kingdom	612	695	23.0	10.7
Canada	480	735	15.7	14.8
Hong Kong	408	163	0.1	0.1
Mexico	337	337	-20.6	-10.5
Korea	315	477	12.0	1.1
Taiwan	243	280	-1.5	-2.1
Singapore	242	87	8.1	1.4

Notes: *Sum of exports (fob) and imports (cif); euro area data exclude trade within euro area.
**Data for 2002–4 span the period from end-December 2001 to 19 May 2004; data for 2003-4 span the period from end-December 2002 to 19 May 2004.
Source: IMF, *Wall Street Journal,* and Republic of China (Taiwan) Government Information Office.

<u>5.4</u>   Reforming the management of the adjustment process

For more than a quarter of a century, the finance ministers and central bank governors of the G7 countries have sought to oversee the global adjustment process – the manner in which they might modify their countries' policies to deal with imbalances between their economies and with the effects of external shocks, such as the oil-price shocks of the 1970s. During that long period, however, the ability of the G7 countries to manage the adjustment process has been impaired by three developments.

5.4.1 Changing views about the roles of policy instruments

There has been a major change in views about the efficacy or proper use of the main policy instruments that were once the candidates for policy coordination. The change was discussed in Chapter 2 and can therefore be summarized briefly. The discretionary use of fiscal policy has fallen out of favour, for good and bad reasons alike, although defenders of the recent US tax cuts have belatedly sought to cloak them in an old-fashioned Keynesian costume. In many countries, moreover, the use of fiscal policy is strongly constrained by high levels of public debt and by the need to anticipate the huge increase of pension and health care costs that will soon be imposed by demographic trends. The conduct of monetary policy has been entrusted to independent central banks, and the European Central Bank (ECB) is committed strictly to maintain price stability, which limits its ability to use monetary policy for balance-of-payments adjustment, except insofar as it concludes that recent or prospective exchange rate changes pose risks to the maintenance of price stability.[37]

5.4.2 Crises and other distractions

Policy-makers who used to focus on policy coordination among the key currency countries have been otherwise engaged. The G7 finance ministers and central bank governors were, of course, heavily involved in resolving the debt crisis of the 1980s. In recent years, however, as Chapter 4 describes, their meetings and communiqués have been devoted even more heavily to the management of emerging-market crises and building better defences against them. Furthermore, many of the problems facing the major industrial countries and, indeed, the whole world, differ in nature and complexity from the problems they used to tackle. Some, such as pension and health care reform, require deep and politically difficult changes in national regimes. Others, such as climate change, epidemic diseases and terrorism, require close cooperation by very large numbers of national governments, because national borders are far too porous to keep them at bay.

5.4.3 The advent of new actors

Finally, it is no longer sufficient for the G7 countries to agree among themselves on managing balance-of-payments adjustment. On the one hand, three of the G7 countries, France, Germany and Italy, are members of the euro area yet cannot speak for it, and another G7 country, the United Kingdom, can no longer be regarded as a key currency country, although London is one of the world's pre-eminent financial centres. On the other hand, one key currency country, China, is not a member of the G7. There have, of course, been many bilateral discussions between Chinese officials and those of the G7 countries, but much of the recent discussion about the renminbi and related matters has taken place too publicly and been confrontational rather than consultative. Sensitive matters of this sort, monitored closely by financial markets, cannot be managed by megaphone diplomacy.

5.5 The need for a new key currency group

The G7 countries still have important work to do. Until the euro area countries consolidate their membership in the IMF (a matter discussed in Chapter 6), the G7 will still be the appropriate forum for coordinating the views of the main industrial countries on matters pertaining to the policies and operations of the IMF and those of other multinational institutions. Furthermore, the G7 countries must continue to collaborate closely in matters pertaining to the functioning of the international financial system. A different group of key currency countries is needed, however, to manage balance-of-payments adjustment and coordinate national policies so that balance-of-payments adjustment does not damage global growth. It is therefore time to create a new, smaller body to oversee adjustment among the world's principal currencies – the dollar, the euro, the yen and the renminbi.

To do that, of course, the finance ministers of the 12 euro area countries must devise a better way to represent the views and interests of the euro area. At present, the chairmanship of the Euro Group, comprising the finance ministers of the euro area countries, rotates semiannually, just like the chairmanship of the larger, more formal ECOFIN Council comprising the finance ministers of all 25 members of the EU. Under the proposed EU constitution, the Euro Group would be given more formal recognition, and its chairmanship would rotate less frequently, but the constitution faces an uncertain fate. The Euro Group, however, need not wait for ratification of the constitution. It could decide on its own to depart from the practice of the ECOFIN Council. It could choose its own chairman for a longer term, thereby providing for greater continuity in the representation of the euro area in the proposed group of key currency countries.

It must, of course, be acknowledged that the chairman of the Euro Group cannot make binding commitments on behalf of the euro area governments – nor can the Euro Group itself. Although the fiscal autonomy of those governments is constrained in principle by the Stability and Growth Pact, there is no mechanism to coordinate those governments' fiscal policies.

For the most part, however, the management of balance-of-payments adjustment among the key currency countries will fall short of full-fledged policy coordination, which involves the mutual modification of national policies. It cannot even involve the close or continuing coordination of monetary policies, given the rather rigid way which the ECB defines and pursues price stability. There may nevertheless be instances in which exchange rates appear to be moving too fast or too far and official intervention may therefore be justified. Intervention is less likely to be effective if it is undertaken unilaterally than if it is conducted jointly by the key currency countries and thus testifies to their unity of purpose. There may also be instances in which the size and timing of interest rate changes can and should be influenced by events in foreign exchange markets, and there will surely be instances in which some key currency countries will want to exercise influence over their partners' exchange rate policies – something that can be achieved most effectively in the context of continuing consultation rather than public confrontation. To that same end, the new four-member key currency group, called hereafter the G4, might be well advised to depart from the recent practice of the G7, which has issued a communiqué after every meeting, even when it had nothing new to say. Because the new G4 will include the key currency countries, it will rarely need to offer advice to outsiders and may not need to issue a communiqué after every meeting. In some instances, indeed, there may be no need for the world to know that it has met.

The new key currency group should be as small as possible to foster candid conversation, but membership should be open ended. India and Brazil may qualify for membership during the next decade. Analytical support for the G4 should be provided by the IMF, and its Managing Director should participate fully in its deliberations. The presence and participation of the Managing Director will add a disinterested voice to the group's deliberations. It may also serve to assure other countries' governments that balance-of-payments adjustment by the key currency countries will not be achieved in a fashion detrimental to the interests and concerns of those other countries.

<u>6</u> Achieving Effectiveness, Legitimacy, Accountability and Representativeness

This Report has discussed the issues that have shaped the agenda for international financial and economic cooperation since the Second World War. They cover four broad and overlapping subjects. One recurrent issue has been traditional macroeconomic cooperation, which has typically focused on balance-of-payments adjustment and the promotion of sustainable and balanced growth. In the last 25 years, relations between debtors and creditors engaged in cross-border transactions and the rules that shape them before and after all too frequent crises have also emerged as important issues. More recently, the agenda has been broadened to include the preservation of the safety, soundness and efficiency of the international financial system, together with a miscellany of political and economic issues that have an international financial dimension, ranging from support for post-communist Russia to reconstruction in Bosnia and Afghanistan.

<u>6.1</u> Accommodating change in the world economy

6.1.1 Where we have been

In order to achieve international cooperation, the nation states active in the international financial and economic system have developed, usually in an ad hoc way, various bodies for discussion and consensus building, as well as instruments for implementation. The bodies have included both formal institutions and organizations, and informal groups and clubs. Their membership has usually been drawn from representatives of states or state organizations, and those memberships have often overlapped, as have the functions of the institutions, organizations, groups and clubs. Although, however, these bodies are in the same business of international cooperation, they usually act individually and zealously guard their independence. Without strategic direction, this unwieldy group of institutions, organizations, groups and clubs will never fully achieve harmonious international financial cooperation, which is their common objective. Over the last 30 years, this strategic direction has been provided by the main industrial countries. They began meeting as the Library Group in 1973 and evolved into the G7, which meets at various levels and in various formats. The G7 has served as an agenda-setting body for most of the other bodies, provided essential political momentum, and has often provided financial support. The G7 has used the IMF as its main instrument, working in conjunction with the World Bank, the OECD and other bodies.

Despite disappointments and some failures, this arrangement has worked reasonably well. Yet this is no reason for complacency about the status quo. Patterns and structures of cooperation suited to the latter part of the twentieth century are unlikely to suit the new world emerging in the first part of the twenty-first century. Too often, innovation in international financial cooperation has had to await the spur of crisis – the Bretton Woods System in reaction to the inter-war depression, the G5/G7 in reaction to the global economic turmoil of the 1970s and the enhanced G7 cooperation, described in this Report, in reaction to the various financial crises of the last 20 years. The nature and timing of future crises are difficult to foresee. One response in the face of such uncertainty is to delay innovation and 'hope that all will be right on the night'. Yet as this Report has made clear, there are some (almost) certainties amidst the future uncertainties. Those certainties are the appearance of new issues and new actors. They present the international financial community with a clear choice. It can await the spur of crisis or it can begin the sensitive, contentious and complex task of adapting its patterns and structures of cooperation so as to accommodate the new issues and new actors. The purpose of this Report is to encourage the decision-makers to foreswear the defence of the status quo and to choose the route of adaptation. That, in its authors' view, is the way, at best, to avoid and, at worst, to mitigate future financial crises that could so beset the immensely complex international financial system. As the Introduction to the Report emphasized, good outcomes require good processes.

6.1.2 Where are we going?

Earlier chapters of this Report have outlined the fundamental changes that are taking place in the world economy. New states and groupings of states have emerged. The emergence of the euro area and the growing importance of China were strongly emphasized in Chapter 5. They are altering fundamentally the global balance of economic and financial power; they are or ought to be key players in achieving balance-of-payments adjustment and fostering global growth; and they may be followed by other new players, such as India and Brazil. New issues are also emerging. Chapter 3 of this Report stressed the need to sustain cooperation between creditors and debtors as the number and diversity of creditors increases and new financial instruments emerge. Chapter 4 stressed the need to maintain the integrity of the global financial system. Cooperation among the G7 countries can no longer manage these issues effectively, nor can the G7 expect to claim the legitimacy, accountability and representativeness required to set the agenda for the various institutions, organizations, groups and clubs that have roles to play in fostering international financial cooperation.

It is therefore time to reflect on ways to improve present arrangements and develop them further. This development has to be an evolutionary process, and it must engage the new players in the international economic and financial system. Sixty years have passed since Bretton Woods, when a small number of governments were able to design an institutional structure for the world economy. Today, we are not dealing with a green field site – a world due to be rebuilt in the aftermath of war – but one that is already functioning. Powerful vested interests, both national and bureaucratic, are embedded in the present constellation of international organizations and bodies. Change has thus to be gradual and studied. Metamorphosis, not revolution, has the best chance of success.

6.1.3 What we need to bear in mind

It is also necessary to acknowledge a powerful political reality. Despite the increasing integration of the world economy and financial system reflecting the process of globalization, the power to make political decisions and the responsibility for them ultimately reside in nation states or, to a limited extent, the group of states that constitute the EU. Concomitantly, the legitimacy of international bodies, formal and informal, derives from those nation states, and there is little appetite in the national capitals of the states active in the world economy for the transfer of decision-making power to supranational bodies. That is the lesson to be drawn from the rejection in 2003 of the proposal made by the Management of the IMF for a Sovereign Debt Restructuring Mechanism (SDRM), even in diluted form. It proved impossible to reach agreement on amending the Fund's Articles of Agreement even for the rather limited purpose of preventing a small minority of creditors from disrupting debt negotiations or blocking a debt restructuring acceptable to a large majority of creditors. The route chosen instead on that occasion typified current attitudes; it relied on national securities' laws allowing the inclusion of collective action clauses in bond documentation rather than the broadening of international law.

It is perhaps paradoxical that, in a world of rapidly integrating economies, the politics of the nation state still prevail. The reason may reside in the old adage 'holding on to nurse for fear of something worse', where the nurse is the nation state and the something worse is the profound uncertainty produced by the rapidly changing global economy.

<u>6.2</u>   Three recommendations

There are nevertheless cogent reasons for considering a further evolution of the present arrangements for the governance of the international financial system. Those reasons derive from the need for effectiveness, coupled with the need for legitimacy, accountability and representativeness. In that spirit, this chapter makes three recommendations:

- It calls for a review of existing institutions, organizations, groups and clubs, with a view to assessing their actual and potential contributions.
- It suggests ways to strengthen the institutional structure of the IMF.
- It proposes the creation of a new body, a Council for International Financial and Economic Cooperation, to assume the agenda-setting role of the G7.

Taken together with the proposal made in Chapter 5, the creation of a new G4 with a mandate to foster timely balance-of-payments adjustment among key currency countries, the three proposals made in this chapter should enhance the legitimacy, accountability and representativeness of the arrangements available to oversee the functioning of the international economic and financial system. The review of existing institutions and groups should help to reduce overlap and duplication. The strengthening of the IMF's institutional structure should improve the Fund's effectiveness and strengthen its links with national capitals. The new Council should enhance the legitimacy of the agenda-setting process by better reflecting the heterogeneity of the global community. And the proposed G4 should improve the balance-of-payments adjustment process by bringing together representatives of the four currency areas that have the greatest impact on the world economy.

<u>6.3</u>   A review of existing institutions, organizations, groups and clubs

A plethora of governmental and semi-governmental institutions and organizations, groups and clubs is involved in international economic and financial cooperation. Many fall under the broad umbrella of the UN system. They include the United Nations Conference on Trade and Development (UNCTAD); the United Nations Development Programme (UNDP); several regional economic commissions; related agencies, such as the World Trade Organization; and UN specialized agencies, such as the IMF and the World Bank Group. The specialized agencies are autonomous organizations working with the United Nations and with each other through the framework provided by the United Nations Economic and Social Council (ECOSOC). The list also includes the Organization for Economic Cooperation and Development (OECD); regional development banks for most of the world's regions; various groups of like minded countries (the G7, G8, G10, G20, G24, G77, and some more); the Financial Stability Forum (FSF); several important committees, the most important of which are the Development Committee and the International Monetary and Financial Committee (IMFC); and the Paris Club of creditor country governments. And this list is not comprehensive. Many of the bodies, moreover, have large administrative and operational staffs, and at the national level they involve the ministers, deputies and other officials responsible for their governments' participation.

It is difficult to devise a metaphor that properly describes this maze of bodies. It is in part a cobweb. It is in part a solar system with a powerful core. It can perhaps be best described as resembling an old fashioned English garden, overgrown, somewhat disorderly and without obvious form or pattern. The maze of bodies has evolved, often in response to particular events. It has always proved easier to create new bodies than wind up old ones. Relationships among the bodies are complex, but that is inevitable in a complex world. In some cases, their functions duplicate and overlap. Sometimes there are frictions and turf fights. Their administration uses up significant resources, not only in their headquarters but also in national capitals. Yet it would be naïve to expect that the plethora of institutions will suddenly embark upon an era of mutual spontaneous cooperation and thereby obviate the need for the sort of strategic direction hitherto provided by the G7.

The changing economic weights of countries and country groups and the new challenges of international financial and economic cooperation make it timely to ask whether this overgrown garden should be pruned so that it can flourish in the future. There is no body obviously able to take on that task. The G7 is not sufficiently representative. Existing institutions, such as the IMF, would be regarded as *parti pris*. The G20 may be the most appropriate group to initiate such a review. It has a widely drawn membership and is not associated with any single institution. It should therefore establish an 'Independent Wise Persons' Review Group' and charge it with reviewing the need for, and the roles of, the various governmental institutions and organizations, groups and clubs and of making recommendations. The Review Group should ask five questions in its review of each institution, group and body:

- What is its contribution to international cooperation?
- Is it the widely recognized leader in its field?
- What is the body's comparative advantage over other bodies in the field?

- Would international cooperation be damaged if the body did not continue to exist?
- Could the body's functions be assumed by another body?

If the answers to these questions do not demonstrate a clear justification for the continuation of the body, the Review Group should not hesitate to recommend that the body go out of business entirely. For example, answers to these five questions are likely to show that there is little justification for the perpetuation of the G10 in either of its incarnations – as a group of finance ministers or a group of central bank governors – other than to discuss matters directly related to amendment or activation of the GAB, which in practice would require meetings very occasionally, if ever. The work of the G10 should be taken over by the FSF. The value added by some of the United Nations' economic bodies, including some of the regional economic commissions, is hard to discern, and the financial resources that they now consume could probably be better used elsewhere in the UN system. It may likewise be useful to review the activities of the OECD with the aim of focusing its resources on the tasks it performs most effectively.

The review group's recommendations cannot be binding, but if they obtained the strong endorsement of the G20, they could not be ignored. Of course, any member of a group could, if it remained unconvinced of its value, withdraw from membership on its own volition. There is likely to be opposition to the abolition of even the most insignificant group. 'Old groups never die.' They tend indeed to expand their membership and are reluctant to ask members to leave when the original reasons for their membership have disappeared. Expanding the membership of a group, however, can reduce its effectiveness. For example, it might be suggested that, rather than create the G4 proposed in Chapter 5, it would cause less trouble to invite China, and India perhaps at a later date, to join the existing G7 finance ministers' and governors' group. Such an expansion of numbers, beyond countries with systemically important currencies, would reduce the group's effectiveness.

A second Review Group might be convened to review the mandates and activities of the multinational development banks. There has been renewed recognition of the need for development assistance, including assistance to combat HIV/AIDS and other diseases threatening whole populations in the developing world. The issues are somewhat different from those posed by the maze of institutional arrangements concerned with macroeconomic problems and the governance of the financial system. There is, however, the same need to ask whether certain institutions have outlived their usefulness or should refocus their efforts and their financial resources.

<u>6.4</u>   Strengthening the institutional structure of the IMF

The IMF has been the butt of much criticism, but few of its critics continue to argue for its complete abolition. Most have questioned the way it does its work: the nature and extent of the conditions it attaches to its loans, the size of its lending packages and the efficacy of its surveillance. Whatever the force of such criticisms and the Fund's success in responding to them, the Fund seems destined to remain at the centre of international financial cooperation in the years to come. Chapter 5 of this Report suggested that the IMF might play a supporting role in the work of a new G4 concerned with balance-of-payments adjustment among key currency countries. Chapter 3 identified the Fund as the linchpin in preventing and resolving currency and financial crises and in managing relations between creditors and debtors. And Chapter 4 described the Fund's efforts to improve the supervision and functioning of financial systems in emerging markets by promoting adherence to various codes and standards.

In view of the Fund's central role, now and in the future, it is worth asking how it could be strengthened as an institution. Two reforms are proposed below: upgrading the role of the Executive Board and rationalizing the representation of the EU. They are not intended to address the concerns of those who believe that the Fund and other multinational institutions should be more directly accountable to civil society, which raise other issues. They are intended to strengthen the Fund's legitimacy, accountability and representativeness. Above all, they are intended to help put the IMF once again at the centre of the debate on policy-making.

6.4.1 Upgrading the Executive Board

In formal institutional terms, the Fund comprises a Board of Governors, with each member state eligible to nominate a Governor (usually its finance minister or central bank governor), an Executive Board of permanent representatives in Washington representing its member states and organized on a constituency basis, a management comprising the Managing Director and his deputies and a staff organized into several departments. The Board of Governors has delegated most of its powers to the Executive Board and plays no real role in steering the institution. This apparent lacuna in formal governance at the highest level would at first sight appear to provide the Executive Directors with an opportunity to decide the policies and strategies of the institution. Yet this has not happened, at least in recent years. The role of the Executive Board has been crowded out by activities elsewhere. Although the Interim Committee and IMFC are not even mentioned in the Fund's Articles of Agreement, their communiqués have been filled with recommendations to the Fund's Executive Board, asking it to elaborate and implement various initiatives. This might suggest that the Interim Committee and the IMFC have been the main source of policy guidance for the work of the Fund, including its work on relations between creditors and debtors. As Chapter 3 argued, however, the G7 has in practice provided strategic direction and proposed many of the policy initiatives that have then emerged from the two Committees and thus guided the work of the Executive Board. The Executive Board has been neither the crucible for new policies nor the forum for debating the principal issues of international financial policy.

The shrinkage of distance and time provided by modern communications explains why, at least in recent years, the Executive Board has not provided policy leadership. Forty years ago, officials in a European finance ministry had to book telephone calls to the United States a full day in advance, and journeys to Washington for the Annual Meetings of the Fund and Bank took almost a week if European officials travelled by transatlantic liner. Today, cheap and easy telephone communication, e-mails and faxes permit the rapid transfer of information, while the speed and convenience of air travel have grown even as the cost has fallen. At the press of a button, moreover, IMF documents can be sent to the relevant official in a national capital, and detailed instructions can be sent back quickly to the Executive Director's office, sometimes after clearance with the finance minister. Direct electronic contact between national capitals half a world away have thus tended to elbow Executive Directors out of the policy-making loop.

These developments have much reduced the freedom of action of Executive Directors, and,indeed of diplomats generally, while raising the influence of policy-makers in national capitals. Agreements on Fund policy, new IMF facilities and important programmes are often reached by 'deputies' (senior officials from capitals who 'deputize' for their ministers) meeting in groups of like-minded countries, such as the G7, G10 and G20 or, in the case of the EU, in committees of senior officials meeting in Brussels. Creditor countries have developed these modes of inter-capital consultation to a much greater extent than have debtor countries. Those modes of consultation have, however, constrained the ability of the Executive Board as a whole to formulate policy for the Fund.

This migration of power away from the Executive Board is undesirable. It is inefficient, because those who shape IMF policy in national capitals do not have direct contact with those who present and debate it in the Executive Board. It also cuts off the skilled and knowledgeable Fund staff from the key decision-makers. Finally, it diminishes the representativeness of the IMF. The international community created the IMF by a formal treaty and meant it to steer work on international financial cooperation. Yet informal groups have arrogated to themselves much of that important work.

One way of reversing this migration is to change the present arrangement whereby Executive Directors reside in Washington. It would be both feasible and desirable for the senior official dealing with Fund issues in a country's capital to serve as that country's Executive Director. He or she would travel to Washington once every six weeks, to participate in major policy discussions for, say, two days. The Alternate Executive Director, the Executive Director's second in command, would reside in Washington, as is the case now, and would deal with the day-to-day business of the Fund. It might also be possible to reduce some of the burden of travel by using modern video-conferencing facilities like those used in the private sector.

If a multi-country IMF constituency preferred to have a resident Executive Director, it should be allowed to do so. Some members of a multi-country constituency might fear that they would have difficulty communicating readily with a non-resident Executive Director busy with the affairs of his or her own country, especially in cases where the member countries of a constituency are dependent on their Executive Director for concentrated expertise in IMF matters. Some might also be reluctant to burden a senior official with additional duties. Nevertheless the Board agendas should be shaped to facilitate the participation of non-resident Executive Directors in the policy debates, which rarely take place on the spur of the moment.

Some Executive Directors would not welcome such a change, but the Fund and its Board do not exist for them. The change would have the great advantage of bringing to the table the most powerful officials below ministerial level who regularly deal with IMF matters. The Executive Board would once again wield real power. Furthermore, Fund staff responsible for advancing the policy agenda would have the benefit of direct contact with the national officials having the main policy responsibility. This should help the staff to reflect the wishes of national capitals and to influence thinking in those capitals. When this change had been implemented, the meetings of the IMFC deputies, which take place before IMFC meetings, could be discontinued.

6.4.2   Rationalizing European representation in the IMF

A second change to the functioning of the Executive Board, already overdue, would bring the composition of the Board into better alignment with the relative economic importance of individual IMF members. The Fund and its members have made gradual progress in reducing the sizes of the differences between individual members' quotas and their calculated quotes, which are meant to reflect the members' economic weight as well as their potential need for balance-of-payments financing. Nevertheless, a number of anomalies remain. Furthermore, the Fund has failed to act on the recommendations made by a committee of experts appointed to consider a revision of the formulae used to derive calculated quotes, and it has not agreed to raise the number of so-called basic votes, which would have the effect of raising slightly the voting power of small developing countries. The most significant anomaly in voting power, however, cannot be addressed without rationalizing the representation of the EU countries.

The 25 EU members hold some 32% of the votes of the Board of Governors. In the Executive Board, however, those EU members can often exercise even greater voting power. That is because an Executive Director who represents a multi-country constituency casts the votes of all the countries in that constituency, and four of the multi-country constituencies are currently represented by Executive Directors who come from EU countries. Thus, a Dutch Executive Director represents a constituency that contains two EU countries – Cyprus and the Netherlands – but also contains 10 non-EU countries; therefore, he casts a number of votes twice as large as those of the Netherlands itself. Furthermore, a Spanish Executive Director represents a constituency that does not contain any other EU country but does contain Mexico and Venezuela, so he casts a number of votes three times as large as those of Spain itself.[38] In all, seven of the 24 Executive Directors and eight of the 24 Alternates currently come from EU countries.

This level of European representation, as well as the EU's large share of the votes on the Board of Governors, is impossible to justify on objective grounds. It reflects history rather the weight of the EU countries in today's global economy, and it makes for an unrepresentative Executive Board.

The advent of the euro presents a further reason for some rationalization of EU representation at the IMF. The IMF is a 'monetary' institution, concerned at its most fundamental level with currencies and their relationships. The Fund's relationships with the members of the euro area have been transformed by the introduction of the euro. Instead of 12 currencies, members of the euro area now share a single currency, supported by a single monetary policy, managed by the European Central Bank. There is therefore strong logic in seeking to group members of the euro area in one constituency so that the euro area can 'speak with one voice' in the IMF.

The rationalization of EU representation might best be achieved in two stages. Initially, the representation of EU countries in the Executive Board might be consolidated into a smaller set of constituencies containing few, if any, non-EU countries. Thereafter, those EU constituencies could be consolidated into two EU constituencies, one for the members of the euro area and one for the rest of the EU countries. Table 6.1 shows how this two-step reform might be reflected in a reorganization of the entire Executive Board.[39] A third reorganization might be necessary, however, depending on the development of the EU itself, which could result in a further consolidation of EU representation.[40]

The zero-sum nature of redistribution of quota and voting shares will make it exceedingly difficult for the Fund's members from the EU to propose, on their own volition, a reconfiguration of the Executive Board. Any proposal might have to be set in a broader negotiating context with other elements thrown into what in the end will no doubt look like a messy compromise. Indeed, there may be negotiating linkages between some or all of the four proposals made in this Report – the creation of a G4, the review of existing bodies, strengthening the institutional structure of the IMF and the creation of a new body, a Council for International Financial and Economic Cooperation, to assume the agenda-setting role of the G7. The role of the Fund's other large members, notably the United States and Japan, will be critical and sensitive in any negotiation. Europe is likely to react adversely to any heavy handed persuasion. Yet the United States, Japan and other Fund members have a strong interest in the outcome. Reconfiguration of the Executive Board also is likely to require a change in the Fund's Articles of Agreement, which would involve national legislatures. It would probably lead to a change in the ministerial membership of the IMFC, which would be a natural outgrowth of the consolidation proposed above.

It is hard to believe, however, that other governments will continue indefinitely to tolerate the over-representation of Europe in the IMF and elsewhere. It would therefore be sensible for European leaders to obtain the best possible outcome by 'leading the end game' rather than fighting a rear-guard action. One way or the other, moreover, the EU would have to resolve a number of practical problems. Who, for example, would choose the Executive Directors, their alternates and staff for the new European constituencies? It might be best to give that task to an independent nominating panel, drawn from the relevant member states and enjoined to nominate the very best people for those jobs, regardless of nationality. That is, however, far from standard practice in the EU.

Rationalization of representation in the IMF is likely to generate pressure for reforming EU representation in other international institutions Decisions on representation in the IMF should not, however, be taken as providing exact precedents for other instiions. The circumstances of the IMF are special, at least in one respect. As a monetary and currency-based institution, the IMF is affected in a unique way by the decision of 12 of its members to adopt a single currency. So decisions on representation in the IMF would not provide exact precedents for other institutions.

Table 6.1 Reorganizing the IMF Executive Board

Country or country group*	# countries Actual	# countries Proposed	Share of total votes Actual	Share of total votes Proposed	Notes
EU euro area	–	12	–	22.94	
Unites States	1	1	17.11	17.11	
EU other	–	13	–	8.97	
Japan	1	1	6.14	6.14	
Germany	1	–	6	–	Merged with euro area
France	1	–	4.95	–	Merged with euro area
United Kingdom	1	–	4.95	–	Merged with EU other
Saudi Arabia	1	1	3.23	323	
China	1	1	2.94	2.94	
Russia	1	1	2.75	2.75	
Belgium, Austria, Hungary and others	10	–	5.14	–	Redistributed
Netherlands, Ukraine, Romania and others	12	–	4.85	–	Redistributed
Italy, Portugal, Greece and others	7	–	4.19	–	Redistributed
Sweden, Norway, Denmark and others	8	–	3.51	–	Redistributed
Switzerland, Poland, Uzbekistan and others	8	–	2.85	–	Redistributed
Ukraine, Romania, Turkey and others	–	19	–	3.41	New country group
Australia, Korea, New Zealand and others	14	14	3.33	3.33	No change
Canada, Jamaica, Bahamas and others	12	11	3.71	3.31	Ireland moved to euro area
Indonesia, Malaysia, Thailand and others	12	12	3.18	3.18	No change
South Africa, Nigeria, Zambia and others	20	20	3.18	3.18	No change
Kuwait, Libya, Egypt and others	13	13	2.95	2.95	No change
Switzerland, Norway, Israel and others	-	5	5	2.91	New country group
Mexico, Venezuela, Guatemala and others	8	7	4.28	2.86	Spain moved to euro area
Brazil, Colombia, Trinidad and others	9	10	2.46	2.47	Timor-Leste added
Iran, Algeria, Pakistan and others	7	7	2.45	2.45	No change
India, Bangladesh, Sri Lanka and others	4	4	2.4	2.4	No change
Argentina, Chile, Peru and others	6	6	2	2	No change
DR Congo, Cote d'Ivoire, Cameroon and others	24	24	1.41	1.41	No change

Note: *Country groups denoted by group name or by the names of the three countries with the largest numbers of votes.
Source: IMF (2003), *International Monetary Fund Annual Report 2003*, Appendix VII.

<u>6.5</u>   The need for a new body

This Report has praised the leadership role exercised for more than 25 years by the various emanations of the G7, including the annual Summits of the heads of state or government and the more frequent meetings of the finance ministers and central bank governors. In recent years, however, geopolitical issues, such as turmoil in the Balkans after the breakup of Yugoslavia, nuclear proliferation, protecting the marine environment and combating terrorism, have found their way onto the Summit agenda. The work on international financial and economic matters, other than trade, has been carried forward by the G7 finance ministers, whether in preparing the Economic Summits or in the regular meetings of finance ministers and central bank governors. These G7 processes have helped to advance international financial and economic cooperation.

It was argued earlier, however, that the ability of the G7 to foster that cooperation has begun to wane. The past successes of the G7 reflected capacity and therefore effectiveness, rather than legitimacy, accountability or representativeness, and the capacity of the G7 has been diminished by the advent of new issues. When the international agenda was dominated by currency crises and debt problems, the G7 was able to lead because its members were large and wealthy, but size and wealth do not necessarily confer effectiveness when, as now, the resolution of international financial problems requires the active cooperation of many other countries. The G7 recognized this challenge to its leadership when, as described in Chapter 3, it convened the G20. It has now to go a step further by conferring its agenda-setting role on a new body – one that has greater legitimacy, accountability and representativeness.

It is worth recalling briefly the ways in which the G7 has provided strategic direction. It has hammered out common positions, often after intense debate at senior official and ministerial levels. Its members have then followed through by supporting those positions in the various other bodies involved in financial and economic cooperation and have sought to exercise informal oversight of the work carried out in the multilateral forums described in Chapter 2. Some of this work has been of a technical nature, such as the efforts to combat money laundering and tax evasion. Other work has had a strategic element, such as the effort to strengthen the international financial architecture. And other work has had a high humanitarian content, such as the HIPC initiative and the support provided for programmes in Bosnia and other crisis-torn countries ('failed states'). In most cases, moreover, the G7 has sought to enlist and enhance the roles of multilateral bodies. It also provided a degree of assurance in times of financial crisis that someone was 'minding the shop'.

The G7's several successes have rested on its members' strong commonality of interest in the smooth functioning of the international financial and economic system. Out of this commonality of interest, there developed solidarity, despite differences in political ideologies and occasionally in personalities. When that solidarity disappeared, so did cooperation, and the operation of the system was the worse for it. The G7 has invariably operated by consensus and has typically sought to mobilize broader support by informal suasion. It has been less successful when it has acted in a heavy-handed way or failed to elicit broad support from the international community. Its internal processes have been informal, even to the extent of abjuring the services of a secretariat.

The creation of the G20 followed a decision taken at the Cologne Economic Summit in 1999. The generous would say that the decision reflected the G7's statesmanship and foresight; the cynical would say that it reflected grudging

> **BOX 6.1** The United Nations Economic and Social Council
>
> The Economic and Social Council coordinates the work of the 14 UN specialized agencies, 10 functional commissions and five regional commissions; receives reports from 11 UN funds and programmes; and issues policy recommendations to the UN system and to Member States. Under the UN Charter, ECOSOC is responsible for promoting higher standards of living, full employment, and economic and social progress; identifying solutions to international economic, social and health problems; facilitating international cultural and educational cooperation; and encouraging universal respect for human rights and fundamental freedoms. ECOSOC's purview extends to over 70% of the human and financial resources of the entire UN system.

recognition on the part of the G7 that its ability to carry out its traditional financial and economic role is already ebbing and will continue to ebb in the years ahead. The creation of the G20 undoubtedly conferred greater legitimacy, accountability and representativeness on the arrangements for governing the international financial system. Nevertheless, there are grounds for doubt about the ability of the G20 to replace the G7, even if given more time for its role to develop. Some 40 people, central bank governors as well as finance ministers, sit around its table – too many to permit the intense debate and, at times, hard bargaining required to give strategic direction to the operation and development of the system. Some of its members, moreover, do not play a significant role in the system itself and thus lack the commonality of interest required for developing the solidarity essential to ensure the smooth functioning of the system. Finally, the deliberations of the G20 have focused mainly on a subset of the economic and financial issues that the G7 have sought to address. It has been chiefly concerned with matters closely related to the activities of the IMF – preventing and managing crises in emerging-market countries. In short, the G20 as presently constituted cannot readily replace the G7, and it would be difficult for the G20 to transform itself.

Could one of the other existing bodies take on the agenda-setting role presently played by the G7? Two such bodies come to mind, the IMFC and the UN's ECOSOC, but they cannot be readily adapted to replace the G7. The remit of the IMFC is rightly concentrated on the IMF. It should not be made to assume wider and more complex responsibilities. Furthermore, its membership must continue to bear some relationship to the membership of the IMF's Executive Board if the Board is to continue to accept the de facto suzerainty of the IMFC.

The UN's ECOSOC would appear at first glance to be a better candidate than the IMFC, given the role assigned to it by the UN Charter. Its remit is described in Box 6.1. It would not, however, be capable of developing in the required direction. Although it is supposed to coordinate the specialized agencies of the UN, including the IMF and World Bank, those institutions have always operated independently of ECOSOC, and members of the Fund and Bank need not be members of the UN, and vice versa. Furthermore, some of the bodies involved in international economic cooperation have no formal relationship whatsoever with the UN. Finally and most importantly, ECOSOC does not have a strong track record in matters of international financial cooperation. The bodies and tasks that would concern a successor to the G7 fall within the ambit of finance ministries and central banks, while much of the work of ECOSOC has typically fallen within the ambit of foreign ministries and development ministries. Much more than bureaucratic turf is at issue here. The approaches of the two sets of ministries are quite different. The objective of most finance ministries is to maintain open and stable international capital markets, whatever the vicissitudes and bitterness of international politics which foreign ministries have the difficult task of managing. Occasionally, a balance has to be struck between the financial and the diplomatic interest, and that task has often fallen in the G7 to the heads of government.

There is thus need for a new body fit for the opening decades of the twenty-first century – one that can take on the tasks now performed by the economic parts of the G7 process and can emulate the G7's well-tried methods of operation, described above. Those who design this new body will have to name it. It will deserve something better than an alphanumeric designation. Hereafter, however, it is described provisionally as the Council for International Financial and Economic Cooperation (CIFEC).

6.6   The mandate and membership of the new council

Like the G7, the new Council for International Financial and Economic Cooperation should serve as an agenda-setting body, providing strategic direction for the functioning and development of the international financial system. Therefore, it should be a forum for the governments whose actions have the largest impact on the functioning of the international financial system. Its members would meet to debate and concert national positions with the aim of maintaining a financial system that is open, robust and stable. The Council would also exercise informal oversight over the work of the various multilateral institutions and forums involved in international economic cooperation.

6.6.1   The mandate of the Council

The Council would not be empowered to issue instructions to any other international body. Its ability to influence the activities of other bodies would depend in part upon the character and cohesion of its own membership. If, however, it included the countries that play leading roles in other bodies and its recommendations reflected consensus within the CIFEC itself, it could expect its own members to back its recommendations regarding the priorities and policies of other bodies. And because its membership would be broader than that of the G7, its recommendations would presumably have more legitimacy than those of the G7, which is too often seen as a self-appointed group of international creditors, unrepresentative of the international community at large. Although no other body would be formally accountable to the CIFEC, there should be a two-way link between it and others. When an issue relevant to a particular institution is to be discussed by the CIFEC, the head of that body should be invited to attend and participate in the CIFEC's deliberations. Furthermore, the CIFEC could invite other bodies to respond in due course to its recommendations although it could not compel them to do so. Finally, the CIFEC would make its recommendations in the same way that the G7 does now – by issuing communiqués after its meetings. It can and should be open about its work – a requirement not easy to avoid in a world of 24-hour news. Using the terminology introduced in Chapter 2, the practices of the CIFEC would entail 'reporting accountability' in that the whole international community would be made aware of its views and recommendations, and the actions taken by others in response to its recommendations would entail an element of 'response accountability'.

The Council's relationship with the new G4 proposed in Chapter 5 would be especially important. The G4 would be wholly autonomous, having no formal relationship with the CIFEC apart from its members' own membership in it. Furthermore, the G4 might find it appropriate to operate quietly, without always issuing communiqués after its meetings. Nevertheless, the CIFEC could keep track informally of its work, because the members of the G4 would also belong to the CIFEC.

The Council would have also to enjoy a close working relationship with the Financial Stability Forum, the body chiefly responsible for coordinating the work of those directly involved in supervising financial institutions and promoting the efficient functioning of financial markets. The political leadership provided by the CIFEC may sometimes be needed to balance the technocratic biases of participants in the FSF, but it would not extend to political involvement in the development of the standards and practices that lie within the purview of the FSF.

More generally, the CIFEC would seek to mitigate overlap and duplication between other bodies and achieve the coherence necessary to secure consistent, concerted action in the pursuit of common objectives. The CIFEC should also identify gaps – activities that need to be carried forward but are not being undertaken – and seek to ensure through its members, as participants in the relevant bodies, that those gaps are closed.

6.6.2 Council membership

Effectiveness requires that the CIFEC include among its members the governments whose actions most strongly affect the functioning of the international economic and financial system. It also requires that the CIFEC be small enough to foster candid discussion and generate consensus. Legitimacy and representativeness, however, require that the CIFEC be widely regarded as being responsive to the needs and concerns of the whole international community. There is no easy way to achieve these competing objectives fully, and the proposals made below reflect an attempt to strike an appropriate balance. It is suggested that the CIFEC have no more than 15 member countries and that each member be represented by its finance minister or closest counterpart (for example, its Treasury or economics minister). No country would be barred from nominating its central bank governor instead, but central bankers should not ordinarily serve on the CIFEC. It would not have operational responsibility for the matters with which central bankers typically deal, and they do not have the political responsibility for setting priorities and striking the cross-issue bargains that may sometimes be needed to reconcile conflicting views held by national governments.

The CIFEC would elect its chair for a two- or three-year term, and officials from the chair's own ministry would serve as the secretariat of the CIFEC. The Secretary General of the UN, the Managing Director of the IMF, the President of the World Bank, and the Director General of the WTO would be invited to attend the group's meetings and participate in its deliberations. In addition to contributing the expertise of their own institutions, they would help to ensure that the recommendations of the CIFEC took account of the interests of the wider international community that cannot be heavily represented in its ranks.

While the CIFEC would normally meet at the ministerial level, it would perhaps be useful for it to meet periodically albeit infrequently at the level of heads of state or government. Those meetings would serve to enhance the authority of the CIFEC and to assess its effectiveness.

How might the 15 members be chosen? The indicators in Table 6.2 suggest that a rather small number of countries are candidates for standing membership. When the euro area is treated as a single entity, it joins the United States and China in the first ten-country group, regardless of the metric used to weigh economic importance, and only five more countries appear uniformly in the first or second ten-country group: Brazil, India, Japan, Mexico and the United Kingdom.[41]

Table 6.2 Measures of relative economic importance, 2002

Country rank	Gross domestic product Unadjusted	PPP-adjusted	Merchandise trade (exports + imports)	Population
1 to 10	United States	United States	Euro area	China
	Euro area	Euro area	United States	India
	Japan	China	Japan	Euro area
	United Kingdom	Japan	China	United States
	China	India	United Kingdom	Indonesia
	Canada	United Kingdom	Canada	Brazil
	Mexico	Brazil	Mexico	Pakistan
	India	Russia	Rep. Korea	Russia
	Rep. Korea	Canada	Singapore	Bangladesh
	Brazil	Mexico	Switzerland	Nigeria
11 to 20	Australia	Rep. Korea	Malaysia	Japan
	Russia	Indonesia	Russia	Mexico
	Switzerland	Australia	Sweden	Vietnam
	Sweden	South Africa	Australia	Philippines
	Norway	Turkey	Thailand	Turkey
	Poland	Thailand	India	Ethiopia
	Saudi Arabia	Iran	Saudi Arabia	Egypt
	Turkey	Argentina	Brazil	Iran
	Denmark	Poland	Denmark	Thailand
	Indonesia	Philippines	Poland	United Kingdom
21 to 30	Thailand	Pakistan	Norway	Dem. Rep.Congo
	Israel	Colombia	Iceland	Myanmar
	Iran	Saudi Arabia	Indonesia	Ukraine
	South Africa	Egypt	Turkey	Rep. Korea
	Argentina	Bangladesh	Czech Rep.	Colombia
	Malaysia	Ukraine	Hungary	South Africa
	Venezuela	Sweden	Philippines	Poland
	Egypt	Malaysia	Israel	Argentina
	Singapore	Switzerland	South Africa	Tanzania
	Colombia	Vietnam	Iran	Sudan
31 to 40	Philippines	Algeria	Venezuela	Canada
	Czech Rep.	Norway	Vietnam	Kenya
	Hungary	Denmark	Chile	Algeria
	Chile	Czech Rep.	Argentina	Morocco
	Pakistan	Chile	Ukraine	Afganistan
	New Zealand	Romania	Slovak Rep.	Peru
	Peru	Hungary	Romania	Uzbekistan
	Algeria	Peru	Algeria	Venezuela
	Bangladesh	Venezuela	New Zealand	Malaysia
	Romania	Israel	Nigeria	Iraq
41 to 50	Nigeria	Nigeria	Egypt	Nepal
	Ukraine	Morocco	Kuwait	Uganda
	Morocco	Singapore	Colombia	Dem. Rep. Korea
	Vietnam	Kazakhstan	Morocco	Romania
	Libya	New Zealand	Pakistan	Saudi Arabia
	Kuwait	Slovak Rep.	Slovenia	Ghana
	Ecuador	Sri Lanka	Belarus	Australia
	Kazakhstan	Tunisia	Tunisia	Sri Lanka
	Slovak Rep.	Sudan	Kazakhstan	Yemen
	Guatemala	Syrian Arab Rep.	Croatia	Mozambique

Use of these indicators is not meant to imply that they deserve equal weight or that are the only ones relevant for measuring economic importance; none of them speaks to the size or international importance of a country's financial sector, A country that is home to a major international financial market, such as the United Kingdom, may have a stronger claim to standing membership than countries that have larger economies or populations or participate more heavily in international trade. Furthermore, the desiderata cited above, especially representativeness, may call for the inclusion of countries that do not appear in the first or second ten-country group. It might therefore make sense to grant standing membership to the United States, the euro area, China, Japan and the United Kingdom, and to grant term membership to ten other countries, grouped perhaps by region, on a rotating basis. Countries such as Brazil, India and Mexico might qualify eventually for standing membership, in which case it would perhaps be wise to accommodate them by increasing slightly the size of the CIFEC rather than reducing sharply the number of term members.

6.6.3   Creating the new council

It is not hard to outline the functions of the CIFEC or propose ways of choosing its members. It is much harder to decide how it might be created. The IMF could not be asked to create the CIFEC, because the IMF subscribes to a different principle – representation by constituency rather than rotation.

It might likewise be impossible for the G7 or G20 to sponsor the creation of the CIFEC, because some members of those groups would be disadvantaged by the introduction of rotating membership. It might therefore be necessary for a group of like-minded members of the G7 and G20 to take the initiative in proposing for wider discussion a scheme to establish the CIFEC. It might also be necessary for the G7 and G20 to function in parallel with the CIFEC until the latter had established itself. In fact, the G7 might continue to function indefinitely, if only for the more limited purpose of achieving internal consensus on matters pertaining to the work of the IMF and other multinational institutions of which they are the principal creditors. And the G8 Summit might also survive in order to develop common positions on geopolitical and other matters outside the domain of the CIFEC.

<u>6.7</u>   Conclusion

This Report has put forward proposals reforming the institutional framework for the governance of the international economic and financial system. It is an agenda, not a blueprint. It is meant to suggest how the international community might, over time, reshape the governance of the system in response to the tectonic pressures for change in the global financial and economic system. It aims to make governance more effective, but at the same time more legitimate, representative and accountable. Other models can, no doubt, be suggested. It is very clear, however, that the present arrangements will not endure. It is therefore time to begin the debate on their replacement.

Discussion and Roundtables

Session 1: Successes, Failures and Principles

Philippe Maystadt
European Investment Bank, Luxembourg

Philippe Maystadt took a broad view of the evolution of economic cooperation and the lessons that can be drawn for the future. When looking at the history of economic and financial cooperation since 1945, Maystadt suggested that four characteristics in particular are worth highlighting.

First, glancing over these sixty years it is difficult to find a grand design, a broad wide structural strategy. Changes have essentially been driven by economic, financial, and political developments that have required finding an appropriate solution to the problem of the moment. The central challenge to economic and financial cooperation has itself changed substantially over time, but in a way that would have been very difficult to predict accurately *ex ante*.

Second, the changing political geography of the world has led to a proliferation of country groupings (see Appendix 1A) that have come in various shapes, and with varying degrees of formalism in their structure and recognition. International institutions, meanwhile, have adapted to changing conditions most often by extending their reach to new issues.

Third, economic and financial cooperation has not developed independently from wider political considerations, a fact probably best demonstrated by the developments that followed the end of the Cold War or by the emergence of global terrorism.

Fourth, and this is a point that Maystadt felt was not stressed enough in the Report and yet which is very dear to EU citizens, is the emergence of regional arrangements for cooperation. This particular development raises the question of whether regional cooperation comes at the expense of wider economic cooperation or whether it is a suitable, possibly interim solution on the way to achieving wider cooperation.

Altogether, these four characteristics provide an adequate framework within which to assess past developments. They also serve as a point of reference to gauge the appropriate changes that may be worth considering in order to reform the framework for international cooperation.

In the last decade, there have been recurrent calls for a new financial architecture and for the development of global rules and standards. However, Maystadt argued that it would be imprudent to expect, any time soon, the emergence of a truly wide master plan that would cover all issues at the same time in an integrated way. Indeed, the cost of building the necessary consensus is very high. It is only when the pressure of events is high enough that decisions can be reached, suggested the speaker.

Maystadt explained that we should not lament the absence of any such wide-ranging blueprint, but that we should instead accept that the spur for advances in economic cooperation will continue to be driven by events which are difficult to predict. Maystadt was certainly not against the emergence of global standards, such as the new Basel II package or current efforts to harmonize accounting and reporting standards. These are indeed appropriate responses to clearly identified weaknesses, he maintained. The point is rather that issues should be taken as they arise and that a problem-solving attitude should be adopted in resolving them.

Even if we accept this cautious approach, Maystadt emphasized that action should be taken to restrain and hopefully redress the proliferation of country groupings of different shapes and sizes, as well as the 'mission creep' of international institutions. The Report clearly points out that cooperation bodies are easily created but hardly ever disbanded, even if it is clear to all that they have become obsolete. We need then, urged Maystadt, to take a hard look at all these country groupings and strive to streamline them so as to establish one such grouping for each main issue – trade, development, banking regulation etc. The country group should be large enough to be representative of the stakeholders but small enough to remain effective.

The same is true for international institutions. They were all given a reasonably clear mandate when they were created. Over time, as conditions have changed, they have extended their reach to deal with new issues, some of which are clearly being covered by other institutions. There is no evidence of any value added gained through such institutional overlap and duplication. On the contrary, it seems reasonable to conclude that having the same issue discussed over and over in various fora and dealt with by different international institutions adds costs and makes it more difficult to reach the necessary compromise for international cooperation. Hence, there is a need for establishing clear task-based demarcation lines between international institutions. Of course these demarcation lines will have to be reviewed regularly to take into account the emergence of new issues.

Maystadt was thus very much in favour of what can be termed the 'specialization' of international institutions. Such a specialization would furthermore contribute to raising the accountability of these institutions, since it will be easier for stakeholders to pass a judgement on the way a specific institution fulfils its mandate.

Edmond Alphandéry
CNP-Assurances, Paris

Edmond Alphandéry focused his comments on the issue of regionalism. He took as his starting point the 'renewed interest in regionalism' that the authors of the Report assert is one of the four main features of today's international economic and financial arrangements.

Alphandéry began his comments by asking why, since Bretton Woods, regionalism has not been a driving force in the evolution of the international financial architecture. Agreeing with the motto put forward by the Report authors, 'remodelling yes; rebuilding no', he took the additional step of asking what place regionalism could play in discussions relating to any future remodelling of the system. Despite the recognition by the authors that 'the creation of the EMS in 1974 was a regional systemic change of far reaching importance', he noted that the Report did not touch in any commensurate way on the systemic impact of the emergence of the euro on the future of global monetary and financial architecture, nor comment on the lessons that can be drawn from this unique experience for other regions of the world (East Asia comes first to mind), and nor, finally, provide any reflection on the type of global model it could help to design for the decades ahead.

Alphandéry's first question was thus the following: how can we explain that after the war, while living in a world much less open than today, in which globalization was much less pervasive, we nonetheless laid the foundations of a system where the regional level was neglected, and why has its potential remained underestimated during 60 years, with the notable exception of the euro?

Alphandéry acknowledged that the creation of institutions like regional development banks or organizations like Mercosur or NAFTA, have punctuated the march towards the present architecture. But no construction has any real significance or global impact comparable whatsoever to the European Union and EMU. Mercosur, for instance, did not prevent Brazil and Argentina from following divergent monetary routes with, as a consequence of the sharp strengthening of the dollar in the late 1990s, the breakdown of the currency board in Argentina and the subsequent collapse of its economy. The Japanese proposal to establish an Asian Monetary Fund in 1997 was effectively neutralized by the United States acting together with China.

There are clear explanations for the lack of focus on the regional level in the post Bretton Woods framework. In the first decades after the war, the dollar-based, fixed exchange rate system, which lasted until the early 1970s, together with the undisputed American leadership of the so-called free world in the face of the Soviet Union and its satellites, precluded the establishment of any significantly fragmented organization. Needless to say, interwar trade policies which in the 1930s had an appalling impact on economic activity and employment, further acted to prevent the emergence of any type of organization that could have been considered as facilitating a return to protectionism.

But what of today? Times have considerably changed. The European Union cannot seriously be held up as any form of protective shield for its members against external competition. Furthermore, the countries of the former Soviet empire have adopted free market economies. And finally, the world's current monetary configuration, based on a system of floating exchange rates (at least among the major currencies) has opened the door to a multipolar order.

Nevertheless, few countries in other parts of the world seem willing to follow the path forged by the European Union, and no new significant step towards a structured regional organization of the economic and financial architecture is in the offing.

This observation led to a second, related question: in this era of globalization, which is daily becoming more intrusive, is there a contradiction between the evidence that 'the list of issues of collective interest is expanding' and that so many issues are to be considered within a world perspective on the one hand, and the argument in favour of regionalism on the other? Alphandéry argued that this is not the case. On the contrary, he claimed that enhancing and strengthening the regional level in other parts of the world should facilitate the resolution of global issues. An example is given by current world trade negotiations. Far from being an obstacle to the promotion of free trade, the fact that European trade policy is in the hands of the European Commission clearly helps defend against moves to protectionism. Furthermore, it cannot be denied that during the recent monetary and financial crises that plagued South East Asia and Latin America, stronger regional relationships and better local arrangements (in the area of trade, currency or financial surveillance) would have, in the very least, contributed to mitigate the impact of the international financial turbulence on these countries. The same applies to Turkey which has, during this period been much more vulnerable than those other Central and Eastern European countries that have effectively received protection from their expected entry into the European Union.

Alphandéry further noted that, using the criteria suggested by the Report to judge the quality of international governance – effectiveness, legitimacy, accountability and representativeness – it can be argued that the regional level represents a better quality playing field; assuming of course that it is supranationally structured (at least in so far as the three key EU dimensions, namely economic, monetary and financial, are concerned).

He thus wondered whether, when the authors call for a 'new, smaller body' to oversee adjustments among the world's four main currencies – the dollar, the euro, the yen and the renminbi – they are ready to acknowledge that better organized regional areas might help deal with current global imbalances.

From here, Alphandéry turned to his second main question: what lessons can be drawn from the European construction project and from the creation of the euro? Indeed, if asked to select three milestones events in the history of international financial relations since the war, Alphandéry made the following choices: Bretton Woods in 1944, the suspension of dollar gold convertibility in 1971 and the birth of the euro in 1999. However, in their nevertheless remarkable review of the period, the authors of the Report did not lay any emphasis on the creation of this new currency, and on its far reaching implications for the future of the world monetary and financial architecture.

In 1999, with the help of leading European personalities, Alphandéry created a group, the Euro 50 group, which looks at the issues raised by the emergence of the euro as well as the possible avenues opened by creation of this common currency. In a meeting in 2003 with their Asian counterparts, the lessons of the European experience for Asia were debated. South East Asia, where most transactions on the foreign exchange market are carried out in dollars and where the bond market is still largely underdeveloped, has been the theatre of two regional initiatives since the 1997–8 crisis which are worth highlighting: the Chiang Mai initiative which has created a network of bilateral swap arrangements and which can be considered as a first (albeit modest) step toward a coordinated exchange rate policy in the region, and the establishment of an Asian Bond Fund by the East Asia-Pacific Central Banks. Since the ASEM Finance Ministers' meeting in Copenhagen in July 2002, it seems clear that there is presently a desire in this region to improve the framework for the stabilization of local currencies, to strengthen regional surveillance and to deepen local financial markets. The consensus that emerged from the Euro 50 discussions, however, emphasized that there is still a very long way to go before anything comparable to the EMU is to emerge in East Asia. Indeed, the creation of the euro required vision and leadership from a pioneering group of countries.

Alphandéry concluded by reiterating a question posed at the end of Chapter 1 of the Report. 'What changes, the authors ask, are needed to get the right structure for effective economic cooperation to deal with the most important issues of today?' Earlier, in the same chapter, the authors rightly pointed out that for the evolution of international economic cooperation, gradualism has been the rule, with change driven by immediate problems rather than by a vision of a better world. Today, who could deny that global trade imbalances, mainly between the United States and South East Asia, are one of the major economic challenges of our present time? Appreciation of the renminbi has been claimed by the US Administration as being the best solution to this crucial issue. But it seems every day more obvious that no satisfactory answer will be found outside regional arrangements among Asian countries themselves. Is there any chance that a systemic change be driven in the Asian case, as it was for the EMU, not only by the immediate problem at hand, but also by a vision of a better world?

Giorgio Gomel
Banca d'Italia, Roma

Giorgio Gomel raised two key points: he first looked at the characteristics of the international monetary system today, following which he analysed the four principles of governance put forward in the Report.

International monetary relationships today, began Gomel, display highly complex structures and governance arrangements. This new order has been shaped by three interacting developments, some of which are well highlighted in the Report: 1) the primacy of private financial markets; 2) the increase in the number and variety of actors; and 3) the increase in the breadth, diversity and complexity of the range of functions performed through international cooperation.

The primacy of private financial markets is the first characteristic of today's international monetary relationships. The effects of global, stateless, finance's domination of the nation-state and the constraints it imposes on national sovereignty in two fundamental areas – the powers to govern its currency and to tax its citizens – are the object of serious reflection and controversy. Abstracting from the thorny 'welfare economics' question of whether the impact of global finance is beneficial overall, and given the significant risks of systemic instability, the fact remains that the primacy of private markets will remain a distinguishing feature of the system. No conceivable institutional or regulatory reform whether the imposition of a Tobin tax on international financial transactions or the creation of a world central bank can alter this state of affairs for the decades ahead. However, just as the national banking and financial crises of the 1930s made it necessary to create public institutions to regulate and supervise private agents within national borders, so today globalized finance is forcing the international community to establish international rules and standards that can be applied uniformly in supervision.

In addition, we see today a large number and variety of actors involved in international monetary relationships. The IMF and the World Bank have nearly universal membership. At their inception they had 29 members; they now have almost 200. This near-universality is a historically significant achievement. The ranking of countries by economic size has, however, changed considerably in the last 50 years, but the composition and relative power of countries in IFIs and decision-making fora have not kept pace. Here Gomel took issue with the assertion in the Report that the governance of the IMF, World Bank, and WTO still appropriately reflect the relative economic weight of countries.

The sweeping changes in political and economic geography have been accompanied by changes in the forms and arrangements of international cooperation. The Report illustrates the changes that occurred in the 1970s and 1980s when traditional institutions, such as the IMF, the World Bank and the OECD, were joined by other organizations, including intergovernmental groupings (G7, G10), concertation bodies bringing together the central banks of the leading developed countries in monitoring financial markets, supervising banks and overseeing the payment system (the BIS system of Committees), 'self-regulatory' organizations charged with establishing uniform rules and codes of conduct (the International Organization of Securities Commissions (IOSCO), the International Association of Insurance Supervisors (IAIS)) and private cooperative groupings, especially among internationally active banks (the London Club, the Institute for International Finance). More recently and importantly, the FSF and the G20 have joined the foray.

Finally, today the range of functions performed through international cooperation is very diverse and complex. Various functions are performed cooperatively. Gomel identified the following: 1) the choice of the exchange rate regime and exchange rate policy; 2) coordination of economic policies; 3) management of financial crises; 4) financial stability.

Essentially, what these changes mean, argued Gomel, is that international cooperation is no longer limited to the traditional macroeconomic sphere but now extends to the institutions of economic policy, operating rules for the markets, supervisory regulations, relations between banks, corporations and the public sector.

In this domain, there is a broad consensus today that one necessary condition for preventing or containing financial instability is the adoption and observance, especially by emerging countries, of internationally uniform standards, rules and codes of conduct.

If we move beyond this general enunciation, the theme of financial stability is complex both technically and politically. Technically, it is difficult to set internationally accepted rules or standards, given the abundance of arrangements, legal systems and cultures in such fields as banking supervision, securities market regulation, bankruptcy law, accounting and auditing methods. To take an obvious example, outlined Gomel, corporate governance entails a series of issues – contract enforcement, shareholders' rights, property rights, and dispute settlement machinery – all of which raise complicated questions legally and politically which continue to be the domain of nation-states.

Rule-making should remain the responsibility primarily of the specialized self-regulatory organizations – the Basel Committee for banks, IOSCO for securities markets, IAIS for the insurance industry, IASC for accounting standards. Effective rule enforcement should be the job of the governments that choose to incorporate the rules into their national legal systems. Between these two moments, international institutions have a key role to play – the IMF in particular. It can exert strong pressure on countries if the rules and standards agreed are embodied in specific recommendations endorsed by the Fund, because this would give the rules a political legitimacy they now lack insofar as they are the product of bodies whose membership is restricted to a small number of countries. The Fund could also make observance of some standards an essential element of conditionality. Even when no financing is at issue, the Fund could make a judgment of observance of international standards as part of its ordinary surveillance activity.

Gomel then turned to the issue of governance and its four principles as analysed by the Report. Discarding such ideas as 'world government' and a 'world central bank' as utopian, he noted that the international community has embarked upon the path of cooperation, often ad hoc, informal and moving forward in an incremental fashion. He agreed with what he referred to as a wise dose of pragmatism, namely the Report's assertion that 'The practice of responding in an ad hoc fashion to problems as they arise within a changing framework of formal and informal institutions has been untidy but often effective'.

The governance of the world financial system, according to the Report, should conform to four principles: effectiveness, legitimacy, accountability, representativeness (LAR). The list of issues of common (global) interest is expanding. Alternative solutions to this development are either setting up new institutions, or delegating new tasks to one or more existing institutions, or putting in place an informal structure. The criterion for judging any new proposal for change is to secure effectiveness with as much 'LAR' as possible.

Gomel offered a few comments on these suggestions, turning first to governance and democracy. International cooperation has operated in the latter half of the 20th century more or less like a 'club'. A small number of rich countries got together and agreed to make rules. Trade ministers dominated GATT; finance ministers ran the IMF; defence and foreign ministers met at NATO; central banks at

BIS. The G7 was the epitome of such process. The lack of transparency to outsiders, under the old club model, was key to its political efficacy.

For a number of reasons – growing number and heterogeneity of states, new participants in the policy process such as NGOs, labour unions, business firms, the demand by democratic societies for accountability and transparency often based on a domestic analogy that conflicts with club practices – the club model has been put into question. Yet, democracy as a government by the majority of the people who regard themselves as a political community has no easy meaning at the global level: who are 'the people of the world' when there is no sense of political identity and community, and the world is organized largely around a system of unequal states? Still, governments can do things to respond to the concerns about a 'global democratic deficit': increased transparency (for example NGOs deserve a voice, not a vote); open markets, against monopolies; better accountability of the IFIs, and so on.

Gomel thus proposed a detailed analysis of the 'soft law' approach to international cooperation. Financial regulation was left out of the picture at Bretton Woods but with today's technology and degree of financial and economic integration, it has gained prominent ground. Since the creation of a supranational regulatory body endowed with enforcement powers is unfeasible, the only option left is the adoption of standards and codes, arrangements of a non-binding nature, internationally promulgated but nationally implemented, and guided by incentives. This is the 'soft law approach', as its elements have neither the strength of ordinary law nor the weakness of international conventions. As financial stability has grown as an international issue and public good, the FSF, an informal network, was set up, which represented a concrete departure from Bretton Woods. It is rather unique in its configuration since it is the only body specifically devoted to improving coordination between the authorities responsible for financial stability, and overseeing action to address vulnerabilities.

What is specific and important about the FSF? In terms of content, the FSF has identified key standards for sound financial systems; in terms of governance, enlarged participation in the FSF would be needed, by co-opting emerging markets into the process (more or less like the G20); as regards incentives, two different sets exist: those that flow indirectly from market reactions to lack of observance and those that result directly from the official community. The FSF has been actively involved in designing the latter, for instance, by publishing a list of offshore financial centres which failed to comply with world standards of financial regulation.

A final question is whether soft law is sufficient or if it needs some hardening. Do we need a formal declaration of the principles and goals the strategy is meant to pursue? Probably yes, and the European experience is illuminating in this respect.

The European approach cannot be replicated at the world level without modifications, concluded Gomel. But the method adopted in Europe holds the key to the success of the financial integration strategy. On the one hand, standards were turned into legally binding rules through the use of the so-called directives, which are legal texts setting the principles that member states are required to implement. But member states enjoy wide freedom with regard to the means they select in order to enact those principles, and an appropriate transition period is provided for. On the other hand, the whole edifice was built on the idea that what is needed for the approach to work is a critical mass of countries, not unanimity. The European experience shows that soft law and hard law are in the end complementary, not substitute, tools.

Richard Portes
CEPR, London

Richard Portes articulated his discussion around the four following points: the new global issues; the principles; the changing environment and the need for innovation drawn from experience.

According to Portes, globalization and international financial integration are the two new key issues, although they are often confused. They are typically represented as a significant increase in cross-border transactions, although economists might prefer to think of them as the application of the law of one price and market integration. The macroeconomic and financial interdependence that they trigger is not as new as is often suggested. The period 1870–1913 was a period of very substantial economic integration which operated reasonably well without the immense proliferation of institutions that we have seen since the Second World War. Much in the same way, contagion is not a new phenomenon; the history of sovereign defaults during the interwar period is a very strong example of contagion that has never been quite repeated on such a scale.

Moreover, globalization should not be exaggerated since it has not entirely overcome the forces of distance and regionalism. Data on both trade and financial integration show that we came back only recently to the level of globalization that was achieved by 1913. Distance still matters if we look at the way in which interaction decays with distance, whether it is trade or cross-border flows of equity, foreign direct investment or technology flows.

The problem identified by the authors could be called a 'trilemma aversion'; that is to say, an aversion to the conflict among the three desiderata: monetary autonomy, fixed exchange rates and capital mobility. In the earlier period of globalization, in 1870–1913, it was monetary autonomy that was given up. Today governments want all three and refuse to choose, except in the case of the EU, where governments have given up monetary autonomy for the sake of capital mobility and exchange rate stability. But capital mobility might have some undesired consequences from time to time, as might floating exchange rates. In these cases, the tendency is to seek solutions through international institutions. Portes argued that there might be alternatives, such as regionalism.

The second issue tackled by Portes refers to the four principles of governance. Accountability is not straightforward, he asserted. To be accountable, an institution must be sufficiently transparent so that one can see what it is doing and the basis on which it is doing it. One must also be able to compare the outcomes with the objectives that have been set for the institution, and this is part of the problem with some of the existing international institutions. An obvious question is also, accountable to whom? To the NGOs? But to whom are the NGOs in turn accountable? This is an important question to which less attention has been paid than is merited.

Furthermore, one should precisely define the criteria for representativeness. The authors raise the issue but concrete examples are missing. For example, the attempt to construct a framework for representativeness has been extremely difficult in an organization like the EU, as demonstrated by the immense difficulties in coming up with an appropriate voting formula for qualified majority voting.

In addition, there are conflicts among the various criteria. Effectiveness may require some degree of secrecy in the proceedings of the institution. Central banks are very familiar with the issue and the importance of not giving out details of internal discussions that would be too sensitive for the markets to handle. Representativeness can also impair the effectiveness of an organization, as may be witnessed now with the enlargement of the European Union.

Third, Portes commented on the changing economic environment. The point about Central Bank independence and its consequences is absolutely right, he noted. However, Portes moved on to disagree with the Report authors on the ineffectiveness of sterilization. Recent academic research goes in an opposite direction, he claimed, and policy-makers who are keeping their exchange rates more or less fixed against the dollar (i.e. China and other East Asian countries and India) but still intervening and sterilizing substantially (as in India) seem to think that sterilization works. Casual observation suggests that this can be the case for quite a long time at least. The inefficacy of fiscal policy is not validated by the experience of the United States – the economic recovery was brought by the tax cuts (and, of course, stimulative monetary policy). As for the twin deficits, the graphs from Chapter 2 of the Report show that they are hardly twins and do not even seem to come from the same family. There is obviously an accounting relationship, but they are both endogenous.

To conclude, Portes tried to draw lessons from this experience. While the authors suggest new institutions and informal structures, explained Portes, he noted rather that the IMF has been a very successful and opportunist organization in finding new tasks for itself. In 1973, it lost the role it was given in Bretton Woods but immediately took up surveillance of the financial flows associated with petro-dollar recycling. Then, it shifted very quickly into managing the Latin American debt crisis. The IMF also moved quickly into transition issues when they came along. That said, there is certainly a case that the IMF should return to its core competences.

In a concluding note, Portes agreed with two of the previous discussants on the point that the Report should devote more attention to regionalism. Possibly in that context, more currency unification is desirable. There will always be some countries left outside but they can be shielded from the consequences of the interaction of these large tectonic plates by some degree of capital controls.

General Discussion

Karen Johnson
International Finance, Federal Reserve Board, Washington, DC
Karen Johnson noted that both the authors and the discussants took a general understanding of the term 'effectiveness' for granted, even if the other criteria were discussed in more details. She suggested perhaps a deeper discussion of this particular notion. In the complex and changing world described in the Report, perhaps what is needed, she continued, is a system that maximizes the capacity of markets and individual decision making to deliver good outcomes. This is a different kind of international cooperation than crisis management which may require different groupings or different strategies. These two elements are discussed in the paper but Johnson regretted that they were not separated clearly enough. Johnson wondered further whether it wouldn't pay to think hard about what is meant by effectiveness and distinguish different kinds of effectiveness in terms of *creating* a framework versus *operating* a framework.

Bernhard Winkler
European Central Bank, Frankfurt-am-Main
Bernhard Winkler detected a hint of nostalgia in the Report, particularly when it notes that the peak of effectiveness of the G7 has passed and that the Bonn summit in 1978 and the Louvre in 1987 are examples of effective good old-days cooperation. Winkler was doubtful on this point. As concerns the Bonn Summit, the consensus in Europe has since been 'never again', while Japan has since become highly sceptical of the Louvre agreement. For Winkler, the most successful period

was the 1990s when there was little cooperation and when the G7 was at a low point in terms of impact, mainly because the major focus was domestic price stability and sound policies. Perhaps, he suggested, we should look forward to a low level of cooperation as a sign that the countries are doing their homework.

Ariel Buira
G-24 Secretariat, Washington, DC
Ariel Buira picked up on something that Maystadt mentioned in his talk, namely that the basic desirable approach is to adopt a problem solving attitude or to address the problems as they arise rather than look at systemic issues and look for global reforms. Indeed, Maystadt said that rather than addressing the problems as they arise, problems are generally dealt with as they reach crisis point. This approach is problematic in the sense that because some problems may not reach a crisis point at the systemic level, they will not be addressed. He illustrated his point by referring to the commodities problem and the implementation of counter cyclical policies in emerging markets.

There are 50 or 60 countries whose exports consist of three commodities or less for more than half of their merchandise export earnings and who are consequently subject to horrendous periodic price shocks, with a direct impact of 2–3% to 7% of GDP (and of about 20% of GDP, if the overall effects through multipliers are taken into account). These are low income countries, with incomes of less than $ 1000 per capita, who do not pose a systemic threat. Consequently, there are no serious attempts to deal with their problems. In much the same way, the problems of financial crises in emerging market countries, are only addressed when the crisis poses a systemic problem and threatens the system.

Similarly, the issue of counter cyclical policies in developing countries and emerging market countries has not been addressed. All industrial countries can follow countercyclical policies and have done so over the last few years to address the international recession. However, these countries accounted only for around 45% of world GDP measured in purchasing power parity terms. The rest of the world could not implement such policies and hence were forced to follow pro-cyclical policies in order to maintain market confidence. It would have been much better for the world economy if all countries could have followed counter cyclical policies. However, the problem was not addressed because it did not seem to create a major problem for the G7.

Marc Büdenbender
UBS AG, Zurich
Marc Büdenbender found it interesting to read this overview of international cooperation for the public sector, but deplored that the perspective of the private sector was missing and argued that there was a good case for thinking about ways to incorporate it. The structure of capital flows has changed, he argued. In addition, the share of private flows has continuously increased and the topics have shifted from macro issues to micro issues, such as banking supervision, accounting, etc. When dealing with these complex issues, it would be interesting to bring in the private sector which is not only concerned by the issues but also possesses a different type of knowledge. Furthermore, there exist, in the private sector, some good examples for international economic cooperation that work well without public sector intervention, such as the Wolfsberg group which came up with the principles for dealing with money laundering.

Jens Thomsen
Danmarks Nationalbank, Copenhagen
Jens Thomsen argued that when looking at matters of international economic governance, one realizes that it is easier to be an economist than a diplomat. Diplomats have numerous difficulties in relation to decision-making on the global scene (in the context of the UN, for example). For instance, he suggested, is it possible for a country to intervene without the consent of the Security Council? Diplomats in that way encounter significant legal problems, which economists are spared. Economists have an international organization managing their affairs with universal representation – the IMF, which has a more efficient decision mechanism. However, in this case, the most important decisions are often hijacked by the G7. And within the G7, one member may have a special role.

Christian Pfister
Banque de France, Paris
Christian Pfister briefly mentioned his doubts on the idea that the focus on price stability of Central Banks complicates policy coordination. The Report writes that exchange rates are shared variables and that they are taken into account by Central Banks to the extent that it affects their objectives for price stability. Balance of payment developments are also taken into account. For example, the ECB explicitly refers to it in its assessment of economic developments. For Pfister, contrary to what others might argue, this creates a clear allocation of responsibilities and should, in his view, make policy coordination much simpler.

Session 2: International Payments: Key Currencies and Debt

C. Randall Henning
American University and Institute for International Economics, Washington, DC
Randall Henning commended the authors of the Report for offering a digestible history of macroeconomic, exchange rate and financial cooperation, a thoughtful diagnosis of the strengths and weaknesses of existing institutions, and a robust set of recommendations for reinforcing existing institutions and creating new ones. In his remarks, he focused on three key themes – first, the relationship between domestic politics and institutional effectiveness; second, the recent reserve accumulation in East Asia and the possible consequences for the IMF; and finally, the rationalization of European representation and quota shares in the IMF.

Looking first at the relationship between domestic politics and institutional effectiveness, Henning noted that a common approach to the problem of institutional design and reform tends to abstract from the role of domestic politics and competing domestic coalitions. Rather we tend to approach the issue by creating a rational set of international groups and organizations, hoping that domestic politics will then allow them to operate effectively. The Report leans towards this approach – it identifies the important players in a substantive area, groups them in a small, consultative forum, and tries to ameliorate the legitimacy problem by placing the group in the context of a larger, more inclusive institution. As a starting point, Henning said, this approach is certainly useful and reasonable. However, as with other studies of this nature, it is incomplete in its treatment of a key element in the analysis, namely, domestic politics.

Stanley Hoffman, Henning referenced, observed early on that economic interdependence does not simply intrude on state autonomy; it also causes domestic politics to intrude on international relations. Thus, as groups and institutions are designed, we need to consider the mechanisms of this intrusion and seek to channel the effect in constructive ways. Similarly, we need to consider the mechanisms by which international institutions work through domestic politics to effect policy change. Rather than constraining powerful states through rules and obligations, in particular, successful international institutions create cooperation through other channels, which may include the exchange of information, the monitoring of agreements, the creation of bargains across different issues areas, shifting the balance between competing domestic coalitions on macroeconomic policy, and perhaps over time, the convergence of analytical ideas and norms. In the presence of domestic politics, these mechanisms operate by facilitating Pareto-improving bargains among states.

The episodes of active, though perhaps somewhat disputed, cooperation highlighted in the Report – namely, the Bonn Summit and the Plaza-Louvre period – witnessed considerable iteration between international bargaining on the one hand, and domestic politics on the other. Indeed, the leaders in Bonn effectively used the Summit process to manage their domestic politics for constructive policy changes across different issue areas (Putnam and Henning 1989). Similarly, the Plaza-Louvre process was driven in no small measure by the desire of the Reagan administration to blunt protectionism in the US – a task that it achieved.

The implications are twofold. On the one hand, as we approach the problem of institutional design, rather than lamenting the intrusion of domestic politics in international cooperation, we should seek to make international institutions relevant and responsible to domestic constituencies in a constructive way. How this should be done is, of course, the tough question. There are no easy or transcendent answers. Nonetheless, the problem deserves more thought – quite certainly, all solutions have not been exhausted.

Perhaps one method is to 'bring the Congressman to the Summit meeting', as is often done within the context of the WTO, successfully generating support in the US Congress for multilateral trade negotiations. Perhaps parliamentary committees could be involved more systematically across different issue areas and processes. More generally, international organizations could be given contact with domestic political actors other than through the national bureaucracies that often mediate the relationship. Domestic political support for the IMF, for example, may be too important to be left to the management of mid-level officials within the Treasury or finance ministry. For example, the IMF Managing Director could testify directly to the US House and Senate Banking committees. Indeed, there are many other ways in which the connection between international institutions and domestic politics may be reinforced. Because international institutions often run afoul of domestic politics, the payoff to creative analysis of this general problem could be substantial.

The second implication relates to those prospective members of new groups. Both the Bonn Summit of 1978 and the Plaza-Louvre process resonated with democracies in which macroeconomic policy was contested among societal groups and political parties. How, on the other hand, would such processes resonate within one-party democracies or authoritarian governments? How would a new G4, as proposed in the Report, resonate within China? How would inclusion in key groups resonate within Saudi Arabia or Russia, or even, for that matter, within the democracies of Brazil, Mexico and India? Whether international bargaining and agreements actually produce policy reform or policy adjustments that are internationally consistent depends on the answers to these sorts of questions.

The second topic that Henning focused on deals with the recent, meteoric rise in reserve accumulation in East Asia. He postulated that this is likely to alter the financial terrain in ways that have not yet been fully appreciated, in particular with respect to the role of the IMF. Today, he pointed out, the combined reserves of China, Japan and the Republic of Korea are roughly 1.3 trillion dollars – more than four times the size of total IMF quotas (and of which only 80 billion is available for lending over the coming year). The implication is that East Asians could easily decide to lend to each other rather than seek crisis financing from the IMF, in turn raising serious questions about the relevance of the IMF in the region in the long term (Henning 2002).

Of course, Henning pointed out, financial resources and financing in general is not the only contribution of the Fund to crisis prevention and management. Indeed, these large reserve holdings suggest that over the long run, the relevance of the Fund will increasingly rest on its expertise and analysis, and on the credibility that the Fund can bestow on country policies in the eyes of financial markets. This suggests that investment in information and the analytical resources of the Fund's staff, as well as insulation of its analysis from political pressures should be priorities.

The long-term future of the Fund also rests on better aligning voting strength with the overall economic importance of members and regions. The Report, Henning pointed out, discusses the over-representation of Europe in the Fund and the need for this to be rationalized. The Report further notes the political resistance that any rationalization attempts will engender, but ultimately observes, as Henning quoted, that 'it is hard to believe that other governments will continue indefinitely to tolerate this situation'. Henning, however, argued that the redistribution of quotas and voting shares is inescapably a zero-sum game, making self-reform of the governance structure within the Fund exceedingly difficult. Resolving this problem would consume a good deal of time and energy, he argued, and serious consideration needs to be given to exactly how to move towards a comprehensive solution.

Henning suggested that a comprehensive solution would require, among other things, a broader context as well as a broker. Indeed, to secure agreement on the part of some countries to reductions in their shares, negotiations will need to be wrapped in a larger set of negotiations in which compensation can be provided across issue areas, thus sweetening the deal for those countries losing quota share. Such compensation could be, for example, the promise of sites for new organizations. Furthermore, Henning suggested, the United States, Japan and the larger European countries will be the ones that will have to take a leading role in brokering such an agreement. The incentives are there for the United States, in any case, as the US government has an interest in preserving the relevance of the Fund over the long term. However, the key point to be made, Henning emphasized, is that because of the highly political nature of the decision, as well as the potentially difficult trade-offs that will need to be made, reform will not take place at the instigation of the IMF itself. The IMF will not be able to reform itself alone.

Carlo Monticelli
Ministry of the Economy and Finance, Rome
Contrary to the claims of the Report, Carlo Monticelli argued, 'The news in the Report of my death [as G7 DD] is greatly exaggerated'. Rather, he suggested, the G7 will continue to be the core of an international governance framework.

In fact, asserted Monticelli, no group is ideally suited to delivering global governance. No group provides all the public goods required today, particularly as globalization and innovation generate evolving needs. Nonetheless, a hard core of decision makers is needed to provide strategic direction, ensure continuity, provide efficiency in crisis management and allow for balance and trade-offs across issues. Conceding that the G7 may well not be the optimal hard core, Monticelli looked at historical examples to bolster the case that the G7 is *de facto* the only grouping capable of providing a hard core for international economic governance. Indeed, the G7, he maintained, is a well-functioning process. Its constituents remain top-ranking in most economic dimensions and have demonstrated (mostly) strong and long-dated political cohesion. It is, furthermore, a well-oiled coordination machine.

How can the G7 continue to maintain its strategic leadership? Monticelli outlined four factors, which he felt were important. First, a sincere openness to new ideas and groups, including a bent for honest brokerage. Secondly, flexibility and support to other fora and events. Thirdly, focus and cohesion, including sticking to economic priorities and maintaining the process and network. And finally, economic performance – the G7 countries must continue to deliver strong growth performance to maintain leadership.

Monticelli did concede that cohesion with the G7 had sometimes proved wanting. As he noted, informal decision-making has its drawbacks. He suggested in response that two facets of the G7 leadership were worth reconsidering in the light of a possible lack of cohesion. The first is the role of the US as a 'first among equals'. Indeed, the special role of the United States is subject to a fundamental ambivalence by its closest partners that is difficult to resolve, namely an attitude we can characterize as 'damned if you do, damned if you don't'. The second is the representation of Europe within the G7. Here Monticelli thought that a stronger role for Europe within the G7 was merited and urgently needed.

Monticelli closed his remarks by briefly touching on the role and relevance of the G8. He noted that the primacy of economic issues in this group has been lost. In its place, a disparate set of issues is currently being treated. Furthermore, the process has shown much less systematic relevance, and has become rather too 'Summit-oriented' in the eyes of Monticelli – 'G8 Presidencies in search of a splash', he stated. Nonetheless, argued Monticelli, the news of the death of the G8 has also been exaggerated. The G8 does fulfil a role that no other 'G' is capable of replacing, at least for the time being. In this respect Monticelli referred to two points. The first is that the G8 provides a useful and unique opportunity to endorse initiatives (for example, the HIPC initiative) – this can be considered as a mere 'rubber-stamping' role but generates momentum to get things done. The second is that the G8 helps generate personal contact between key leaders – and some leaders openly declare that personal contacts are essential to foster mutual trust, in turn smoothing the functioning of international politics.

Jean Pisani-Ferry
University of Paris-Dauphine, France
The assessment of the G7 to date is generally positive, but for its failure to meet the criteria of legitimacy, accountability and representativeness, said Jean Pisani-Ferry. Indeed, it cannot be said that the G7 has any particular legitimacy when addressing global issues. It is certainly not accountable – it is a relatively narrow group of countries, and in particular, only one side of those involved in debtor-creditor issues are represented.

Pisani-Ferry shared the general assessment made in the draft Report on the G7. He noted that the bottom line problem as presented is essentially the following: where the G7 is legitimate (e.g. on exchange rates and macroeconomic coordination), it is not efficient; and yet when it is efficient (e.g. as an agenda-setter for the IMF), it is not legitimate. On this basis, explained Pisani-Ferry, the Report made several proposals: on the one hand, to downsize the G7 to increase its effectiveness as a player, while bringing China into the fold (for exchange rate and balance of payments issues); and on the other hand, to expand the G7 in order to maintain its role as an agenda setter. In both cases, Pisani-Ferry noted, the implications are particularly significant for the representation of the Europeans, and especially the eurozone countries.

Following his baseline analysis of the Report's diagnosis and proposals, Pisani-Ferry brought three questions to the fore. First, he outlined, the proposal essentially implies that the same body would not be dealing with on the one hand, macroeconomic and monetary/exchange rate cooperation and the broader issues of debtor-creditor relations, and on the other hand, all the other issues that the G7 touches on. In other words, the proposal put forward by the Report essentially suggests that the G7 transform itself into two different bodies. Is it a good idea to have two bodies rather than one?

The second question relates to the agenda-setting role of the new enlarged G(x) – CIFEC to use the name proposed in the Report. Would this new enlarged G(x) retain the agenda-setting role that currently falls under the responsibility of the G7? This is essentially a problem affecting the functioning of the global governance regime.

The third and final question Pisani-Ferry raised relates to the problem of European external representation. Would the recommendations made by the Report provide a solution to the European representation problem?

Pisani-Ferry answered his first question with a 'qualified' yes. Qualified, he argued because there are good arguments both for and against transforming the G7 into a G4, and creating a new agenda-setting body. The key disadvantage of having two bodies is that when both macroeconomic and other issues are dealt with by the same grouping, meetings will tend to be more frequent, the membership more continuous and the ability to act as a group with a common culture is enhanced. Separation will tend to limit the advantages that can be reaped from having one body deal with all issues.

Pisani-Ferry spent some time discussing the inclusion of China. Yes, he argued, China is a big country. China's trade is, without doubt, a significant part of world trade, and the RMB is clearly a systemic variable in the world economy today, even if, as Pisani-Ferry pointed out, the floating currencies of the G7 still represent two thirds of exchange market transactions. GDP rankings and other statistics, particularly as regards trade and population, certainly call for China's inclusion. Still, Pisani-Ferry questioned whether the inclusion of China will solve the current shortcomings of G7 cooperation, but nonetheless concluded that it is certainly better to have China in, and avoid recourse to 'megaphone diplomacy'.

One argument in favour of two bodies relates to Pisani-Ferry's third point. He pointed out that the solution to the problem of European representation is likely not to be the same as regards macroeconomic and exchange rate matters on the one hand, and as regards the management of international financial interdependence on the other. In a way then, the two-body solution may be an interesting one in the context of the European representation problem.

With regards to Pisani-Ferry's second question – the role of the G7 as an agenda setter – he began by remarking that global governance today relies on a series of specialized agencies. These agencies derive their legitimacy from an explicit mandate, their specialization, and from the formal agreements that form the basis of their actions. The upside with the kind of arrangement thus proposed by the Report is that legitimacy may be enhanced, and accountability ensured with respect to the particular mandate foreseen. The downside is that the creation of a G(x) would serve to contribute to the much-maligned proliferation of agencies. Indeed, Pisani-Ferry highlighted the high degree of inertia affecting international organizations – within the institutions themselves, with respect to their mandates, and with respect to the instruments at their disposal. There is thus a resultant lack of flexibility, and as a consequence, overall guidance is very much needed to enable the international community to address new issues and design desirable reforms. This is very much a role that a G(x) can retain in the future.

Pisani-Ferry's final question, relating to European representation, received a 'maybe' in response. He outlined three main models that characterize European external representation. The first, Pisani-Ferry referred to as 'unconditional delegation'. This characterization applies to the ECB today. The ECB has received a precise mandate, it is entrusted with the authority to implement it, and it is clearly accountable to Parliament on the fulfilment of its mandate. It can act as a full player within its functional domain. The second category is that of 'supervised delegation'. This currently applies to the area of trade, where the Commission (the agent) receives a mandate to conduct negotiations on trade from the Council (the principal). The principal delegates responsibility to the agent, and then checks that the outcome is in conformity with the mandate. The final model is that of 'coordination', as applied in G7 negotiations. Different countries participate together and endeavour to consult reciprocally or adopt similar positions. This is a soft form of external representation in which no delegation is involved. It is also the least effective in terms of representing the euro area externally, argued Pisani-Ferry. But it is often the only mode of representation possible when internal domestic policies are part of the discussion. If the discussion should turn to fiscal or structural reform issues, as discussions in the G7 frequently do, the 'coordination' model would be the only possible solution to European representation. Indeed, it would be the only applicable solution to any G4-type meetings. The 'supervised delegation' model of representation could, however, be appropriate for debt and financial issues, where decisions taken do not impact so directly on internal policies and where positions can be agreed on in advance and thus a mandate identified by the member states and given to an agent.

Thus, in a way, the separation solution envisaged by the Report could possibly facilitate the solution of the European representation problem. The G4 would not, however, be a G4. Rather, ministers from different European countries would still want to participate individually.

Jean-Jacques Rey
National Bank of Belgium
Rey's first point concerned the title of the Report. Economic cooperation, he felt, extends naturally to trade matters, which are however deliberately left out of the Report itself. Furthermore, issues in development finance received little emphasis, with the exception of the HIPC initiative, and while multilateral development banks were generally positively endorsed as institutions relevant to the global economic governance system, the substance of their challenges is not clearly specified. Rather, for Rey, the focus of the Report seems to be on financial stability issues, broadly speaking, or, viewed from the institutional angle, on the bread and butter of Treasuries and Central Banks, as witnessed over the last 15 to 20 years. The rest is treated as 'distractions', to quote the Report. Rey's suggestion to possible omissions was rather to keep the substance unchanged, but fix the title. There are enough reasons to accuse treasurers and central bankers of imperialism; they should not be involuntarily added to.

Rey proceeded to analyse in somewhat greater depth the chapter on balance of payments adjustment, which he characterized as 'refreshing', largely because it calls for rejuvenating attention to balance-of-payments equilibrium and exchange rate management. He strongly endorsed the comments made on exchange intervention, particularly the distance taken from pure monetary theory about sterilized or non-sterilized interventions. He similarly endorsed the need to combine domestic with external adjustment if one is serious about correcting imbalances. However, he was less convinced that balance of payments could or even should regain regular priority, be it in the context of a new institutional arrangement such as the G4. In his view, while policy coordination should address clear cases of misalignment, it should not be seen as a regular ex ante tool to fine tune developments in the economy. In the presence of free capital movements, balance of payments do not tell much today, unless there is, at the same time, some domestic problem to be addressed. And it has been demonstrated that the system can cope with fairly wide swings in major exchange rates, although the limits in volatility and swings should be recognised.

Rey's third point focused on the creation of a G4, which he strongly endorsed insofar as it involves a single representation of the euro area. He clearly positioned himself among those in Europe who feel that the international representation of the euro is presently inadequate and thus welcomed the pressure from outside in this respect, even if he did not wholeheartedly buy the argument of the 'over-representation' of Europe. The current dispersion of votes is, in Rey's view, a source of weakness rather than one of strength, as there is virtually no such thing as a European voice on the international monetary scene. Obviously, achieving such a merger calls for more work within Europe, but it also calls for some understanding and flexibility from outside, as the asymmetry between a centralized monetary policy and decentralized economic policies – including fiscal policies – will not soon be eliminated, and as the relative size of the euro area and the EU non-euro area is bound to change over the next 10 to 20 years.

Rey noted, with reference to the G4 discussion, that further reflection was perhaps needed before labelling the renminbi a 'key currency', even if he agreed that discussing the behaviour of that currency without involving the responsible authorities in multilateral consultations is a mistake.

Fourth, turning to the chapter on debt, Rey expressed a word of mourning for the near-death of the SDRM. If the Report is correct in identifying the objections to the SDRM as coming from 'strident private sector opposition' and the need for changes in the IMF Articles of Agreement, Rey believed that the SDRM will receive new consideration at some point, as the views of the private sector do fluctuate (note the experience with CACs) and the need to work out changes in the Articles of Agreement will anyway be needed if the suggestions made in this Report are sustained.

Rey's last point was to note that much credit is given to the G7 for engineering the various substantive and institutional steps, which have allowed the international financial system to withstand successive crises. While he did not dissent from this view, except for the argument that 'without the G7, it is difficult to see from where that leadership would have come', Rey argued that one should not under-estimate the extent to which the self-appointed G-7 has contributed to prevent other existing bodies, the IMF in particular, from providing the efficient governance needed, from the roots of their own legitimacy.

The G7 did not inaugurate the parallel structures to discuss major international monetary issues. Back in the 1960s, the G10 did much the same. But, at least, when it came close to conclusions on a new liquidity creation scheme, a new arrangement involving all Fund members was put in place to carry on the negotiations, not just to ratify a pre-cooked agreement. Later in the 1970s, when a comprehensive reform of the international monetary system was contemplated, Jeremy Morse was fairly successful in conducting the work under an IMF mandate, until it had to be cut down to what eventually became the second amendment to the Articles of Agreement. In the early days of the Interim Committee, when the Ministers and Governors of all member countries took the trouble to sit through the meetings, the Fund was thought to be the real and effective locus of the decisions taken. When the 1982 Mexican debt crisis erupted, in mid-August, the Managing Director of the IMF effectively took the leadership: he did not wait for G7 guidance.

Rey's point here is that the G7 has done good work, but, in the process, may have choked good work which might have proceeded under more legitimacy-sensitive conditions. He thus welcomed the fact that the Report emphasizes legitimacy in looking at possible reforms, but noted that legitimacy comes bottom up, not top down, a fact that is not often appreciated.

General Discussion

Richard Portes
CEPR, London
A first point in the general discussion raised by Richard Portes concerned the definition of a 'key' currency. There must be a story to bring in the yen and the RMB, said Portes. This story is certainly not about financial centres – the decline of the yen on the international scene has been in part due to the perceived decline of Japan as a global financial centre. Is the story then about being a large reserve holder? Perhaps yes – China is indeed big in that regard, and so is Japan. In general, suggested Portes, more could be said on what it means to be a key currency.

Portes continued to argue that greater emphasis should perhaps be put on private sector involvement and the failure of the G7 to organize and induce private sector involvement in dealing with debt. As a corollary, Portes suggested that it would be interesting to explore how the official sector can better deal with so-called representative private sector organizations. What is the role of the official sector in organizing the private sector? Right now, pointed out Portes, a rather chaotic mess appears to be unfolding in Argentina, partly due to the fact that there is no organization representing the interests of the private creditors, but rather a self-appointed organization of bond-holders covering only 50% or so of outstanding bonds. If one looks at history, continued Portes, the official sector took on the critical role of stimulating the creation of the Council of Foreign Bondholders (UK, 1868) and the Foreign Bondholders Protective Council (US, 1934).

Portes then cautioned against any proposal that involves amending the IMF Articles of Agreement. Indeed, he warned, there is an inherent hostility in the US Congress, and bringing anything before them is fraught with danger. The last quota increase, he outlined, went through only because of the Brazilian crisis and the willingness of the administration to see the Meltzer Committee set up. When the Meltzer Committee finally reported, Summers had to resort to immense efforts to keep the findings within committee and ensure nothing would come out which might end up on the floor of Congress. Any suggestion then of amending the IMF Articles of Agreement, Portes underlined, opens up the process to a panoply of Congressional reactions.

Jens Thomsen
Danmarks Nationalbank, Copenhagen
Jens Thomsen posited that if a G4 were to be created, the G7 would nonetheless be maintained, if only because all created groups have continued to exist. Indeed, the only way to get a new grouping is effectively to introduce one more. The inescapable conclusion is then that when one is introducing a new group onto the international playing field, one is essentially contributing to group proliferation in turn.

Gavin Bingham
Bank for International Settlements, Basel
Along similar lines to the point made above, Gavin Bingham highlighted an inherent contradiction in the Report. While lamenting the proliferation of official groupings and arguing that there are currently too many of them, the Report proposes to deal with this by creating still more official groupings. Bingham also noted that the focus of much international cooperation was shifting from the official sector to the private sector. Indeed, the private sector is really at the cutting edge in some of the most important areas of international financial cooperation such as accounting and auditing, though there was the constructive involvement of former, eminent central bankers and other officials who promote this form of cooperation. Bingham suggested the existing official sector groupings welcome and endorse the work of these quasi-private groupings but refrain from creating yet another new grouping of officials. The integration of the private sector into the managing global cooperation would, moreover, fulfil a fifth possible criterion for judging the value on any grouping. This is the criterion of relevance, to supplement the four criteria of effectiveness, legitimacy, representativeness and accountability cited in the Report. Indeed, proposals for action stemming from bodies, whether they be official or private, will only be accepted and implemented if they are widely seen to be relevant and Pareto improving without side payments.

Tommaso Padoa-Schioppa
European Central Bank, Frankfurt-am-Main
Tommaso Padoa-Schioppa made a distinction between institutions such as the IMF and the World Bank and global leadership, such as is encapsulated within the G7 and other G_is. He noted that the two are both necessary and complementary, and have to be measured according to their specialist abilities. Thus the G7 must be measured on its ability to assert leadership and its ability to relate constructively with institutions rather than trying to replace them.

With this in mind, Padoa-Schioppa maintained that too little emphasis is given to institutions and their role in the international financial governance system. One important factor is that the IMF is virtually absent from G7 meetings, even when what is being discussed is entirely in its field of expertise. A second important point to note is that the G7 has no permanent staff, no secretariat. As a consequence of this, there is no one preparing the work of the G7 that has the interests of the world or even, for that matter, the collective interests of the G7 in mind. What we often see, then, is a direct jump into negotiation without the voice of the general interest being elaborated in a satisfactory way.

A second point raised by Padoa-Schioppa relates to the G20, which is slowly taking shape and which may turn out to be a very promising body that would merit greater attention. He noted that, in general, G20 meetings are more interesting than G7 meetings, which rather resemble looking at oneself in the mirror. During G20 meetings, one has the impression, instead, that the entire world is sitting around the table – points of view and issues are voiced that would never arise in a G7 discussion. Nonetheless, the G20 is complementary to the G7 and cannot be seen as a substitute. In fact, Padoa-Schioppa asserted, if events and creations were better planned, the G20 membership should probably coincide with the IMFC membership and be viewed as a way to restructure the constituencies of the IMF.

Two additional brief points were made. First, Europe is quite simply not present in the G7. There are, of course, four European countries involved, but under no pretext does that imply that Europe is present. Suffice it to ask any of the other 21 countries in the EU whether they feel represented at the G7 level. The answer will consistently be negative. What we see then is that Europe has chosen to be absent of the G7 process, and this is a major problem.

As a final point, Padoa-Schioppa commented on the missing element – trade – in the Report. Indeed, why consider including China in a possible G4, if not for trade reasons. Certainly not for direct financial reasons. The real economy and particularly trade is still very significant and as such, must figure in any discussion of international interdependence.

Ulrich Kohli
Swiss National Bank, Zurich
Ulrich Kohli raised two important issues – the need for cooperation with respect to key currencies, and the debtor-creditor relationship. On the first item, Kohli felt that collaboration on currencies should be left to Central Bankers. He agreed that trade policy or fiscal policy may have an impact on exchange rates, but argued that it would be a mistake to conduct trade policy with the aim of correcting exchange rates. Similarly, for fiscal policy. Thus, what is needed is a forum for Central Bankers, which is to an extent already offered under the aegis of the BIS. Kohli also noted that we would do well to stay away from talk of exchange rate management. There is certainly a need to talk about exchange rate issues, but management is not the way forward.

On the other item, namely the debtor-creditor relationship, Kohli felt that there did not necessarily exist a need for a new G(x). Indeed, he argued that the IMFC currently does a good job in this domain, and a new group would not contribute much. What there is a need for, arguably, is a creditor grouping – a group of like-minded countries. At the moment, the G10 offers such a grouping. Thus, he agreed with Monticelli that any news of the death of the G10 is somewhat premature. Indeed, the G10 offers a forum for creditor countries, and it furthermore represents those countries which have the world's main financial centres. In addition, the G10, unlike the ad hoc G20, is a grouping based on an international agreement – the GAB. Envisaging the disappearance of the G10 would further put the GAB, which is really the last line of defence of the IMF, into question.

Gerd Haeusler
IMF, Washington, DC
Gerd Haeusler took the opportunity to illustrate a 'mathematical conundrum', linked in part to the point made by Portes in an earlier session on the fact that capital flows are today largely private and exacerbated by the increasing number of official groups and unofficial groupings. Indeed, many think that the former – the various G_is – have mushroomed. Alongside this, one can argue that the private sector is not doing so much better – indeed, there are countless lobbying groups today, making it difficult sometimes to identify who is representing whom. With this twin proliferation, one can only imagine how efficient any dialogue between the two will be. The number of mathematical possibilities of interaction is almost without limits. This can certainly be seen in the process of debt restructuring, which has proved to be increasingly difficult, in part due to the fact that, unlike in the 1980s, debt-restructuring issues are left to creditors and the country concerned.

Ariel Buira
G24 Secretariat, Washington, DC
Buira agreed with the authors of the Report in their diagnosis of key problems relating to legitimacy, representativeness and accountability of the G7. The main

difficulty, Buira added, was that since the G7 was created, the world economy has changed very fast. The G7 used to represent most of world economic output, and included the world's major capital exporters. Today, the G7 represent something in the order of 44% of world GDP in PPP terms, which means that the rest of the world represents over 50 per cent. The problem is thus that, while the economy is fast changing, economic decisions reflect the present, investment decisions look to the future, but the governance structure is backward looking and reflects the situation as it was 40 or perhaps 60-odd years ago, when the Bretton Woods institutions were founded. Quite obviously, this raises a number of problems. First, it is not so easy to manage the global economy when you represent only 44% of global output. Furthermore, this 44% represents only 15% of the global population; from whence stem the problems of representativeness and legitimacy.

In this regard, stated Buira, the over-representation of the EU is dramatic. In the case of the IMF, for example, there are nine European Executive Directors and one European Central Bank observer at the Executive Board. The EU as it was constituted until enlargement holds some 74% more voting power than the United States, yet has a somewhat smaller GDP. If European quotas were adjusted for the fact that there is a single currency among 12 members and that trade between members of a single currency cannot be considered to give rise to balance-of-payments problems, European calculated quotas would fall by some 40%. If European representation were to be adjusted, this would allow considerable room for improving the representation of developing countries, which are currently excluded; particularly those that are more dynamic and would have an ability to contribute.

A related issue concerns the continued relevance of the Fund. Buira pointed out the following. Europe moved away from the Fund some 25 years ago and Asia has recently moved away from the Fund. This is partly the result of the size of the Fund and partly the result of its non-representative governance. The current members of the G7, who no longer resort to Fund financing, and control the size of the Fund are not willing to contribute to it, nor are they willing to let others contribute, because they would lose their relative share of power. This essentially means that the Fund resources have declined from a position in which it accounted for 58% of world trade to a little over 3% of world trade today. This decline in resources has led to a hardening of conditionality, a combination that makes it largely irrelevant for most countries – the amount of money that the Fund can offer is quite simply not enough.

As a consequence, and we have seen this recently, special packages and agreements are needed that very often have additional conditions of a frankly questionable nature. What is needed, Buira stressed, is to put things in perspective – see that the world is moving and that unless governance moves in step with the world, the whole structure becomes increasingly irrelevant and ineffectual.

Jon Cunliffe
HM Treasury, London
Jon Cunliffe drew attention to the fact that representation at the IMF is not just a question of EU representation. Indeed, there are a number of other so-called 'relics' from 1945 that do not make sense in today's world. An example is the US veto on key changes to the Fund. This has effectively put the Fund under the control of US Congress at key points in time, and, in times of crisis, quite dangerously so.

Session 3: Proposals for a New Framework

Jon Cunliffe
HM Treasury, UK
Two quotes highlighted what Jon Cunliffe thought were at the core of the issues at stake in international economic governance. 'Global economic governance without global economic government' encapsulated, Cunliffe stated, what the Report was striving for. Indeed, today, there is a need for global economic governance. However, there is no global government to provide global governance, essentially creating problems of legitimacy and accountability in any type of institution devised to provide such a good. The second quote, 'it is not surprising that people worry about process; process is about power' provides the clue into the difficulties of reform of global institutions.

He agreed with two key conclusions in the Report. First, he concurred that the G7 role is changing and in some ways becoming less dominant. Not in the sense of 'falling empires' but rather because of the increasing complexity of both the environment in which it is operating and of the issues that it must deal with (including number of players, types of players, range of issues). Secondly, Cunliffe felt that the key message contained in the Report, albeit implicit, was important and true – things must change and things will indeed change.

The question, he countered, is how will things change and what will they change into? In providing an insight into this question, Cunliffe laid heavy emphasis on the notion of evolution. He outlined the process by which the G7 itself has developed throughout the years. It began as a G5 in the 1970s, with both Italy and Canada joining early on in the process. Following the collapse of communism, Russia was brought into the G7 Summit process. With the subsequent growth in political importance of the G8, the non-G7 G10 countries slowly moved off the radar screen of international governance. In 2000, we witnessed the creation of the G20, which itself is interesting in several respects. Notably, the G20 was not created as is straight away – the G20 solution emerged with the failure of the G22, the 'Willard Group', and the G33. Furthermore, it emerged through crisis. The creation of the G20 reflected in a sense the notion of evolution through crisis.

The last G7 meeting itself heralded some new elements. Cunliffe explained that the number of meetings that were held around the last G7 meetings was extraordinary. He cited a meeting involving the G7 deputies and the Chinese deputies, outreach events with NGOs, a conference involving development ministers and entrepreneurs to promote private sector activity, a terrorist financing activity, and so on. On the one hand, Cunliffe argued, this represents the proliferation of bodies, which so many have talked about – the 'overgrown English country garden' metaphor in the report draws its evidence from examples such as this. On the other hand, he explained, this also represents evolution (in the sense of metamorphosis). The 'English country garden' metaphor might then be better replaced with a metaphor of 'biological evolution'. Indeed, Cunliffe highlighted how very apt the notion of biological evolution is to the evolution of global economic governance. Biological evolution is a messy, painful process, creating much waste, and often quite cruel and pointless. Furthermore, it is a process that does not happen steadily over time, but rather takes place in bursts of evolutionary change. In a way, Cunliffe explained, this is what happens in the world of international financial bodies. There are turf battles; there is competition; bodies evolve; bodies change; bodies die. Evolution and the notion of strong, powerful periods in which competition, waste and destruction exist provide a better approach to understanding global economic governance today.

A further point about evolution was put forward by Richard Dawkins. He believed that metaphors like 'inherent force' or 'inexorable momentum' have no validity. Rather, each evolutionary development pays its way. Each evolutionary development has to make sense and be of value in its own time otherwise it effectively turns into an evolutionary dead-end. This is also true in the world at large, and reflects what was said by Maystadt earlier – that we change things by solving problems. Thus, any new developments must pay their way at the time in question by doing something useful. Along the way, any new institutions or bodies that are created may well evolve into something else and that is part of the process. As an example, Cunliffe outlined the experience of the IMF – since its founding, the institution has evolved into something else and moved into areas it was never intended to move into. Nonetheless, at each stage and in each new development, the IMF had a particular role to play.

Cunliffe felt that the recommendations put forward by the Report were perhaps not as innovative and creative as they might be. With respect to the proposed establishment of CIFEC, Cunliffe felt that this was a somewhat 'tried-and-tested' solution. It rightly represented, he felt, a recognition that a more complex world could no longer be managed by the G7, but provided a solution that relied on finding the right grouping and then replicating what was essentially already in being today. The solution, Cunliffe argued, is rather about the proliferation of bodies and organizations. The world we face today, he explained, is one with different actors, different concerns and different issues needing immediate attention. The role to be played by the international community is rather one of managing a 'Darwinian' environment of bodies, and within this, building the consensus needed for change and economic cooperation.

Attempts to create new bodies to manage the process will not garner the necessary legitimacy. In the end, the question will always arise: who gives such bodies authority? And attempts to create new bodies will ultimately fail because such implanted bodies simply cannot manage the complexity of actors today or the complexity of issues that need to be dealt with.

Cunliffe did agree that the financial sector represented a rather special case, however. He outlined a scenario in which the trend is towards 'harder-edged' supranational bodies in the financial arena, largely because of the predominant role of the private sector in this field. Two reasons can be given for this. First, the private sector is a strong proponent of rationalization and tends to move in this direction through its activities. Secondly, while there are of course entrenched private sector interests that may well hold progress up, there are also private sector actors that benefit from progress and that tend to push the process of rationalization forward.

Cunliffe also touched on IMF reform in his remarks. He was heartened by the proposed elevation of the Board to roughly G7 Deputy level, mainly because he felt that deputies have the authority to be able to solve problems. He noted, however, that the proposal missed one crucial point. In his view, the IMF has two functions – surveillance of all its members on the one hand, and the design and management of programmes for some of its members on the other. The evidence today is that these two processes are contaminating each other.

Possibly, Cunliffe proposed, the solution lies in greater political control over the use of resources in programme design and management, and in moving surveillance out of the 'programme' process. In effect, some of the technologies that have been applied to Central Bank functions in an attempt to develop greater credibility and authority may well be appropriate to IMF surveillance functions. The key here is, on the one side, to remove the Executive Board and other political influences out of the surveillance process in order to limit the opportunities for distortion, and on the other side to bring in greater political impetus into programme aspects and those decisions that merit both political and economic input.

As a final note, Cunliffe pointed out that there exists today a significant gap between the high level objectives and aims that the IMF aspires to fulfil on the one hand, and the day-to-day management minutiae that goes on in the Board and among the staff on the other. There is a need to look at how the gap between such high level objectives and what actually goes on can be filled. Perhaps, Cunliffe suggested, government ministers could be responsible for setting medium-term objectives, which the Fund would follow and for which it could be held accountable.

José De Gregorio
Banco Central de Chile, Santiago
José De Gregorio prefaced his comments by commending the Report, which he felt combined academic rigour with political wisdom. He proceeded to focus his comments on strengthening of the IMF and on the proposed creation of CIFEC.

The Report suggests that the objectives of financial cooperation are broad, began De Gregorio. However, he felt that the objectives should in fact be narrower, and suggested that they be restricted to basically two key objectives. First, well-functioning financial markets, and this is about developing standards and practices in financial markets, and how cooperation can be fostered between international financial institutions. The FSAP is one example here. And second, avoiding systemic crises, including both macroeconomic and balance of payments crises. For any other issues, such as dealing with criminal or terrorist activities, argued De Gregorio, there are well-functioning, technically specialized agencies (indeed there has been a proliferation of such agencies), often within countries, that are better placed to deal with the problems and to propose solutions.

It may be a good idea, however, outlined the speaker, to streamline and create, at this stage, a committee of wise men to avoid duplication and increase effectiveness on a global scale. This may not reduce the number of agencies in existence, but will potentially provide more effectiveness.

Now, whether this should be at the level of deputies or principals is really a question of whether it is more important to focus on the political or technical aspects of cooperation. Here, stated De Gregorio, there is a trade-off, and, as almost always, the middle ground often offers the best solution. Political support and legitimacy is needed when tasks are to be accomplished, for this we need the top officials. But technical expertise is crucial to the quality of the discussion and proposed actions, and to ensure that political aspects do not deviate the course of any outcome, and for this we need deputies and technical staff.

As concerns the strengthening of the IMF, De Gregorio strongly emphasized his preference for an independent IMF. It is important to clarify who is responsible for what within the IMF. In itself, steps to make the IMF more independent and accountable will increase its effectiveness. Nonetheless, De Gregorio recognized the difficulties of the task at hand in reforming the IMF. In particular, problems arise if the Articles of Agreement of the IMF require changes – this would in effect mean, for example, having to go to US Congress for ratification.

An evaluation of the IMF's working practices and role in the last few years is positive. He argued that the surveillance process has been relatively effective – a good example has been the recent IMF criticism of US fiscal policy. Surely, within an entirely dominated IMF, such a critique would not have been allowed to pass. On the whole, stated De Gregorio, the IMF has been doing good work. FSAP, which provides detailed assessments of national financial systems, has been a positive development, helping policy-makers in developing countries formulate and promote reforms. This is also an example of good cooperation among the IMF, the World Bank and national authorities.

Key problematic areas remain. The most important is concerned with IMF programmes – programme design, waivers, and approvals. The IMF is, maintained De Gregorio, too dependent on political approval for programme design and approval. Argentina provides a case in point. Perhaps, suggested De Gregorio, there is a need for the creation of 'Chinese walls' between programmes and surveillance within the IMF.

The idea of upgrading the Executive Board of the IMF goes in the right direction, agreed De Gregorio. This would ensure that those responsible for decisions (government ministers) are actually making and discussing the decisions to be taken. This is surely facilitated today, by the ease of transportation and communications.

De Gregorio briefly touched on the proposed creation of CIFEC. While he supported the creation of such an agenda-setting body, he queried the relation of CIFEC to the Financial Stability Forum (FSF). He further raised the question of whether CIFEC should be made up of finance ministers or central bankers. While, the Report argues that central bankers may not have the appropriate expertise, de Gregorio felt that given that CIFEC is rather an agenda-setting body and not an action group, it would be preferable to have the involvement of persons with expertise rather than operational functions.

De Gregorio further felt that it is important to maintain the existence of the G7 alongside CIFEC. While CIFEC is agenda-setting, it is not an actor on the global stage or a main source of funding for the IMF, and as such cannot provide political direction or liquidity assistance when this may be needed. The G7 thus provides a much-needed good. With this in mind, and in order then to make CIFEC fully convincing, it is necessary to relate its existence to that of the existing G_is. And complementing this, more thought should be given to private sector involvement both within and alongside CIFEC.

De Gregorio concluded his talk with two comments. First, he brought up the issue of taxation, arguing that this will be an important future issue in the domain of international financial cooperation. Some form of standards may need to be developed, particularly as double taxation treaties proliferate, and negotiations may be required to look into the allocation of taxation revenue globally. The second issue he briefly alluded to is that of consumer protection. International financial cooperation should play an increasing role in ensuring consumer protection in financial markets alongside producer concerns.

Ngaire Woods
University College, Oxford, UK
Economists, Ngaire Woods began, are usually accused of being blind to political realities. They prefer to supplant the reality of politics with some idealized vision of what political institutions should really be like. She commended the Report for providing a sensitive and nuanced reading of the politics that have shaped international financial cooperation to date.

Following this introduction, Woods proceeded to concentrate her remarks on the three recommendations made in the Report to improve global governance. Before embarking on such an analysis, however, Woods argued that it is absolutely critical to ensure that the problem at hand has been properly diagnosed.

In so doing, the relevant questions we should be asking ourselves in the context of this Report are the following: why is it that the IMF and the World Bank currently exist? What is it that these institutions do that private actors cannot do? Or that governments acting individually cannot do? What public goods are being provided?

The most important public good that both the IMF and the World Bank are mandated to provide, and this appears as a priority in the Articles of Agreement, is the responsibility to ensure balanced growth – balance among countries as well as balance within countries. This is moreover a public good that has gained ever more significance in today's globalizing economy. If we take the World Bank's two big studies on globalization, and we remove China from the analysis, what we see is that those countries that have moved most fervently towards market-friendly policies are simply not reaping the benefits promised by globalization, and are certainly not reaping them evenly. If we look at the global monitoring reports of the IMF and World Bank, we see in fact a very disturbing picture of a world in which a large number of countries are going to be nowhere near meeting the Millennium Development goals. If we look at the impact of recent emerging market financial crises, we are struck by the example of Argentina. As per the former Argentinean Central Bank Governor, almost a half of Argentines are today in poverty and 25% are in absolute poverty. This in a country that fifteen years ago had one of the lowest poverty rates in the Latin American region. The key point here, Woods emphasized, is that we cannot ignore the issues that are arising from the way in which the international financial system is operating.

With this in mind, Woods argues that the gap that emerges in the Report is the following: we all have a long-term vision of how everyone can benefit from globalization – that is largely about convergence; and we all have a short-term vision, which is very much about crisis management. What is missing, however, in the system of international cooperation, is what to do with the most vulnerable countries to protect them in the mid-term phase. What is to be done with countries that do not have perfect institutions, but whose institutional arrangements are certainly not all bad, and who face considerable vulnerability in the world economy today? How can these countries that are asking for real assistance from the international community, ensure exchange rate stability, and how can they manage their capital accounts in a way that promotes their integration in the world economy but does not leave them vulnerable to the treacherous financial crises we have seen all too often in the past decade? Alphandéry posed another question that is on the minds of these countries: how can they benefit from regional arrangements? What are the prerequisites to help insulate them from the ravages of untrammelled global economic activity?

There exists then, Woods stated, a gap in the diagnosis of the problem at hand in reforming international economic governance. Either the Report title must be narrowed to reflect this gap, or the fact that the problem at hand goes further than is outlined in the Report needs to be highlighted.

Woods then turned to the proposals for reforming the IMF. The key point, Woods explained, is that the IMF is completely independent of at least 170 of its members. The Executive Directors representing these 170 or so members virtually never consult the members whom they are representing, and these 170 members, when asked who their IMF representative is will either reply that they do not have one, or explain that they only have an adviser in the office of the Executive Director. They do not say, 'our Executive Director is...'. Thus, the problem with IMF governance, Woods contended, is not so much that it is inadequately representative or that it is unaccountable, but rather that it is unequally or asymmetrically represented. This point is not emphasized in the Report. The IMF is accountable to and representative of the US and other single constituency members, but not to others.

And if we take this argument just a little further, we should note that for the majority of members, there is nothing to stop national representatives to the IMF from doing very little. Indeed, if the Executive Director of one of these 170 members should decide to play golf five days a week and never turn up to a single Executive Board meeting, what are the incentives to stop him or her? Herein lies another problem: there is little incentive or accountability structure beyond the two-year election cycle.

The question that it is important to focus on then, is that of how to reconfigure incentives, and how to reconfigure the structure of each of the Boards of the IMF and the World Bank so as to promote genuine representativeness and accountability.

Perhaps a good starting point, as per Woods, is to ensure that none of the constituencies represent a single country. A constituency with more than five or six members will simply not work in terms of representation, and if the Board is to remain effective (and therefore small), the math ensures that each Executive Director will have to represent a core of countries. Of course, there is then the very real question of which countries each Executive Director should actually represent, and here it is necessary to look at the structure of constituencies, drawing on club theory, coalition theory, and theoretical prescriptions on how best to represent a coalition of interests. Important are the relative weighting of countries within each constituency, their shared interests, and their capacity to act as the collective voice of their members. Constituencies as they are currently constituted are far from effective.

Without amending the articles of the IMF and without major constitutional reform, there is much that can be done, particularly in the rethinking and rewriting of country groupings and representation, to make the institution more representative.

Other reforms may also be useful. Why not involve every Executive Director in at least one parliamentary report to each country they are representing? Indeed, how else can a represented country ever see the Executive Director charged with their representation as 'theirs'?

With respect to the proposed creation of CIFEC, Woods asked what it was in the analysis of current governance that led the Report authors to suggest its creation. Woods argued rather that there are two big gaps in the global governance system today. First, there is no one body that allocates and distributes responsibilities among different organizations. This results in a conflict between specialization and coherence. For example, if the IMF does specialize, it will be criticized for, among other things, ignoring poverty, HIV/AIDS, developmental needs; and with reason, as all issues are today so interconnected. What is needed is for the IMF to be able to say: we have been given this task to carry out. Yet it is quite unclear today who exactly is taking on the role of task distribution. This is a task that the G7 have informally played to date.

The second gap Woods outlined in her talk is a role that the G7/G8 have never played, namely reviewing, monitoring and holding institutions accountable for the task they have been set. The G7/G8 structure makes it difficult for it to fulfil such a role, largely because it is a 'moving feast'. There is no follow-up structure that ensures things are done. In a way, noted Woods, CIFEC could fill that gap. Perhaps, however, the gap could be filled by the G20. Indeed, this is what the G20 has been particularly good for – a peer-to-peer exchange of experience. But the G20 does not function well in times of crisis, for very good reasons. The G20 is a group comprising creditors and debtors. Thus, in times of crisis, when finance ministers are above all focused on restoring market confidence, a frank exchange and discussion about the real problems at hand will simply not happen. Furthermore, during such times, finance ministers face strong and competing demands from the investor and banking communities, rendering it difficult for them to be the point person for a coordinated strategy. This task falls rather to Heads of State.

Herein lies the additional problem with the CIFEC proposal. If CIFEC were to meet at Finance Minister level, the problem faced is that outlined above. If CIFEC were to meet at the Head of State level, it is not clear that the Heads of State of non-vulnerable countries (namely, the G7 and G10 countries) will want to discuss financial crises – for them, this is a finance ministry issue. The key point, Woods explained, is that of clarifying the role and membership of CIFEC, and particularly of CIFEC's role in managing financial crises.

General Discussion

Gavin Bingham
Bank for International Settlements, Basel
Bingham's first question, addressed to Sir Nigel, suggested that if the Executive Board of the IMF was to be upgraded, it might also be a good idea to introduce proper corporate governance principles and separate the function of Chief Executive Officer (CEO) from that of the Chairman of the Board to reduce the risk of conflicts of interest, bureaucratic capture and weak accountability. Sir Nigel responded that he did not feel that this need be the case. He drew attention to current arrangements, in which the Managing Director plays the subtle role of being both CEO and Chairman of the Board. These arrangements have worked well, he contended, and are part of the successful dynamic that makes the institution work well. 'If it ain't broke, don't fix it', he quipped.

Bingham's other three questions related to the need for an agenda-setting body (CIFEC). Is there truly a need? Would it work? Groupings and institutions, particularly international, do not meekly listen and simply do as they are told. And finally, would it make any difference? Would the agenda not continue to be set by the G1?

Shafer responded to Bingham's questions. He pointed out, as an example, that it is difficult to get technicians in Basel to take the problems of emerging market financial systems seriously – a problem that became apparent to most after the Mexican crisis in 1995. With the Asian financial crisis, it took the G7 to concentrate minds. Furthermore, Shafer noted, an agenda-setting body does exist to date – the question is whether it is the right one, given current political realities, in going forward.

Kenen emphasized that he had no doubt that there existed a need for an agenda-setting body. Whether others will always heed its advice is not a given, however. Should this body then be given the power to enforce decisions? This may well be desirable, but it is quite simply not realistic. Indeed, within the international arena, groupings may only lead; they cannot coerce. This is because the other institutions involved are sovereign inter-governmental bodies, which cannot be told what to do, except in some cases by the G1.

Benoît Coeuré
Ministry of the Economy, Finance and Industry, Paris
Benoît Coeuré felt that the Report should outline, with greater deliberation, the precise mission – perimeter so to speak – of the IMF's functions. Indeed, he noted that the first part of the Report referred to problems of 'mission creep' faced by the IMF – problems largely resulting from multi-task monitoring. An agenda-setting body might help mitigate this, he postulated. Indeed, one logical consequence of the proposed agenda-setting body would have to be the creation of reporting agencies with a greater degree of specialization, which in turn would imply a certain streamlining of the IMF's role.

Coeuré also raised a question concerning the role of the OECD in the framework presented by the Report. On this point, Kenen replied that he felt the OECD was performing a largely uncontroversial, effective function that is not in need of supervision or reform.

Jean-Jacques Rey
National Bank of Belgium
Rey raised the issue of legitimacy as concerns the new body proposed by the Report , CIFEC. He felt that an institution should emerge and be given a mandate by a wide body – if not ECOSOC at the UN, then at least a joint mandate by the IMF, the World Bank and the WTO. This would provide the wide base necessary for ensuring legitimacy of any new institutions. This would be a bottom-up process of institution-creation rather than a top-down process.

Alexandre Swoboda
Graduate Institute of International Studies, Geneva
Alexandre Swoboda questioned the usefulness of cooperation, in a setting such as the G4 or the G7 to deal with the type of payments imbalances that we are currently experiencing. Suppose that (a) the US budget deficit were not there, (b) the fiscal and monetary mix in the EU were better and (c) Japan tackled its non-performing assets and various other problems adequately. Would we need G4 cooperation? Indeed, if we are, as the authors of the report seem to be, sceptical about the impact of fiscal policy, or about the possibilities for changing fiscal policy for anything but purely domestic reasons, what improvement in current account imbalances can coordination among the G4 or G7 provide, apart from helping to ratify changes (such as those that took place in Bonn) that are necessary for domestic purposes? If the things that require coordination are anyway immovable, there is not much that co-operation can achieve.

Peter Kenen replied that it would be difficult to envisage a world in which something is not wrong, or going wrong. The examples given by Swoboda above, Kenen thought, are essentially about fine-tuning, which is not what the Report is concerned with. Bonn Summit type deals are also not at the heart of what is being considered. Rather what is needed is a dialogue between countries that are today systemically important. A standing body able to engage in discussion when and if things go wrong, and they will, is beneficial. Furthermore, there will be new sets of problems in the future, and we thus need a body to encourage consultation and policy adjustment when required. Above all, there is a need for episodic coordination when things reach a serious impasse, which they have arguably today.

Ulrich Kohli
Swiss National Bank, Zurich
Kohli pointed out that, in fact, three new bodies are being proposed in the Report – a G4, CIFEC, and a new FSF. Indeed, what the Report is proposing is quite different from the existing FSF. The FSF today is a creation of the G7. It has non-G7 members (Hong Kong, Singapore, the Netherlands, among others), but it reports to the G7, which raises questions in turn about its legitimacy and accountability.

Kohli also made the point that in trying to assess the importance of different countries today, we should try to move away from the standard indicators that are usually proposed (such as GDP, PPP exchange rates and so on). GNP rather than GDP might be of greater value, as GNP is a much better indicator of economic weight. PPP exchange rates may not be ideal measures to use, since there are huge measurement issues involved with PPP exchange rates and furthermore, in the international relations domain, such exchange rates are largely irrelevant. Most importantly, however, the Report is about financial cooperation, and thus it is all the more surprising that no financial indicator has been considered in assessing the importance of different countries. True, there is currently no ready indicator that lends itself naturally to such a task, although perhaps one could look at the weight of countries in financial markets.

Session 4: Round Table: Financial Markets and International Cooperation

Ariel Buira
G-24 Secretariat, Washington, DC
Emerging market countries with access to international financial markets have faced a number of financial crises, often due to the volatility of private capital flows. These countries try to sustain high rates of growth and investment that they cannot finance domestically. They resort to foreign borrowing, often in foreign currency, thereby incurring currency risk. Because the credibility of their institutions and policies is frequently less recognized by market participants than that of governments and institutions of industrial countries, they often get shorter-term financing, thus adding maturity mismatch to currency exposure, giving rise to higher risk. In addition, their exports are often concentrated in a few commodities or products and are subject to commodities and terms of trade shocks, so adding another vulnerability. Furthermore, investor sentiment can change suddenly and unpredictably, provoking large reversals in capital flows and giving rise to severe crises.

The first question that should be asked is: why do crises occur? They may result from poor policies by the country or from exogenous factors; in many cases they are the outcome of a combination of both. They are more frequent than in the past because investors are very pro-active and always seeking to improve their performance. They are always ready to move in and out of markets rapidly, giving rise to rushes for the exit, leading to herding behaviour and self-fulfilling speculative attacks. As markets are freed from restrictions they gain efficiency, but volatility also increases. Empirical studies show that emerging market countries face a much higher volatility and vulnerability to exogenous shocks than both developed countries or low income countries. Emerging markets are all significantly correlated independent of their policies because of the behaviour of investors. Due to the large portfolios many of the investment funds manage, when they move money from one country to another, they may have a significant destabilizing effect on the small financial markets of many countries.

Capital flows to emerging markets are often volatile for reasons that have little relation with a country's policies. For instance, exogenous changes in financial conditions in industrial countries, particularly sharp unanticipated increases in interest rates, as was the case in 1982 with the Latin American debt crisis. Capital flows, including commercial bank lending to developing countries have been markedly pro-cyclical. This pro-cyclical behaviour of capital markets themselves tends to undermine the creditworthiness of countries. Imagine what would happen in the national context if banks were suddenly to cut credit flows to the corporate sector during a recession. The result would be a financial collapse. Market behaviour is often characterized by asymmetries in information and often contagion effects. Country risk analysis is often characterized by herding behaviour, by which a country may lose its creditworthiness very rapidly often without enough time to react.

Logically, the second question that should be asked is: how to deal with these financial crises? Surveillance should be much closer than at present with the application of standards and codes, and good regulation and supervision of the financial system and so on. Since massive capital outflows can inflict great damage to an economy very quickly, the current approach to financial crises, that does not do more to prevent them, must be considered unsatisfactory. We should do something more to prevent crises rather than follow the current approach which may be characterized as one of IMF lending to the countries after the outbreak of the crisis, after capital flight has caused a large depreciation of the currency, a deep recession, causing a severe fall in output and employment, and a sharp rise in interest rates, more often than not leading to a banking crisis. This is very destructive. In the case of the Mexican crisis the cost must have been over 20% of GDP counting the drop in GDP and the cost of the banking rescue (about 15% of GDP). Of course this has a significant cost also for the country's trading partners, because they stop selling.

An approach to crises that would be consistent with the purposes of the Fund, would sustain high levels of employment without resorting to measures destructive of national and international prosperity. If the IMF could intervene in a timely manner, with enough financial support to restore market confidence, it would have a deterrent effect and the crisis could be avoided. Countries with sound policies who would be eligible for immediate Fund support would be countries with a close ongoing dialogue with the Fund.

Looking ahead, Latin America, with substantial external financing requirements and several countries with high levels of external debt, is particularly exposed to the risk of rising US interest rates, that could trigger a reversal of current favourable external financing conditions. One cannot discount the possibility that in the next 18 to 24 months new financial crises may emerge. If we can see the rising risk of a crisis ahead of time, we should be able to act in a timely manner to try to prevent it. Among the early warning signs of risk that should lead the IMF to stand ready to enter the scene are rising spreads on external borrowing, concentration of external liabilities in the very short term, rapid decline in international reserves, commodity price and interest rate shocks, political shocks, etc. What is needed is close surveillance and the Fund to be ready to step in time with substantial financial support. A code of good conduct agreed by lenders and borrowers setting out mutual obligations, could also contribute to enhanced confidence and market stability. To diminish the currency risk, it would be good if institutions could lend to countries in their own currency. Among the unresolved problems to be dealt with by a cooperative approach are the involvement of external creditors and the restructuring of external bond debt when appropriate.

Gerd Haeusler
IMF, Washington, DC
Haeusler focused his comments on the cross-border repercussions of globalized financial markets, i.e. the implications of globalization in financial markets on policy coordination. He focused mainly on the most developed non-US part of financial markets, that is to say the EU, but his remarks applied also to a great degree to other parts of the world, including emerging markets. The glue that binds together these various parts of the world is the risk appetite of investors that move capital.

Haeusler began by exploring the correlation of market interest rates and equity prices across borders and currencies. He then moved on to touch briefly on the channels of that transmission and finally, he proceeded to make a few remarks about the implications for policy coordination.

To begin, then, Haeusler noted that the correlation of market interest rates and equity prices is increasing. Government bond yields between the United States and the EU have become increasingly correlated over the years. For example, the average correlation between the 10-year bullet versus the German bund has been increasing. It used to be around 0.5 in the early 1990s and it has risen to about 0.75 this year. Correlations between major equity indices have generally been even higher than those between government bond yields. The average six months correlation between the S&P` 500 and the German DAX (the largest economy in Europe), for instance, has now reached 0.8 whereas it stood at 0.5 in 1990. Why? And what does it mean?

To make his point Haeusler proposed looking back to the 1980s. In the mid-1980s there were quite wide variations in the US dollar–deutschmark exchange rate and a significant amount of Forex intervention without much effect on the equities and the fixed income market. One could safely say that at that time the different sectors within the financial market were clearly and largely segmented. The major contrast today is that private capital flows are much higher both in absolute terms and relative to the underlying real economy and they arbitrage virtually across all asset classes. The point is that today's capital markets have become more integrated and investors react quickly to price signals emanating from the largest economy and the largest capital market which is, after all, the United States. *De facto*, on a day-to-day basis, the transmission mechanism works even more strongly in equity markets. To a significant degree investors react in a self-feeding and almost instinctive manner. The European evening trade in equities had to be abolished partly because *de facto* it was only a mirror image of what was taking place in New York. Thus there are instantaneous arbitrage opportunities between the United States and the European bond yield levels, equity, etc.

More fundamentally capital markets have undergone a significant structural change, since there is increasingly a single pool of capital. Banks, insurance companies, mutual funds, governments, households, etc. – any market participant in the developed part of the world – can tap into that pool directly. The countervailing forces are therefore much stronger and this is a positive development. This will keep the global pool of capital from moving as abruptly as it did ten or twenty years ago. The bottom line is that the closer we move towards a global pool of capital, the more capital will carry a single price tag. This is what Chairman Greenspan alluded to when he mentioned that the United States could relatively easily finance a current account deficit of US$500 billion a year.

What are the implications for policy coordination? The integration of capital markets is a matter of fact. International interest rates are increasingly driven by US economic data and by the corresponding policy of the Federal Reserve. The evolution towards a global capital market is creating a natural centre of gravity for interest rate determination in the United States. To take an analogy, today the Fed plays globally more or less the role that the Bundesbank played in Europe in the late 1980s and early 1990s. Dictated by national mandate, monetary policy in the United States today follows primarily domestic objectives. This may pose problems for countries which are at a different stage in the business cycle. In the case of the Bundesbank in the early 1990s the situation was particularly untenable given the fixed exchange rate regime in Europe which did not give other countries any room for maneouvre. The transatlantic relationship restrictions are not that stringent given the higher degree of flexibility of exchange rates, particularly the exchange rates relationships between the US dollar, the Euro and the Yen.

Yet, for Haeusler there is an increased perceived need for policy coordination or discussion among non-US countries, as US monetary policy repercussions clearly go very strongly beyond its borders. Nevertheless the high correlation of transatlantic interest rates makes European monetary policy in Haeusler's view less effective, especially in the case of rising rates, as the problem is to some degree asymmetric. At this juncture the growth differential between the United States and Europe seems to be widening and therefore a rise in European bond yields triggered by a rise in bond yields in the United States would be more problematic in Europe than it would be in the United States. As a result, the pressure would rise further to use policies other than monetary policy because in a context of integrated markets, the lever of monetary policy on bond yields is not as strong as it used to be. Fiscal policy in Europe has already gone to a maximum if not beyond, which means that other policies will have to take that part. The prerequisite if a region like Europe or any other would like to decouple to some degree, is that it would have to establish a stronger single regional market of financial services.

The conclusion is that if the growth potential continues to differ between the United States and Europe the implication of having similar market interest rates, not policy interest rates, is not without problems. This is especially true if monetary policy outside the United States is rendered less and less effective and fiscal policy is limited by the Stability and Growth Pact. There is thus no way of escaping the necessity of structural reforms to raise growth rates to a level closer to those of the United States.

Alexandre Swoboda
Graduate Institute of International Studies, Geneva
Swoboda raised three questions with respect to the theme of the panel, 'Financial Markets and International Cooperation': first, how does the growth in financial markets and their increasing integration impact on international cooperation; second, what kind of cooperation is appropriate to help ensure financial market stability; finally, if we think about the mix of institutions that we need in global economic governance, is the mix that was proposed in Bretton Woods, possibly supplemented by some other measures, obsolete or still appropriate in today's 'globalizing' world economy?

The first question, then, is whether increasing financial market integration makes cooperation more or less difficult, effective, or needed. The answer depends in large part on how well or badly the international monetary and financial system at large is functioning. Under a fixed exchange rate regime where the rules of the game are respected, looking for instance, as Portes did earlier, at the end of the nineteenth century and beginning of the twentieth century with its high degree of capital market integration, financial integration should help as capital movements would reinforce rather than hinder balance of payments adjustment. The caveat is of course that national monetary policy autonomy be largely if not entirely surrendered to the requirements of maintaining the fixed parities, with the possible exception of the monetary policy of the system's centre or Nth country. Of course, proper leadership is needed, as was provided by Britain then or by the United States in the Bretton Woods system. In this scenario, capital market integration helps policy coordination. Of course it is very unforgiving to attempts to run an independent monetary policy together with a fixed exchange rate regime.

For the type of flexible exchange rates we have today, financial integration may paradoxically increase the case for explicit international macroeconomic policy coordination. Paradoxically, because exchange rates started floating in 1973 in good part in response to national monetary policies and internal goals that were incompatible with the maintenance of fixed exchange rates. With a high degree of capital mobility, however, spillovers from national policies can be severe and competitive depreciations can have even more devastating external effects than devaluations under fixed. The first response is of course that each country should try to keep its house in order, and IMF surveillance has an important role to play here as well as in trying to deal with spillovers.

Swoboda's second question was: taking financial market integration as a given, what kind of cooperation is desirable? There is, first, the type of cooperation needed to achieve stability within financial markets. Here, stated Swoboda, the Report has it right on the dot with its emphasis on setting standards and codes, and on regulatory harmonization such as Basel I and II. However, there are some caveats concerning the implementation of regulatory harmonization, he noted. Care should be taken to avoid that regulation that seeks to cope with microeconomic shocks be set in such a way that it would amplify the destabilizing impact of macroeconomic shocks. This is one of the dangers with Basel type rules (and, for that matter, with many fixed-ration rules in financial markets): they are fine to reduce the risk of insolvency of individual banks but may amplify the consequences of a macro shock by causing a wholesale liquidation of assets by the whole banking system.

There is, second, the related question of what type of cooperation: should one rely more on rules or on discretion? When discussing the G7 and similar groupings, we have talked a lot about discretion rather than rules. In financial markets, it is quite important to have the right rules and regulation and to use discretion as little as possible. This is where standards and codes and clear regulatory and prudential rules are important. Of course, it is good to have some discretion when destabilizing events such as LTCM occur, but better rules could also lower the probability of their occurrence.

Third, to obtain financial stability, the best tool is to avoid macroeconomic shocks in the first place, as well as minimizing the feedback of financial markets into the real economy and vice-versa. There is a role here for better coordination, not so much in the financial arena and the regulation of financial markets as in the macroeconomic arena, of the type discussed in previous sessions of this conference. After all, the turmoil of the 1930s was not caused by something inherent to financial markets but occurred as a result of a big trade and macro shock, though poor financial regulation did play a role of course. The 1982 turmoil was due to a debt shock; the 1987 stock market problems were at least partly due to disagreements concerning the direction of macroeconomic policy in the major countries; the 1998 LTCM crisis was due to mistakes in the financial management of the company but also to the crisis in Russia. Herstatt is perhaps the one exception, a crisis that originated largely in the financial system itself.

Swoboda's third question referred to the institutional mix. This is somewhat similar to a targets and instruments problem. There are a number of targets that have to be reached and a corresponding number of instruments or institutions are needed to meet them. In addition, the institutions need to be correctly assigned to the targets. Here the basic goal is a well-functioning economic and international monetary and financial system – that is to say, one that would be efficient, stable, and include at least a modicum of equity. It should, first, allow trade to take place according to comparative advantage, both trade at a point in time and trade over time. Secondly, it should ensure price stability and high employment. Third, it should ensure stability in the sense of avoiding systemic crises that are generated by the system itself. Fourth, it would need to have a modicum of equity to make the system acceptable to its members and be incentive compatible with a smooth functioning of the system.

The vision of the postwar economic system that was forged around the time of the Bretton Woods conference, and the type of institutional mix and division of tasks that was foreseen to achieve these goals at the time is still basically correct. Although the World Trade Organization did not see the light of day then, GATT assumed responsibility for trade liberalization while the support of current account convertibility, which went together with allowing trade to take place along the lines of comparative advantage, was one of the main aims of the IMF. The IMF was also created with the aim of facilitating balance of payments adjustment in a way that was not detrimental to others. The IBRD, now the World Bank, was the organization designed to help transfer resources efficiently over time, even though it operated with a strong regional bias (the reconstruction of war-torn Europe). The world employment agency never materialized and responsibility for taking care of employment and price stability has remained that of national governments, although of course price stability becomes a matter of international concern under fixed exchange rates. Three developments have led to ask whether that original mix of institutions is still valid today: the abandonment of a universal system of fixed (but adjustable) exchange rates; the increasing economic integration of the world economy, including that of a significant number of developing countries; and the rising level of financial integration and capital mobility. Floating exchange rates have meant that many tasks are devolved to national governments and that the nature of those of the IMF has changed significantly since 1973, with its surveillance activities taking on increasing importance. The integration of the so-called emerging market economies into the world economy has likewise contributed to the change in the IMF's activities and tasks, and to some blurring of the lines of responsibility between the Fund and the Bank as well as the creation of new institutions such as the regional development banks. The response to increasing financial integration and capital mobility has also been the emergence of new institutions (such as various associations, committees and clubs), and, again, by older institutions taking on new roles and responsibilities, e.g. new lending facilities at the IMF or the Basel Committee and Financial Stability Forum 'at' the BIS. One could argue, however, that with increasing financial market integration, new universal institutions are needed: the more ambitious proposals have included a world central bank, a world lender of last resort, or a world financial supervisory authority.

These last proposals, to Swoboda, are not realistic. What can be done today is to reinforce and better allocate tasks among existing institutions. In this context, there is one institution or set of institutions, the market, about whose role as a regulatory mechanism – in contrast to its role as something to be regulated – we have perhaps said too little at this conference. To harness markets to control imprudent behaviour requires, however, that the proper incentives be provided, among them information provision (through, e.g., standards and codes) and the incentive to use it, that is, a limit on explicit and implicit guarantees and hence on moral hazard.

Finally, who should be doing the assignment of tasks to various institutions? According to Swoboda, to some extent at least the broad tasks should be written in the charters of these institutions to avoid a multiplication of new bodies, new tasks and the generalization of mission creep.

Angel Ubide
Tudor Investment Corporation, Washington, DC
Angel Ubide presented the view that financial markets have had of international cooperation in the last three or four years. He divided his talk into two parts. He first presented a series of stylized facts related to the global economy and policy cooperation. He then presented the market reaction to these facts.

Ubide first noted that the global economy has recently become largely a combination of three regions. The first is composed of China, South East Asia and Japan; the second comprises the EU; and North America forms the third. The second stylized fact he noted was that, at least for the past three or four years, there has been a feeling that in the post bubble global economy the G7 has run out of policy ammunition. Interest rates were basically zero in Japan and in the United States, and very low in the euro area. Budget deficits have also been high and there has been a fear of a risk of deflation for at least a year. The embedded feeling in financial markets has been that the currency was the only remaining policy at the G7 or G10 level.

The third stylized fact concerns the lessons of the 1997 crisis in Asia. Asia has since that episode strived to become independent, at least from a currency point of view. Three initiatives can be distinguished. First, the 'excessive' accumulation of reserves in Asian countries. This is not perceived as myopic or as a policy mistake, but rather as a well-defined policy aimed at avoiding undue reliance on any international institution whenever the next 'sudden stop' arrives. Second, the Asia Bond Fund, where we have recently seen an incipient move towards some sort of reserves independence at the Asian level; the third is the ASEAN + 3 (Japan, China and South Korea) initiative, in which the countries concerned have agreed to allocate an increasing amount of money to a network of currency swaps.

The fourth stylized fact is that the United States at the moment absorbs nearly 80% of the world's savings, defined as the total surplus in the current account.

What has been the reaction of the markets to these stylized facts? The first consequence, and it is in line with the Report, is that in the past, the G7 or G10 meant a lot of small players (with the United States as the key, big player). Today, the world is constituted of three blocs and this could lead to some strategic behaviour at the level of international cooperation. If all three want to be Stackelberg leaders, it will not be possible to reach an optimal solution.

The second consequence is that, unfortunately, the market's assessment of the G7 in the last few months has been essentially that the G7 has said one thing, while its constituents have done another – similar to what has happened with the Stability and Growth Pact. Hence, there has been a decline in the credibility of the G7. This in turn has led to higher policy uncertainty and therefore higher volatility.

The third consequence is that there was indeed some coordinated action in the recent past. It was not, however, what had been expected. In some sense the intervention in currency markets by Asian Central Banks have performed what Ubide calls 'credible quantitative easing in the United States'. In theory, an efficient policy, when facing a risk of deflation, is to lower interest rates and make sure that the yield curve is not too steep. We will never know what would have been the 10-year rate in the United States in the absence of Asian intervention. These interventions were good both for the United States and for Asia, but bad for the rest of the world. It was not an optimal solution but was in some sense informally coordinated. The bottom line, and this has been the market feeling for a long time, is that markets and policies have been distorted as a result of this.

Much in the same way, the debate on the US fiscal deficit is completely inhibited by the low interest rates. The US current account has not been corrected as much as the market expected, despite the 20–30% decline in the US dollar. In addition the world financial system has moved to an extreme position. When the market realized that there was a distortion, it took a bet against the distortion, as usual. Taking an extreme view, the public sector was taking the long side against the private sector taking the short side of a trade in US dollars. This has led to some concentration of risk in credit protection derivatives in the main investment banks. In some sense, as a result of the lack of coordination, the global financial risk is higher at the end of this three or four year period.

Markets have understood that there was a sort of competitive devaluation going on in the world. First the US dollar weakened; then it took the form of a Japanese intervention; then basically every other member of the G7 tried to control the appreciation of their currency. It is thus not surprising that markets rushed to physical assets such as gold, commodities and oil. There were obviously some demand factors relating to the increase in commodity and oil prices, but there was at least an initial kick that came from market sentiment. The result is higher expected inflation in the minds of many market participants.

Finally, as was outlined during the morning session, it is most difficult to foresee what the issues will be in the future, and hence it is not possible to predict what the optimal cooperation should be. However, we can be certain that we are getting older, and very quickly. Given that the G7 has a deficit close to 5% at the moment and given the demographic profile, Ubide wondered whether this is something that the G7, G10 or G-something that the Report is proposing, should take as a medium-term task.

In conclusion, Ubide made the following remark. It can safely be said that higher long-term expected inflation is a consequence of the type of cooperation that we have witnessed in the last few years. In addition, higher financial risk as a result of distortions in some of the prices and some degree of unsolved real imbalances may also be observed. Ubide made the following final comment – how much can we coordinate policies if the main players do not even agree on the philosophy underlying the policies?

General Discussion

Jeffrey R. Shafer
Citigroup, New York
Jeffrey Shafer said that he is very pessimistic about the prospects for reducing the risks of occasional financial crises in emerging markets until the countries themselves decide to adopt consistently more conservative financial policies. There is a consistent failure to undertake timely adjustment, although this might be changing in Asia. Shafer took two examples to make his point about dealing with external problems and finding a balance between financing and adjustment. In 1974 the United States launched a nearly year-long campaign to convince Mexico to undertake adjustment. Their failure to do so did not, however, dissuade the United States from actively trying to generate support after the crisis erupted and appropriate Mexican policies were put in place. The same thing can be said for Argentina where despite large volumes of pre-emptive IMF lending, a problem that was clearly identifiable and well known was still allowed to develop. Finally, Shafer lamented the problematic case of countries with good policies but which might still be facing crises because of problems or events which they cannot influence. It is desirable, but can be still be difficult in these cases, to engineer cooperation.

Ariel Buira
G-24 Secretariat, Washington, DC
Buira agreed substantially with Shafer. The only point of difference, he noted, is that one should be ready to support countries that have good policies and to maintain confidence in these cases. If countries have bad policies and end up in a crisis, no help can be brought. However, in situations where the countries have sustainable, reasonably good policies, the international community, and certainly the country itself, would greatly benefit from avoiding a crisis.

Gerd Haeusler
IMF, Washington DC
Hauesler noted that everyone acknowledges that emerging markets are today in better shape than some time ago – exchange rates are more flexible, reserve ratios are higher, etc. This is good news when entering a tightening cycle of interest rates. Unfortunately, these improvements are not equally shared among the emerging markets. While Asia and Eastern Europe are doing well, in Latin America the improvements have not taken place to the same positive degree as they have elsewhere. The situation looks fine while the current commodities price boom off-sets higher interest rates. But there remains a lot of work to be done in moving for-ward, and there might be hiccups along the way.

Bernhard Winkler
European Central Bank, Frankfurt-am-Main
Winkler commented on the data for correlations between the euro area and US bond and equity markets that was presented by Haeusler. The data ironically gives the message that due to globalization and the integration of capital markets world-wide, the ECB is much less able to run an independent monetary policy than the Bundesbank was able to do in the 1980s and 1970s. For Winkler, this is somewhat disappointing, and he offered the following alternative interpretation of the data. These correlations were taken with the early 1990s as a reference when business cycles were desynchronized after German unification. By contrast the following decade has arguably been characterized by shocks of a far more symmetric nature. Moreover, there has been policy convergence on both sides of the Atlantic, with monetary policies being more stability-oriented and also for this reason looking more similar than in past decades. Looking forward, there should certainly be scope for European monetary policy to follow a different course to the Fed. One piece of evidence is that although nominal bond yields are highly correlated, if one looks at index-linked bonds and the break-even inflation rates in the United States and in Europe, the correlation is a bit weaker. In addition, also the level of bond yields could differ substantially under floating exchange rates even in glob-alized markets, as shown by Japan. All this should still leave scope for autonomous control of inflation in Europe.

Charles Wyplosz
Graduate Institute of International Studies, Geneva
Charles Wyplosz noted that there has recently been a lot of discussion on the orig-inal sin problem as a source of vulnerability and a number of proposals have been made, particularly by Barry Eichengreen and Ricardo Hausman. Obviously there are no takers for these kinds of ideas while it is generally acknowledged that for-eign currency indebtness is a key source of vulnerability.

Alexander Swoboda
Graduate Institute of International Studies, Geneva
Swoboda mentioned that there exist today world surveillance bodies like the press, the markets, the brokers, Citibank, UBS, etc. In addition, many of the problems are identified. However, the problem of having an independent surveillance body is that it is not much good unless it has some teeth. There is thus a reason to have such a surveillance body within the IMF. The question then is how, within the IMF, to separate the staff that do the programme work from those who carry out the surveillance work. That done, however, does not solve the implementation problem: the IMF surveillance team was courageous when it stated that the United States should do something about its fiscal policy; it did not have any effect, how-

ever, as the IMF has no programme and hence no teeth with regard to the United States.

Gavin Bingham
Bank for International Settlements, Basel
Bingham raised the question of missing markets. There had been extensive discussion of financial markets during the meeting and product markets had been given the attention they deserved in the discussion of trade. But Bingham noted that it was folly to ignore a third, extremely important market – the labour market. It was not possible to understand the dynamics of the international adjustment process unless the need to integrate 2 1/2 billion Chinese and Indian people into the global economy was given due weight. The need to absorb these vast reserves of labour is a significant factor affecting exchange markets and the accumulation of foreign exchange holdings by countries that by rights would be expected to have a shortage of capital. Any thorough discussion of the international adjustment process and international cooperation should not ignore this important missing market.

Endnotes

1   The Alternate Executive Director, the Executive Director's second in command, could reside in Washington to deal with the day-to-day business of the Fund.

2   In many ways we are designing a process to carry forward the sort of policies described by Williamson (2003) for the post Washington Consensus world.

3   Respectively: International Organization of Security Commissions, International Accounting Standards Board and International Association of Insurance Supervisors.

4   For a good review, see Baldwin (1997).

5   This chapter relies heavily on Solomon (1977) to pin down dates and sharpen hazy recollection of events that are a matter of public record, as well as for a very clear presentation of the international financial policy process during the period it covers. For the later period, and especially for the history of G7/G8 Summits, the basic source for facts are a number of papers by Nicholas Bayne available on the Website of the G8 Information Center, University of Toronto (www.g7.utoronto.ca). A more comprehensive history and analysis can be found in Putnam and Bayne (1987), and Bayne (2000). Citations in the text are limited to documentation of specific recollections concerning matters that would otherwise not be matters of public record.

6   Fully developed in Triffin (1960).

7   As recalled in Solomon (1977), pp. 53-5.

8   Solomon (1977), p. 212.

9   Solomon (1977), p. 202.

10 The amended version of Article IV, concerning exchange-rate arrangements is reproduced in Box 3.3 of Chapter 3.

11 The German banking authorities closed Bank Herrstatt at the end of the German business day following the settlement of the deutschemark side of its foreign exchange trades but before settlement of the dollar side, leaving the failed bank's counterparties with large losses and throwing the global payments system into chaos.

12 Brady (2003).

13 International Monetary Fund (2003b).

14 Agreement was reached for a special one-time allocation of SDRs three years later in the IMF Board of Governors, but the United States has not, as yet, followed through on ratification. It holds a de facto veto by virtue of its 17% voting share and the requirement of an 85% majority for adoption.

15 Condensed from International Monetary Fund (2003a).

16 The 'G7 system' is not limited to the Summits. See below for a discussion of the G7 meetings of finance ministers and central bank governors.

17 These numbers reflect the economic weight of countries. Adjusting for purchasing power parity provides a different measure meant to evaluate the standards of living. The corresponding ranking for 2001 is: the United States, China, Japan, India, Germany, Italy, the United Kingdom, France Brazil, Russia, Canada, Mexico, Spain, Korea, Indonesia, Australia, South Africa, Netherlands, Argentina and Thailand.

18 For a comparison, see De Gregorio et al. (1999).

19 Similarly, the Chairman of the Federal Reserve Board cannot commit the Federal Open Market Committee.

20 Chapter 4 provides a more precise assessment of the G7, in particular distinguishing between the meetings of heads of states and governments level and those that deal with economic issues and that bring together finance ministers and/or central bankers.

21 The story is nicely presented in Blinder (1998).

22 According to Obstfeld and Rogoff (2001), however, the benefits from price stability are likely to outweigh the costs of the loss of coordination.

23 Dominguez and Frankel (1993).

24 Cecchetti et al. (2000).

25 Blanchard and Perotti (2001), for instance, show that the effects of fiscal policy are uncertain and materialize with variable delays.

26 France is one country that would like to see cooperation develop. Its governments regularly propose to establish an 'economic government of Europe', a rather foggy concept that suggests an institutional approach.

27 Williamson (2000) offers an excellent discussion of many of these reports.

28 ILO is International Labor Organization, ITU is International Telecommunication Union, WIPO is World Intellectual Property Organization, WTO is World Trade Organization.

29 The term 'London Club' was used initially to denote the steering committees of commercial banks that dealt with the syndicated loans of the 1980s. But here it is used generically to denote all groups negotiating on behalf of private-sector creditors, regardless of the way in which they are organized and the sorts of claims they hold – loans or bonds.

30 This box draws upon Dixon and Wall (2000).

31 A comprehensive treatment of the rationale for and the modalities of Sovereign Debt restructuring Mechanisms is to be found on the IMF web site at http://www.imf.org/external/np/exr/facts/sdrm.htm This box draws upon that material.

32 IMF Board Paper (2003), 'The Restructuring of Sovereign Debt - Assessing the Benefits, Risks, and Feasibility of Aggregating Claims', http://www.imf.org, external/np/pdr/sdrm/2003/090303.pdf, September 2003

33 The material in this appendix is drawn from Box 1 of the IMF Board Paper, 'Crisis Resolution in the Context of Sovereign Debt Restructuring: A Summary of Considerations', January 2003 at http://www.imf.org/external/np/pdr/sdrm/2003/012803.pdf.

34 At the time of writing this Report, this still remains the position.

35 The term 'key currency' is often used to denote a currency that is widely used in commercial and financial transactions between countries other than the issuing country. It may also be used as a vehicle currency by foreign exchange traders and for various purposes by the official sector – defining the external value of a country's currency, intervening on foreign exchange markets, and accumulating reserve assets. The renminbi is not used extensively for any of these additional purposes, but it is systemically important because of the size of the Chinese economy and its foreign trade and the extent to which the external value of the renminbi appears to influence the exchange rate policies of other Asian countries.

36 China's reluctance to revalue, however, may derive in part from concern that other Asian countries will not let their currencies appreciate along with the renminbi and will then gain a competitive advantage vis-à-vis China.

37 Truman (2004) argues, however, that the prospects for policy coordination would be improved if the Federal Reserve and ECB adopted inflation-targeting regimes like that of the Bank of England. That would improve their ability to communicate with markets and, more importantly in the present context, their ability to communicate with each other and their finance ministry colleagues.

38 Taking account of arrangements like these, Truman (2004) calculates that Executive Directors from EU countries effectively control some 12% of the votes of non-EU countries, in addition to the 32% held by the EU countries themselves. Truman goes on to propose a 'gradual' reform of EU representation. First, the EU countries should agree to drop from their own multi-country constituencies all non-EU countries. Next, they should gradually consolidate their representation until they have only one Executive Director. As they presently have three appointed Executive Directors (for France, Germany and the United Kingdom), two of the five chairs permanently reserved for single countries would be vacated and could be reassigned to Canada and China, which would be next in line, given the sizes of their quotas. Truman's proposal, like the one proposed in the text, would also reduce the size of the Executive Board.

39   The rearrangement of multicountry constituencies shown in Box 6.1 is based largely on geographic propinquity and linguistic affinity; it takes no account of the bargaining process by which multi-country constituencies are actually formed. It does not, however, involve an arbitrary or dramatic rearrangement of existing constituencies, apart from those which presently include EU countries.

40   Box 6.1 also shows that the euro area itself would have huge voting power on the Executive Board. Its IMF quota and voting power would be reduced, however, if the calculation of benchmarks for quotas employed the most relevant measure of euro area trade – not the total trade of the euro area countries, but their trade with countries outside the euro area. In 2002, the total trade of the euro area countries – the sum of their exports and imports – amounted to $3,909 billion. Their trade with their euro area partners amounted to $1,965 billion, however, which accounted for half of their total trade. It should perhaps be noted that the rationalization of EU representation in the IMF would require an increase of IMF quotas. That is because the euro is one of the currencies usable by the IMF in its transactions with its members, and the rationalization of EU representation would reduce the supply of euros available to the IMF unless accompanied by an increase of total quotas.

41   Australia, Canada, Korea and Sweden rank with them by GDP and trade but not by population.

References

Baldwin, R. (1997), 'The causes of regionalism', *The World Economy* 20 (7), pp. 865-88.

Bank for International Settlements (2004) 'International Financial Statistics', *www.bis.org/statistics/index.htm*.

Bayne, N. (2000), *Hanging in There: The G7 and G8 Summit in Maturity and Renewall*, The G8 and Global Governance Series, Aldershot, UK: Ashgate Publishing.

Blanchard, O. and R. Perotti (2001), 'An Empirical Characterization of the Dynamic Effects of Changes in Government Spending and Taxes on Output', unpublished, MIT.

Blinder, A.S. (1998), *Central Banking in Theory and Practice*, Cambridge, Mass.: MIT Press.

Brady, The Hon. N.F. (2003), 'Address to Latin Finance Gala Charity Dinner, June 26, 2003', Darby Overseas Investments, Ltd.

Cecchetti, S.G., H. Genberg, J. Lipsky and S. Wadhwani (2000), 'Asset Prices and Central Bank Policy', *Geneva Reports on the World Economy 2*, London: CEPR.

Cooper, R.N. (1968), *The Economics of Interdependence: Economic Policy in the Atlantic Community*, New York: McGraw-Hill.

De Gregorio, J., B. Eichengreen, T. Ito and C. Wyplosz (1999), 'An Independent and Accountable IMF', *Geneva Reports on the World Economy 1*, London: CEPR.

Dixon, L. and D. Wall (2000), 'Collective Action Problems and Collective Action Clauses', *Financial Stability Review* 8: pp. 142-51, Bank of England.

Dominguez, K. and J. Frankel (1993), *Does Foreign Exchange Intervention Work?*, Washington, D.C.: Institute for International Economics.

Eichengreen, B. (2000), 'Can the Moral Hazard Caused by IMF Bailouts be Reduced?', *Geneva Reports on the World Economy Special Report 1*, London: CEPR.

Feldstein, M. (1998), 'Refocusing the IMF', *Foreign Affairs*, March/April: pp. 20-33.

Financial Stability Forum (2003), 'Ongoing and Recent Work Relevant to Sound Financial Systems (September 2003)', *www.fsforum.org/publications/publication_24_67.html*

Frankel, J. and K. Rockett (1988), 'International Macroeconomic Coordination When Policymakers Do Not Agree on the True Model', *American Economic Review* 78 (3), pp. 318-40.

Hamada, K. (1976), 'A Strategic Analysis of Monetary Interdependence', *Journal of Political Economy* 84 (4), pp. 677-700.

Henning, C. R. (2002) 'East Asian Financial Cooperation', *Policy Analyses in International Economics* No. 68. Washington, DC: Institute for International Economics.

International Monetary Fund (2003a), 'A Guide to Committees, Groups, and Clubs', *www.imf.org/external/mp/exr/facts/groups.htm*.

International Monetary Fund (2003b), 'IMF Borrowing Arrangements: GA Band NAB', *www.imf.org/external/mp/exr/facts/gabnab/htm*.

Kenen, P.B. (1991), *The International Financial Architecture: What's New? What's Missing?* Washington, DC: Institute for International Economics.

Obstfeld, M. and K. Rogoff (2001), 'Global Implications of Self-Oriented National Monetary Policies', unpublished, University of California at Berkeley.

Olson, M. (1965), *The Logic of Collective Action: Public Goods and the Theory of Groups,* Cambridge, MA: Harvard University Press.

Putnam, R.D. and N. Bayne (1987), *Hanging Together: Cooperation and Conflict in the Seven-Power Summits*, Revised edn, Cambridge, Mass.: Harvard University Press.

Putnam, R. D., and C. R. Henning (1989) 'The Bonn Summit of 1978: A Case Study in Coordination' in R. N. Cooper, R. D. Putnam, C. R. Henning, and G. Holtham, *Can Nations Agree? Issues in International Economic Cooperation,* Washington, DC: Brookings Institution.

Rodrik, D. (2000), 'How Far Will International Economic Integration Go?', *Journal of Economic Perspectives* 14 (1): pp. 177-86.

Rogoff, K. (1985), 'Can International Monetary Policy Coordination be Counterproductive?', *Journal of International Economics* 18, pp. 199-218.

Solomon, R. (1977), *The International Monetary System 1945–1976: An Insider's View*, New York: Harper & Row Publishers.

Stiglitz, J. (2002), *Globalization and Its Discontents*, New York, NJ : W.W. Norton & Company.

Triffin, R. (1960), *Gold and the Dollar Crisis*, New Haven: Yale University Press.

Truman, E.M. (2004), 'The Euro and Prospects for Policy Coordination,' paper prepared for the conference on 'The Euro at Five: Ready for a Global Role', Washington D.C., Institute for International Economics, 26 February.

Wallich, H.C. (1984), 'Institutional Cooperation in the World Economy,' in Frenkel, J.A. and M.L. Mussa (eds), *The World Economic System: Performance and Prospects,* Dover, Mass.: Auburn House.

Williamson, J. (2000), 'The Role of the IMF: A Guide to the Reports', *International Economic Policy Briefs* 00-5, Washington, DC: Institute for International Economics.

Williamson, J. (2003), 'From Reform Agenda to Damaged Brand Name', *Finance and Development* 40(3), pp. 10-113.

DATE DUE